DELEUZE AND

FIGURES OF THE UNCONSCIOUS 14

DELEUZE AND DESIRE

Analysis of *The Logic of Sense*

Piotrek Świątkowski

LEUVEN UNIVERSITY PRESS

ISBN 978 94 6270 031 4
D/2015/1869/28
NUR: 777

Cover design: Griet Van Haute
Lay-out: Friedemann BVBA

For Carla, Noah, Sarah en Ella

TABLE OF CONTENTS

Acknowledgements

This book aims to be a systematic, rigorous and at the same time accessible analysis of one of the most difficult of Deleuze's texts, *The Logic of Sense*. This English version is a translation and adaptation of the Dutch original that was published and defended as a thesis in 2013. This version was finished in 2014, during a research period graciously funded by the Radboud University Nijmegen.

I am grateful to all my friends and colleagues who helped me during the long process of writing. First of all, I would like to thank my former PhD supervisor, Philippe van Haute. His sharp critique was of immense value for the development of my arguments. I also want to express my gratitude to other members of the Centre for Contemporary European Philosophy of the Radboud University Nijmegen. The numerous conversations, reading groups and seminars have been a source of tremendous philosophical joy and development. I particularly appreciate the help and advice of Gert-Jan van der Heiden, Benda Hofmeyr, Veronica Vasterling, Ben Vedder, Haydar Öztürk, Arjen Kleinherenbrink and Herman Westerink. I would also like to thank my various colleagues from the Dutch-Flemish Centre for Philosophical Anthropology and Psychoanalysis, the International Society for Philosophy and Psychoanalysis and Rotterdam Centre for Art and Philosophy, I was meeting on various occasions. I would further like to express my gratitude to all of my friends I have been discussing philosophy, art and politics with in the recent years. Thanks a lot to Tina Rahimy, Aetzel Griffioen, Sjoerd van Tuinen, Rick Dolphijn, Maurice Specht, Jeroen Timmermans, Piet Molendijk, Catarina Pombo Nabais, Michel Banabila, Henk Oosterling, Wim van Binsbergen, Damian O'Sullivan and many others. I also appreciate the help of Heleen Schröder and David Levey who edited the manuscript. They could not have been better qualified for the task.

Finally, I would like to express the highest gratitude to my family. Carla, Noah, Sarah and Ella, you are a true miracle. I enjoy every crazy moment I can spend with you.

Piotrek Świątkowski
Rotterdam, March 2015

ABBREVIATIONS

Works by Deleuze, Gilles

PSM	(1967), *Presentation de Sacher Masoch* (French version)
DR	(1968), *Différence et Répétion* (French version)
LdS	(1969), *Logique du Sens* (French version)
DF	(1977), *Dialogues* (French version)
CC	(1989), *Coldness and Cruelty* (English version)
LoS	(1990), *The Logic of Sense* (English version)
CeC	(1993), *Critique et Clinique* (French version)
DRE	(1994), *Difference and Repetition* (English version)
ECC	(1997), *Essays Critical and Clinical* (English version)
LID	(2002), *L'île Déserte* (French version)
DRF	(2003), *Deux régimes de fous* (French version)
DI	(2004), *Desert Islands* (English version)
TRM	(2006), *Two regimes of Madness* (English version)

Works by Deleuze, Gilles and Guattari, Felix

LAO	(1972), *L'Anti-Œdipe* (French version)
MP	(1980), *Mille Plateaux* (French version)
AO	(1983), *Anti-Oedipus* (English version)
ATP	(1987), *A Thousand Plateaus* (English version)

Chapter i

Introduction

1. Debate

Readers of the books *Anti-Oedipus* (1972) and *A Thousand Plateaus* (1980) will be familiar with the vehemence of Deleuze and Guattari's critique of psychoanalysis. The practice and theory of Freud, Lacan and Klein are presented there as a contemporary technique of power that represses the creative and critical potential of desire. The said 'psychoanalysis' produces narcissistic and docile subjects, who participate in a conformist manner in a society dominated by the capitalist mode of production; desire, engaged with social and political problems, is restrained. This fierce attack on psychoanalysis had unwanted consequences for the reception of the work of Deleuze and Guattari. The interpreters have frequently underestimated the importance of psychoanalysis for these authors regarding desire and have also neglected Deleuze and Guattari's will to reform this practice. This is surprising, certainly given the fact that Felix Guattari, one of the most acknowledged participants of the seminars of Jacques Lacan, has been active as a practicing psychoanalyst in an experimental psychiatric clinic *La Borde* throughout his life.[1] It is equally surprising, given the fact that Deleuze himself has made extensive use of psychoanalytic vocabulary in books such as *Coldness and Cruelty* and *The Logic of Sense.*

Drawing a general conclusion about the whole work of Deleuze and that of Deleuze and Guattari about desire and their relationship with psychoanalysis is nevertheless a difficult, if not an impossible, task. The diversity of the texts, or their degree of complexity, is too extensive to provide a reader with both a clear and nuanced analysis. In point of fact, instead of an all-embracing analysis, I provide the reader with a careful commentary on a single text.[2] This book is devoted to the analysis of desire developed in *The Logic of Sense,* one of the most beautiful and complicated books of Deleuze, and, particularly,

---

[1] The nature of the relationship between Lacan and Guattari and of the work of Guattari in *La Borde* is discussed in François Dosse (2007), *Gilles Deleuze et Félix Guattari, Biographie Croisée,* Paris: La Découverte, pp. 50, (Dosse 2010: 40).

[2] The choice for an 'ad litteram' commentary of the text will be explained more extensively below.

of what he calls 'the dynamic genesis of sense'.[3] This precise commentary not only reveals the core of Deleuze's thought about desire, but at the same time also establishes his strong ties with psychoanalysis. This text appears to be particularly interesting due to its extensive engagement with the work of Melanie Klein, one of the key figures of British psychoanalysis. Her work allows Deleuze to criticise Jacques Lacan's structuralist psychoanalysis, the dominating framework for exploring the theory of desire in the France of the nineteen sixties. Deleuze objects to the idea that human desire could be analysed by means of a universal structure. The patterns of our behaviour are constructions, emerging out of the interactions of a body with its surroundings.

The analysis of desire in *The Logic of Sense* stands on its own, but may also be considered as a missing link in the reception of Deleuze and Guattari's work. This analysis sets the groundwork for the cooperation with Guattari[4] and as such, is able to shed a new light on this cooperation. Numerous books have been written about the cooperation of both writers, but very little has been said about the dynamic genesis of sense and particularly about the influence of Melanie Klein.[5] This relative lack of interest is caused both by the relative popularity of *Anti-Oedipus* (1972) and *A Thousand Plateaus* (1980) and by the relative lack of knowledge of the work of Melanie Klein among philosophers.

---

3 This analysis may be found in the following chapters of *Logique du Sens*: '*27e série, de l'oralité*', '*28e série, de la sexualité*', '*29e série, les bonnes intentions sont forcément punies*', '*30e série, du phantasme*'. Chapters '*31e série, de la pensée*', '*32e série, sur les différentes espèces de séries*', '*34e série, de l'ordre primaire et de l'organisation secondaire*' complement this analysis.

4 On 5th April 1969 Guattari writes the following message to Deleuze: '*Une lecture lente, à la loupe, de* Logique du sens *me mène à penser qu'il q a une sorte d'homologie profonde de 'point de vue' entre nous. D'avoir à vous rencontrer quand cela vous sera possible constitue pour moi un événement déjà présent rétroactivement à partir de plusieurs origines*' (see Dosse 2007: 15, 2010: 5).

5 Until the present time, almost no literature about the relationship between the work of Melanie Klein and Gilles Deleuze has existed. The work of Nathan Widder (2009), 'From Negation to Disjunction in a World of Simulacra: Deleuze and Melanie Klein', in *Deleuze Studies* 3(2), pp. 207-231 and of J. Bednarek (2012), 'Logika sensu – najbardziej lacanowska z książek Deleuze'a?', *Praktyka Teoretyczna*, nr 5/2012, are the exceptions to this. James Williams' (2008), *Gilles Deleuze's Logic of Sense*, analyses the dynamic genesis equally brief as does Žižek's (2004: 80) *Organs without Bodies*, London: Routledge. Both neglect the influence of Klein. Sean Bowden (2011), pays some attention to the work of Klein in the chapter about the dynamic genesis in his book, *The Priority of Events, Deleuze's Logic of Sense*, Edinburgh: EUP. He nevertheless, pays more attention to the influence of Lacan and structuralism on *The Logic of Sense*. This relative lack of attention to the analysis of dynamic genesis is striking, certainly given the fact that Michel Foucault considers it to be of vital importance for understanding of the whole of Deleuze's philosophical project and is, for example, very impressed by his analysis of the phantasm. *Cf.* Michel Foucault (1970), 'Teatrum Philosophicum', *Critique* 282, pp. 885-908. A careful analysis of the notion of the phantasm is developed in Chapter six.

In *The Logic of Sense* the analysis of desire is not a fierce critique but rather a fundamental contribution to further development of psychoanalysis. Such analysis could therefore be of great importance to both psychoanalysts and philosophers interested in desire.[6]

The engagement with Melanie Klein's work as a means to criticise structuralist psychoanalysis originates from Deleuze's broader philosophical ideas. To the majority of philosophers, Deleuze is known for his frequently extravagant contributions to the analysis of philosophical systems of key figures of Western philosophy. I lack space to pay sufficient attention to these aspects of his work. For our understanding of the dynamic genesis, a brief mentioning of few influences and concepts must suffice. It is Spinoza, Bergson, Nietzsche and, to a lesser extent, Leibniz who have significantly influenced the work of Deleuze.[7] Spinoza is even described by Deleuze as the messiah (*christ*) of the philosophers, the only thinker capable of accepting immanence as the starting point of a philosophical system.[8] Spinoza allows him to reject any ontology that would take a privileged, transcendent point as departure for philosophical analysis. No higher instance constitutes immanence. God, Ideas, or subject do not form the fundamental basis that is able to explain the functioning of reality. Immanence is always the starting point.

---

[6]   The popularity of *Anti-Oedipus* has unfortunately, led many psychoanalysts to neglect the contribution of *Logique du Sens* to their field. For a critique of Deleuze and Guattari by various psychoanalysts refer to the contributions to the seminar *Anti-Oedipus*, Edouard Privat (ed.), (1974), *Les chemins de l'anti-œdipe*, Toulouse: Bibliothèque de Psychologie Clinique. For us, the text of Jean Bégoin 'L'Anti-Œdipe ou la destruction envieuse du sein' (pp. 139-159), where Klein's initial influence on his work is greatly admired, is of major importance.

[7]   Deleuze wrote a number of books about the work of other philosophers: on Hume (*Empirisme et Subjectivité*, 1953), on Nietzsche (*Nietzsche et la philosophie*, 1962), on Kant (*La philosophie critique de Kant*, 1963), on Bergson (*Le Bergsonisme*, 1966) and Spinoza (*Spinoza et le problème de l'expression*, 1968 and *Spinoza – Philosophie pratique*, 1970). Later in his career, he wrote about his deceased friends Foucault (*Foucault*, 1986) and Châtelet (*Périclès et Verdi: La philosophie de François Châtelet*, 1988) as well as about Leibniz (*Le pli*, 1988). All those books analyse the work of philosophical friends, with the exception of Kant, whom Deleuze considered to be one of his philosophical enemies. (*cf. Dialogues*, 1977). For an analysis of the true influence of Kant on Deleuze, refer, for example, to Kerslake (2009), *Immanence and the Vertigo of Philosophy: From Kant to Deleuze*, Edinburgh: Edinburgh University Press.

[8]   *Cf.* Deleuze & Guattari (1991: 59), *Qu'est-ce que la philosophie?*, Paris: Les Éditions de Minuit. For an interesting analysis of the concept of immanence and on the influence of Spinoza's, Bergson's and Nietzsche's work on Deleuze, refer to a short essay by, Quentin Meillassoux (2007), 'Subtraction and Contraction, Deleuze's remarks on *Matter and Memory*', in *Collapse III*, pp. 63-108.

Concepts from Bergson's work assisted Deleuze to develop the philosophy of immanence further. Bergson is an inspiration for the concept of the virtual and the actual.[9] Each object consists of a virtual and an actual part. The actual part of an object may be observed and known. The virtual part, despite being fully real, remains hidden. It precedes the actualisation of an object. Deleuze understands the separation between these two realms by characterising the virtual as the realm of problems, while the actual, he described as one of solutions. The actual is hence a solution provided for the problems characterising the virtual. An actual object is an expression of a problematic field.[10] A similar distinction plays a role in *The Logic of Sense*. Sense belongs to the realm of the virtual. It is real but at the same time never fully actualised. It does not consist of pre-determined relations between various structural elements but may be understood as a dynamic realm of problems. Individual patterns of behaviour are not an expression of universal and determined structures. Rather, they are an actualisation of the possibilities emerging in the realm of the virtual. The influence of Nietzsche's thought of the eternal return is also directly visible in these brief characterisations. Reality, if not chaotic, is contingent on nature. Sense is continually changing. It is an expression of events (*événements*) which continually undermine the actualised patterns or structures. Influence of Nietzsche allows Deleuze to emphasise the importance of the individual relation towards chance. Its affirmation in the production of sense is possible, but only within precisely defined conditions.[11]

These philosophical influences allow Deleuze to develop an alternative to the structuralist psychoanalysis which is known from Jacques Lacan's work.[12] For Lacan, the unconscious is structured in a manner that resembles

---

[9] For a brief introduction of the concepts actual and virtual see: Constantin Boundas (2005), 'Virtual/Virtuality', in Adrian Parr, (ed.), *The Deleuze Dictionary*, Edinburgh: EUP, pp. 296-299 and Meillassoux (2007).

[10] Refer, for example, to: *Différence et Répétition* (1968: 269), (DRE: 209).

[11] The influence of the philosophers mentioned will be largely neglected in the further analysis of the dynamic genesis in order for me to concentrate on Deleuze's understanding of desire and less on the influence of other thinkers on his work. I will clarify the reason for this, below.

[12] Deleuze analyses the characteristics of structuralism in the article: 'A quoi reconnaît-on le *structuralisme*', in François Châtelet (dir.), Histoire de la philosophie VIII. Le XXe siècle, Paris: Hachette, 1973 [Édition de poche: coll. 'Pluriel', 2000]. For an analysis of the relation between Lacan's work of the nineteen fifties and structuralism see: Markos Zafiropoulos (2003), *Lacan et Lévi-Straus, ou le retour à Freud 1951-1957*, Paris: PUF. For an introduction to the work of Lacan, refer to the analysis of his famous text: *Subversion du sujet et dialectique du désir dans l'inconscient freudien*, by Van Haute (2001), *Against Adaptation*, New York: Other Press. We must nevertheless remember here that the critique is oriented mainly towards Lacan's earlier work. The later texts of Lacan emphasise the importance of the Real, and partially answer Deleuze's critique.

a language. This structure, called the symbolic order, consists of signifiers, relating in a predefined manner. For Lacan, desire is Oedipal in nature. A child always relates to a symbolic mother and a symbolic father. Lacan assigns a key role to the symbolic father. A child must accept his authority. It must learn to acknowledge the determinations characterising the symbolic order and accept its role in the oedipal triangle. In this way only, is it able to break the imaginary unity with the mother and escape the inevitable psychosis. Deleuze is critical about the quasi-transcendental status awarded to the symbolic order. For him, the Lacanian symbolic order plays the role of transcendence that leads to unjustified judgements of immanence. Structuralist psychoanalysis imposes a pre-given structure upon the unconscious.

For Deleuze, the structures present in the unconscious are always temporary. The meanings of words or the social roles characterising our societies are not an expression of a higher and unchanging order. Sense cannot be reduced to any finite determination. It is not a universal structure. It displays the characteristics of an event (*événement*).[13] The actual possibilities for individual behaviour are a product of contingent interactions. This does not mean that sense is equal to complete chaos. It is a construction of material interactions. Sense is produced by an individual in the interactions of a body with its surroundings. The meaning of a word is equally never predetermined. It is constructed by means of the singular use made of it by an individual or a group. This use of a word leads to the subsequent emergence of actual patterns of speech and language use. A philosopher, interpreting these patterns as a universal structure and not a construction, makes a profound mistake which has severe consequences. The same point may be made about the social position of men and women in a given society. These roles are equally a construction, emerging out of material interactions. Changes in the structure of an economic mode of production or in the technology available to individuals at a given historical moment contribute to the changes in the production of sense and in the subsequent actualised patterns of living. Development of industry, and the subsequent rise of the services sector, have without doubt led to a substantial reshuffling of the symbolic relations between men and women and have produced corresponding actualised behaviour.[14]

---

[13] I concur here with the interpretation of the concept of sense offered by Badiou, A. (2006: 403), *Logiques des Mondes*, Paris: Seuil, Badiou (2009: 381). Badiou points to the connection of sense with the notion of the virtual and event.

[14] For such an analysis, see for example: Michel Tort (2005), *Fin du dogme paternel*, Paris: Éditions Flammarion.

The process that leads to the production of sense is called individuation.[15] The properties of a separate entity cannot be determined by a step from the most general level of sense to the most particular or by an application of form to matter, as is the case in Aristotelian hylomorphism. For Deleuze, each entity is a product of the process of ontogenesis.[16] The entity is produced by its surroundings and expresses the problems characterising it. Individuation is not predetermined. An individual is always able to transcend the given material circumstances and develop their own independent relationship towards the said circumstances. Having the ability to generate sense and change their surroundings, the individual functions within a problematic or virtual field and not solely according to the actualised structures. During the process of individuation they develop partial solutions to the problems encountered, in this manner expressing part of the complexity of their surroundings. An individual actualises the virtual; by realising the immaterial events, they escape the complete determination by the actual, producing new connections between the existing material entities.[17]

The possibility of the production of sense occurring during individuation does not mean that the actualised patterns of behaviour, already present, can easily be overcome. Meanings of words or the social roles are determined. Deleuze's understanding of sense in *The Logic of Sense* is, in this respect, not entirely different from that of Alain Badiou, who is equally interested in the notion of event.[18] An individual generally acts in accordance with the actual structures and is, for example, a perfect narcissistic consumer, addicted to communication technology. Their capacity to express events is very limited. An active involvement with their territory and an active construction of sense is far from being self-evident.

---

[15] For an analysis of the theme of individuation in the works of Deleuze, refer to Alberto Toscano (2006), *The Theatre of Production – Philosophy and Individuation between Kant and Deleuze*, London: Palgrave.

[16] For a critique of Aristotelian hylomorphism see Simondon, Gilbert, (1964), *L'Individu et sa genèse physico-biologique*, Paris: PUF. For secondary literature on this topic consult also Toscano (2006: 14) and Bowden (2011).

[17] Deleuze discusses the problematic nature of sense; for example, in: 'Ninth Series of Problematic,' in *The Logic of Sense* (LdS: 67-73), (LoS: 52-57).

[18] *Cf.* Alain Badiou, (2006: 403), (2009: 381).

2. The dynamic genesis and Melanie Klein

The alternative to the structuralist psychoanalysis developed by Deleuze in *The Logic of Sense,* consists of two elements. Deleuze emphasises not only the dynamic nature of sense but also the fundamental role played by the body during the production of sense. The body produces its own signs in the direct physical interactions with external objects. These exact signs contribute to the emergence of sense and to changes on the level of the actual. The body is not an empty container, destined to receive the signs proper to the symbolic order. Its activity allows for the emergence of sense. This interest in the original production of signs by the body explains Deleuze's fascination with the work of Melanie Klein, an attentiveness that has, surprisingly, been largely neglected in the secondary literature on Deleuze. This interest is not coincidental. Her work had already been subjected to strong critique by Lacan during his seminars.[19] According to Lacan, Klein unjustly overemphasises the importance of the protection provided by the mother for the development of a child and particularly for its sense of self-confidence. Again according to him, Klein underestimates the fundamental significance of the father. Only the symbolic father can impose the laws of the society (the law of the father) upon a child. Only he can be held responsible for the breaking up of the imaginary and incestuous relationship between a child and his mother and serve as a protection against psychosis.[20] The major criticism of Klein's work is nevertheless more theoretical in nature. In Lacan's own view Klein does not allow for the existence of the symbolic order. Her theory on the phantasmatic life of a child is merely imaginary in nature and does not allow for her to undertake a proper analysis of the structural problems facing a child and tormented adults.[21]

---

[19] The texts of Lacan from the nineteen fifties, may, to a significant degree, be seen as a response to the appearance in 1952, of *Developments dans la psychanalyse* of Klein and her adherents. Refer, for example, to the text 'Fonction et champ de la parole et du langage en psychanalyse', in *Ecrits* (1966: 235) and his first seminar '1953-1954, *Le Séminaire I*. For an analysis of the reasons why Lacan misinterprets the ideas of Klein about the body, refer to van Haute (2008) 'Lacan reads Klein, Some remarks on the body in psychoanalytic thought', in *Philosophy Today*, pp. 54-62.

[20] See i.a. Lacan, Jacques, *Écrits*. Paris: Seuil, 1966. p. 728-9 and Lacan's seminar of 1956-57, '*La relation d'objet*', '12 December, 1956', pp: 47. The exact analysis of the mentioned concepts will be given below.

[21] Lacan, Jacques, 'Some Reflections on the Ego', *International Journal of Psycho-Analysis*, vol. 34, 1953: p. 11.

This criticism is visible in Lacan's critical examination of the case study of a patient of Klein's, little Dick, which he, Lacan, developed in his first seminar.[22] Little Dick engages in analysis with Klein because he is unable to develop meaningful relations with his surroundings. Little Dick is slightly autistic. He lives in a world where people do not differ much from toys and other objects. After several therapeutic sessions Klein establishes contact with the child. Little Dick's capacity for communication develops increasingly. Klein is convinced that her therapy has been successful because she was able to explore the vulnerable, phantasmatic world of the child.[23] The transformation of the phantasms allows the boy to deal with his aggression, which, for Klein, is the primary cause of his mental predicament. Little Dick has overcome his aggressive impulses and corresponding fears, due to the development of the phantasm of a complete and good object. Lacan, on the other hand, is convinced that Klein has entirely misunderstood the cause of the success of her own approach. She did not reach into any kind of hidden phantasmatic life of her patient, but has played the role of the symbolic father. Her analysis has helped Dick to understand his own behaviour. His actions and experiences became meaningful. Little Dick gained access to the symbolic order. He overcame his limitations precisely because he realised that his relationship to the world is mediated by an external structure. He gained understanding of his position within the oedipal triangle and accepted the authority of the symbolic father.

In *The Logic of Sense,* Deleuze embraces Klein's idea of an independent phantasmatic life and uses her conception of a position.[24] In his opinion Klein is correct to emphasise the process of construction of phantasms, an idea not frequently found in psychoanalysis.[25] She must have understood her actions correctly. Her analysis allowed the child to develop a phantasm of what Deleuze would call a good object of the heights, an object that protects the ego against aggression and fears.[26] However, Deleuze and Guattari, in their mutual work, are far more critical about Melanie Klein in their common

---

[22] I schematically present the core of the problem here. For a longer analysis of this case study, see van Haute (2008). A precise analysis of the phantasms discussed here will be given in Chapters two and three.

[23] For the analysis of similar cases, see: Melanie Klein, (1997), *The Psychoanalysis of Children,* London: Vintage.

[24] The status and nature of the early phantasms, as well as the exact meaning of the idea of position, will be analysed in Chapter two.

[25] This position is developed in 'Thirtieth Series of the phantasm', (LdS 246), (LoS 210).

[26] The exact meaning of the content of this phantasm will be analysed in Chapter three.

work.[27] Construction of internal phantasms, made possible in her analysis, is unnecessarily restricted by the continuous reference to the oedipal structure in the analysis. Klein fails to stop interpreting desire by means of an oedipal structure. This is visible in her analysis of little Dick. The train must represent the father. The station stands in for the mother. The child must desire the mother and fear the father. For Deleuze and Guattari, this use of an actualised structure inhibits the full development of desire. The Oedipal interpretation limits it by downplaying the role of the phantasm that is developed out of an engagement with a broader field of relations. Psychoanalysis should therefore focus on the process of construction and not the interpretation of desire. It should engage with various institutions and social practices. Both Deleuze as well as Deleuze and Guattari stress the importance of art, literature, films and political organisations, for the process of construction of desire.[28] Art and literature diagnose the symptoms of our time, allowing us to develop a relationship with them. They allow us to reconstruct desire, to constitute responses to the problems emerging in our surroundings.[29]

In *The Logic of Sense* however, Deleuze is not interested in the oedipal terminology used by Klein in her analysis. Klein's work allows Deleuze to demonstrate that our psychic life consists of various forms of organisation, known as positions. In the account of the dynamic genesis, he adapts her analysis of the working of the paranoid-schizoid and manic-depressive positions.[30] In his analysis, he speaks of the schizoid, depressive and sexual

---

[27] Deleuze (2003: 92), 'L'Interprétation des énoncés', in *Deux régimes de fous*, Paris: Les Éditions de Minuit. (TRM 89).

[28] Deleuze, in 'Thirty Third Series of Alice's Adventures', states it as follows: *'Les cliniciens qui savent renouveler un tableau symptomatologique font une ouvre artiste; inversement, les artistes sont des cliniciens, non pas de leur propre cas ni même d'un cas en général, mais des cliniciens de la civilisation. Nous ne pouvons pas suivre à cet égard ceux qui pensent que Sade n'a rien d'essentiel à dire sur le sadisme, ou Masoch sur le masochisme. (…) Avec le génie de Freud, se n'est pas le complexe qui nous renseigne sur Œdipe et Hamlet, mais Œdipe et Hamlet qui nous renseignent sur le complexe'.* (LdS 277), (LoS 237).

[29] In this book we will analyse various examples of affects or phantasms that are being produced in literature and art. In Chapter two, we will, for example, observe the role of the phantasm (simulacrum) of the body without organs in the case of anorexia. Deleuze seeks to find constructions that provide an answer to the extreme suffering and problems faced by various individuals. He does not romanticise schizophrenia, but fully understands its negative impact on individual life. A critique of a possible romantic nature of Deleuze's work may be found, *inter alia*, in: Jacob Rogozinski, (2008), 'Deleuze lecteur d'Artaud' in *Rue Descartes* 59 (1), pp. 77-91 and Monique David-Ménard, (2005), *'Deleuze et la psychanalyse'*, Paris: PUF.

[30] For a splendid representation of the working of the Kleinian positions and their relation to language, refer to Susan Isaacs (1948), 'The Nature and Function of Phantasy', *International Journal of Psychoanalysis* 29, pp. 73-97. This topic is addressed in Chapters two and three.

positions. The sexual position itself is divided into various phases, including the phase of post-castration that will be of considerable significance for our analysis. The positions are characterised by different topological dimensions; Deleuze speaks of the depths, heights, physical and metaphysical surfaces. The different positions are also characterised by different internal objects or phantasms. Deleuze analyses the working of simulacra, the object of the heights, the images, amongst which are the image of the phallus and in the end, the phantasm proper. We will notice that these positions lead to experiences of pleasure, tension, fear and aggression. We will also observe that they are characterised by different ways in which to deal with the negative experiences. We will see, for example, that the fears of the schizoid position may be overcome by the continuous introjections of good partial objects or by the construction of the simulacrum of the body, without organs. A weak ego, continually threatened by bad partial objects, can introject good partial objects or reject the mechanism of introjections completely.

As we will realise, Klein's ideas are not sufficient to understand the working of desire in all its dimensions. Deleuze is convinced that Klein is not capable of a critical understanding of narcissism. This is a fundamental point for Deleuze, who attempts to develop an understanding of non-narcissistic forms of desire throughout his work. The critique of Klein on that point does not mean that Deleuze embraces the analysis of narcissism as understood in structuralist psychoanalysis.[31] He does make use of the structuralist vocabulary in his analysis of the sexual-perverse position and the phase of post-castration.[32] Deleuze, for example, underlines the importance of the image of the phallus for the development of a narcissistic subject and analyses the consequences of its loss. This analysis is nevertheless far removed from the structuralist one. The story of Oedipus, in *The Logic of Sense,* has its own internal dynamic. As we will see, Deleuze is critical of the severity of the trauma attributed to the loss of this image. The most powerful experiences are proper to the paranoid-schizoid position, as analysed by Klein. Moreover, the image of the phallus cannot be understood as a signifier inscribed onto the body by the symbolic order.[33] The image of the phallus emerges given the development of the previous positions, without mediation of an external structure of meaning. The image of the phallus does not presuppose any primacy of the symbolic or real father. It is an image projected on the genital zone by both a boy and a girl, and is an expression of the good intentions on the side of the ego.

---

[31] For the Lacanian analysis of this topic, see van Haute (2001).
[32] For the Lacanian analysis of this topic, see Žižek (2004: 82) and Bowden (2011).
[33] For the Lacanian analysis of this topic, see van Haute (2001: 157, 181).

Oedipus believes in his good intentions by claiming the possession of the good objects of the heights, an object that allows him to protect others.

We will furthermore observe that the consequences of the loss of the image of the phallus are understood by Deleuze in a very particular manner. This loss is not a structural given, but an event dependent of the direct experience of the subject. This loss of one's own reparative capacities leads to an orientation at the metaphysical surface, where narcissism is overcome. The ego constructs its own proper phantasm and starts to experience itself as a result of events. It develops a more independent relationship towards the external and actualised structures and engages the world in a more open and risky manner. The ego becomes capable of producing sense.[34]

3. Approach and organisation of the text

Why should the reader be interested in perusing an entire book devoted to a systematic analysis of only thirty pages of text? The reason for such a choice is the fact that the original analysis of the dynamic genesis undertaken by Deleuze is particularly dense, extremely precise and systematic. The untangling of his argument proves to be extremely difficult. A similar type of dense analysis of desire is moreover only partially present in other books of Deleuze. The critique of structuralism and of structuralist psychoanalysis is indeed developed in *Difference and Repetition* (1968). This critique, nevertheless, does not form the core argument of that book. Rather, it is an addition to a more general, ontological argument against what Deleuze calls the philosophy of representation, attributed, for example, to the work of Hegel. According to Deleuze, philosophy of this nature unjustly considers identity to be the fundamental ontological concept. It is therefore unable to consider the fundamental importance of the concept of difference.[35] A systematic analysis of desire is also only partially present in *Coldness and Cruelty* (1967), one of the first books where Deleuze explicitly argues against Freudian psychoanalysis. Deleuze, in this book, poses himself a modest goal. He uses Sacher-Masoch's

---

[34] This interpretation of the Deleuzian concept of sense is also to be found in Badiou (2006: 403), (2009: 381).

[35] Deleuze underlined that for dialectics differences must necessarily be united within an identity. Only an identity can be negated and subsequently sublated (*aufgehoben*). For Deleuze on the other hand, identity is just an expression of the primary movement of difference. Identity plays merely a minor role in the process of change found in reality. For a critique of Hegel's notion of contradiction in *Différence et Répétition*, refer to Chapter one (DR: 64), (DRE 44). A critique of the role of philosophy of representation in psychoanalysis may be found in Chapter two (DR 128), (DRE 96).

work as a background to understanding two kinds of perversion, sadism and masochism. Freud unjustly blurs the distinction between those two practices by taking the idea of the reversal of the drives as the starting point.[36] For Deleuze, both perversions express different bodily tendencies and are an answer to different social and political problems. Deleuze shows, for example, how masochist imagination allows for a humorous distance towards the limitations imposed on a subject by the law of the father. Unlike the sadist, the masochist wants to minimise the impact of this law on his own life.[37] Some of the concepts developed in *Coldness and Cruelty*, such as the phantasm, only become part of a more systematic analysis of desire in the analysis of the dynamic genesis in *The Logic of Sense*.

Anti-Oedipus (1972) provides an analysis of the working of desire that is every bit as systematic as the one developed in *The Logic of Sense*. Moreover, in this case, the writers are not entirely dismissive of the whole tradition of psychoanalysis. According to Deleuze and Guattari, desire is not determined by the symbolic order, but consists primarily of a multiplicity of what they call desiring machines. Here the body fulfils a fundamental role; the mouth of a child is understood as a machine that is firstly connected to the breast of the mother and subsequently to larger social machines, constituting, for example, the consumerist society, under a capitalist mode of production. The mouth is capable of receiving the uninterrupted flow of products sent towards it by those machines or it can close itself off, as in the case of anorexia. *Anti-Oedipus* and *A Thousand Plateaus* (1980), the two parts of *Capitalism and Schizophrenia*, nevertheless place more emphasis on the analysis of the political and social dimensions of desire. Both writers analyse the influence of the economic modes of production, of power structures and of the social and political machines on desire and imagination.[38] The analysis

---

[36] An analysis of the critique of Freud, by Deleuze, may for example be found in Geyskens, T. (2006), 'Deleuze over Sacher-Masoch – Literatuur als symptomatologie,' in *Tijdschrift voor Filosofie*, (68), pp. 779-801.

[37] A similar point of departure is taken in a later book, *Essays Critical and Clinical* (Deleuze 1993), where Deleuze analyses the clinical implications of literature. The points made about masochism and sadism, in *The Logic of Sense*, are discussed in Chapter three.

[38] An analysis of the influence of economic modes of production on desire may be found in Chapter three of 'Sauvages, barbares, civilisés' in *Anti-Oedipus*. Deleuze comments on the changes between *The Logic of Sense* and *Anti-Oedipus* in the introduction to the Italian version of *The Logic of Sense*: 'Je crois aussi que ce changement de mode implique un changement de matières ou, inversement, qu'une certaine politique prend la place de la psychanalyse. Une méthode qui serait aussi une politique (une micro-politique) et une analyse (une schizoanalyse) qui se proposerait l'étude des mulitiplicités sur les différents types de corps sans organes'. (Deleuze 1976, cited in Deleuze 2003: 60), (TRM 66). *Cf.* also Deleuze and Guattari (1972: 298).

of the construction of internal bodily phantasms, constitutive of some of the machines, appears to be of lesser importance.

The exclusive focus on the analysis of desire, developed in *The Logic of Sense,* does not mean that the social and political analysis undertaken in *Anti-Oedipus* and *A Thousand Plateaus* is of no interest to us in this book. Ideas developed in those texts will be frequently consulted. As mentioned above, the analysis of the dynamic genesis must also allow for an understanding of the common ground shared by Deleuze and Guattari before they engaged in writing together.[39] *The Logic of Sense* provides a systematic analysis of the topology of desire. The disruption, caused by the social and political structures of power per se, is put between brackets. The advantage of this procedure is twofold. It allows for a thorough analysis of the various ways in which an individual body may invest in similar structures of power.[40] It also allows for an analysis of the reasons why certain kinds of desire are preferred to others by those very structures.

The precise analysis of the way Deleuze thinks of the process of construction of desire in *The Logic of Sense* will also allow us to show that his philosophy is not vitalist in nature.[41] Deleuze's thought cannot be reduced to an ontology of forces. It is not an attempt to understand the conditions under which an inner creative force, repressed and hidden inside our bodies, may be expressed. Deleuze's central aim was to develop a constructivist understanding of desire. Desire consists of concrete activities undertaken within concrete circumstances. It consists of a creation of adequate concepts, affects and phantasms and Deleuze seeks to analyse the conditions under which an individual and a group may become critically engaged with reality.

I will moreover, try to show that the analysis of the dynamic genesis is able to enrich our understanding of Deleuze and Guattari's mutual work. When

---

[39] I have already indicated that Guattari was very enthusiastic about Deleuze's analysis of desire in *The Logic of Sense.* See Dosse (2007: 15), (2010: 5).

[40] Due to having selected *The Logic of Sense* for analysis, I will pay little attention to the changes in terminology that occur with the appearance of *Anti-Oedipus.* The examples from the later work will in the main be used to clarify the analysis of desire undertaken in *The Logic of Sense.* Deleuze himself admits that the cooperation with Guattari has led to some changes of the concepts that are used to analyse desire. I will partially try to show that these changes are of little significance. Deleuze states the following about his collaboration with Guattari: '*Je crois que nous* (Gilles Deleuze and Félix Guattari – P.S.) *avons cherché d'autres directions parce que nous en avions le désir. L'Anti-Œdipe n'a plus ni hauteur, ni profondeur, ni surface. Là tout arrive, se fait, les intensités, les multiplicités, les événements, sur une sorte de corps sphérique ou de tableau cylindrique:* corps sans organes.' (DRF: 60), (TRM: 66).

[41] This point is made by Alain Badiou in Badiou (2000), *Deleuze, The clamour of Being,* Minneapolis: UMP; and by Peter Hallward (2006), *Out of this world,* London: Verso.

we look at Deleuze's work about desire, various periods can be distinguished.[42] Christian Kerslake underscores, for example, that Deleuze had initially, before 1962, been interested in Jung's work. This initial interest changed after 1962 when he wrote *Coldness and Cruelty* and *The Logic of Sense*, where Freudian, and especially Lacanian, concepts seemed to be preferred.[43] His work with Guattari would introduce a fierce critique of the whole psychoanalytic tradition. Many commentators of Deleuze's work take the supposed break between the individual work and the cooperation with Guattari for granted.[44] The individual work is indeed characterised by a generous tone. Psychoanalysis is admired for the extensive vocabulary describing the unconscious. The texts written with Guattari on the other hand are polemical in nature. Even Freud is frequently ridiculed. Against this reading, I focus primarily on the continuity that is to be found in his work on desire. The statements made in *The Logic of Sense* are, according to my position, reconcilable with the later ones made in *Anti-Oedipus*. The work of Deleuze can and should be read in both cases as an attempt to enrich psychoanalysis and is in no sense an attempt to dismiss it in its entirety.[45]

To analyse the various steps characterising the dynamic genesis properly, a specific approach must be followed. This book is not a general introduction to the work of Gilles Deleuze or to *The Logic of Sense* in particular. It is, rather, a precise '*ad litteram*' analysis of one part of the book.[46] This approach should avoid the pitfall faced by the general overviews, that while they may

---

[42] See Christian Kerslake (2006) *Deleuze and the Unconscious*, London: Continuum, but also David-Ménard (2005) and Badiou (2000). Badiou particularly stresses the break between Deleuze's individual work and the work done with Guattari.

[43] Kerslake does not point to the fact that in *The Logic of Sense* Deleuze is greatly interested in the work of Melanie Klein.

[44] Refer, *inter alia*, to Badiou (2000); Hallward (2006: 67) and Žižek (2004: xi). Badiou and Žižek prefer *The Logic of Sense* to the later work, as it places more emphasis on the notion of event.

[45] Deleuze recognises the dual relationship towards psychoanalysis in his work as well as in the time of his collaboration with Guattari. In the introduction to the Italian version of *The Logic of Sense*, he says the following: '*Qu'est-ce qui n'allait pas dans cette* Logique du sens? *Evidement, elle témoignait encore d'une complaisance ingénue suivante: j'essayais pourtant, très timidement, de rendre la psychanalyse* inoffensive, *en la présentant comme un art des surfaces, qui s'occupe des événements comme d'entités superficielles (Œdipe n'est pas méchant, Œdipe n'a que de bonnes intentions....). Mais de toute manière, les concepts psychanalytiques restent intacts et respectés, Melanie Klein et Freud.*' (DRF 60), (TRM 65).

[46] The analysis here concerns the following chapters from *The Logic of Sense: 27ᵉ série, de l'oralité, 28ᵉ série, de la sexualité, 29ᵉ série, les bonnes intentions sont forcément punies, 30ᵉ série, du phantasme*. The series that will be partially analysed are: *31ᵉ série, de la pensée, 32ᵉ série, sur les différentes espèces de séries, 34ᵉ série, de l'ordre primaire et de l'organisation secondaire*.

be extraordinarily good introductions into the work of Deleuze,[47] they, nevertheless, simultaneously tend to break away from the original text. This does little justice to the complexity of the arguments. The overarching general statements necessarily lead to a suppression of various relevant details of the various steps taken in the analysis. The commentators frequently appear to be incapable of correctly and understandably representing the given arguments. Such texts have frequently strengthened the impression that the texts of Deleuze are incomprehensible and unsystematic, if not chaotic, in nature. However, this notion is entirely unjustified. The work of Deleuze and of Deleuze and Guattari is complex and highly systematic. A precise commentary that follows the original text step by step is able to reveal some aspects of the original text that are often hidden from the hasty reader and commentator. Hence, Deleuze's original text is accompanied here with an understandable commentary. I make use of examples from daily life, literature, art and films and frequently refer to various psychoanalysts and philosophers. Nevertheless, I am not interested in whether Deleuze provides us with a precise and true reading of Klein, Freud or Lacan. Those theories are discussed here only in so far as they contribute to the understanding of the analysis of the dynamic genesis itself.

In my commentary, I analyse the dynamic genesis of sense from three different angles. Firstly, I expound the importance of this analysis for the psychoanalytic understanding of desire. Secondly, I try to map the philosophical implications of this analysis and thirdly, I point towards the continuity to be found in Deleuze's work. In the following chapters I analyse the structural and topological characteristics of each position. I also pay attention to the dynamic that leads to the emergence of these positions, analysing their specific unconscious phantasms. In the analysis of the philosophical aspects of the dynamic genesis I indicate the manner in which the different positions imply a different relationship toward the structures of meaning and suggest in which way they contribute to the eventual emergence of the surface of sense.

The book consists of seven chapters. In Chapter two I further discuss the meaning of the concepts that are necessary to understand the process of the dynamic genesis. The largest part of this chapter is nevertheless, devoted to an analysis of the characteristics of the schizoid position. We will see that this most original organisation of the psychic life is characterised by the experiences of pleasure, mingled with aggression and the self-preservation drive. We will also examine swhich role is played by the simulacrum of the

---

[47] A superb analysis of the relation between Deleuze, Guattari and psychoanalysis may be found in Eugene Holland (1999), '*Deleuze and Guattari's Anti-Oedipus*'.

body without organs, a crucial concept also in the later work of Deleuze with Guattari. Chapter three is devoted to the analysis of the depressive position. The primary topological dimension of the schizoid position, the depths, is supplemented by the heights. I analyse the psychopathology introduced in this position and explain why this position is characterised by a higher degree of order than the schizoid one.

The first two positions are followed by the sexual position, discussed in Chapter four. This position emerges due to the defusion of the drives and we perceive how images are produced on the erotogenic zones and learn to understand the role of the image of the phallus in the process of emergence of a unified subjective experience. The analysis of Deleuze's ideas about the castration complex may be found in Chapter five. The development of the good intentions and their loss are discussed here and I explain how the loss of the image of the phallus might lead towards the metaphysical surface. An analysis of the characteristics of the phantasm proper can be found in Chapter six where I show that it can lead to a high degree of independence with respect to the existing, actualised structures. A full production of sense is possible only at this point. Finally, in the conclusion, I briefly discuss the critiques of Deleuze's work by Badiou, Hallward, Žižek and David-Ménard.

CHAPTER 2

Schizoid position

1. Introduction

In this book the analysis of the dynamic genesis of sense will be undertaken from three different angles. It will be treated as a psychoanalytic theory about the nature of desire, as a philosophical theory about the emergence of structures of sense and finally as a specific point in the development of Deleuze's theory. This chapter is concerned with the first position, characterising the dynamic genesis of sense, called the schizoid position. The analysis of this position may be found in 'Twenty-Seventh Series of Orality'. I first introduce the concepts that are crucial to understanding our analysis. After that, I discuss the characteristics of the Kleinian paranoid-schizoid position, as they are portrayed by Deleuze. Subsequently, I analyse the implications of the characteristics of this position for philosophical understanding of the emergence of structures. In the final part I focus on several amendments to the original analysis of Klein, introduced by Deleuze.

2. Fundamental concepts

Deleuze's main aim in his analysis of the dynamic genesis of sense in *The Logic of Sense* is to demonstrate that our desire is not primarily organised by external structures. The body is not an unwritten surface subscribed to a pre-given system of meaning, as it is in Lacan's early work. Rather, it fully contributes to the emergence of sense. Our unconscious is not directly structured as a language; our thought and speech are, first of all, an expression of primary interactions of a body with its surroundings. Structures of sense do not contain any universals; sense emerges in the process of genesis and is the product of a variety of experiences undergone by an individual – it is a construction. While saying that thought and the body are not two entirely separate ontological realms, assuming this position does not lead to a complete annihilation of the difference between both. The dynamic genesis of sense is an analysis of the process during which thought separates itself from the body.[1] Sense has

---

[1] I here refer to the following sentence from the 'Twenty-Seventh Series of Orality': '*Mais, dès lors, nous nous trouvons devant une dernière tâche: retracer l'histoire qui libère les sons, les rend indépendants des corps.*' (LdS 217), (LoS 186).

to liberate itself from limitations imposed upon it by the actual interactions of the body with environment. Sense belongs to a topological dimension that is different to the dimension to which the body belongs. It is a property of a surface, while the body belongs to what he calls the depths.[2] As we will see below, both topological dimensions continually interact. The body produces the surface of sense and at the same time is continually influenced by the events occurring at this surface.[3]

The dynamic genesis of sense is in fact a process of development of various topological dimensions that organise desire. It is an analysis of an 'entire geography and geometry of living dimensions', states Deleuze.[4] The analysis of the characteristics of these dimensions is based upon Melanie Klein's work. In the same vein as Klein, Deleuze describes these modes of organisation of desire as positions, an idea that differs from the Freudian term phase. Position does not refer to a historical moment when a particular erotogenic zone dominates experience. For both Deleuze and Klein, a position is a systematic manner in which the ego relates to the surrounding world.[5] Its interactions are mediated by various internal objects. These objects are not grafted onto the desiring body from the outside but emerge out of the process of continual interaction of the body with the outside world.

In examining the topological dimensions that Deleuze distinguishes we discuss those of the depths, the heights and of two surfaces: the physical surface of the body and the metaphysical surface of thought. The depths, central to the analysis of the schizoid position, are a dimension with hardly any order and with limited possibilities for action. As we will see, a person experiencing the world from the schizoid position is continually torn apart by various tensions and has a limited capacity to distance himself from them. The depths are moreover characterised by a lack of differentiation between language and

---

[2] I here have the following passage in mind: '*Le langage est rendu possible par ce qui le distingue. Ce qui sépare les sons et les corps, fait des sons les éléments pour un langage. Ce qui sépare parler et manger rend la parole possible, ce qui sépare les propositions et les choses rend les propositions possibles. Ce qui rend possible, c'est la surface, et ce qui se passe à la surface: l'événement comme exprimé. L'exprimé rend possible l'expression.*' (LdS 217), (LoS 186). The concept of event (*événement*) is discussed below.

[3] The precise characteristics of those interactions are analysed in Chapters five and six.

[4] Deleuze states this as follows: '*Les remarques que nous proposons concernant certains détails du schéma kleinien ont seulement pour but de dégager des « orientations ». Car tout le thème des positions implique bien l'idée d'orientations de la vie psychique et de points cardinaux, d'organisations de cette vie suivant des coordonnées et des dimensions variables ou tournantes, toute une géographie, toute une géométrie des dimensions vivantes.*' (LdS 219), (LoS 188).

[5] The idea of the position is proposed by Klein in the following article: 'A contribution to the psychogenesis of manic-depressive states', (1935) in Mitchel, J., (ed.), *The Selected Melanie Klein*, (1986), New York: The Free Press. pp. 115-145.

the body. In the schizoid position, the speech is a bodily endeavour.[6] Nothing separates the bodies from propositions.[7] The world is entirely physical in nature and does not yet know any events.

The second topological dimension, characterising the depressive position, is the height. It allows the ego to distance itself from the depths and establishes a first separation between thinking and the body. An initial understanding of the existence of language as different from direct physical experience emerges. The complete separation is nevertheless only accomplished given the formation of surfaces.[8] The first surface to emerge is the physical surface of the body that guarantees the separation between the inner and the outside world.[9] It enables the ego to fully control the swarms of excitations for the first time and allows for the establishment of first connections. The physical surface enables a connective synthesis that forms the first structures of sense. The disorganised experiences are unified into various series that form the first partial surfaces. The original source of the order cannot be found here in any external structure, as is the case in structural psychoanalysis. The experiences are arranged in series due merely to the working of the physical surface. The first attempts to join the various series into a unified experience may be comprehended as an activity of the body. Only the body that develops itself along the path of the dynamic genesis is responsible for the second, conjunctive synthesis, made possible by the emergence of the image of the phallus. The nature of this process will be discussed in Chapters four and five. As we will see, the ego fully adapts itself here to the already existing external structures of meaning.

The fourth topological dimension contributing to the establishment of the separation between body and thought is what Deleuze terms the metaphysical surface. Thought and the partial structures of sense – the series – eventually liberate themselves from the limitations imposed upon them by the body. The ego orients itself at events that transcend not only the physical limitations but

---

[6] Deleuze expresses this as follows: '*parler sera taillé dans manger en dans chier, la langage sera taillé dans la merde, le langage et son univocité…*' (LdS 225), (LoS 193).

[7] I am here referring to the following passage: '*Le langage est rendu possible par ce qui le distingue. Ce qui sépare les sons et les corps, fait des sons les éléments pour un langage.*' (LdS 217), (LoS 186).

[8] I refer here to: '*Ce qui sépare parler et manger rend la parole possible, ce qui sépare les propositions et les choses rend les propositions possibles. Ce qui rend possible, c'est la surface, et ce qui se passe à la surface: l'événement comme exprimé.*' (LdS 217), (LoS 186).

[9] The concept of the surface is fundamental for the whole philosophical project of Deleuze and is developed in most of his books. This book, nevertheless, does not attempt to arrive at a general definition of this concept throughout Deleuze's work. I will concentrate on its use in *The Logic of Sense* only.

31

also those ones imposed by the external structures of meaning.[10] The ego can only now master its desire, by tracing its own path on the metaphysical surface and responding to problems in its environment. It is important to realise that this surface cannot be equated with the symbolic order, as defined by, for example, Lacan's early work.[11] Sense and thought do not form a unified and organised whole, but consist of a variety of partial systems instead. The series is part of a multiplicity that can never be unified.[12] The metaphysical surface is both virtual and actual in nature, consisting of various forms of organisation, which mutually influence each other. In his analysis of structuralism (Deleuze 1972), he discusses a variety of structures, such as various epistemes,[13] economic structures – economic modes of production – or sexuality. For Deleuze those forms of organisation cannot be over-determined by only one of them. Their continuous interactions are not predetermined and can never fully determine the experience of an individual. An important point in the analysis of the dynamic genesis of sense is that, under specific conditions, an individual is able to minimise the impact of the large actualised structures on his behaviour. It is only the access to the metaphysical surface, with its orientation to events by means of a proper form of the phantasm that allows the subject to manoeuvre between the actual and the virtual or between the large- and small-scale systems. The ego accompanies connections between the hitherto unrelated series and amends the actualised structures of sense only in this case. It becomes capable of the disjunctive synthesis.[14]

---

[10] I here have in mind: '*et ce qui se passe à la surface: l'événement comme exprimé.*' (LdS 217), (LoS 186).

[11] Deleuze analyses the properties of the metaphysical surface not only in *The Logic of Sense*, but also in his article on structuralism: Gilles Deleuze (1972), 'À quoi reconnait-on le structuralisme?,' in François Châtelet, (ed.), *Histoire de la philosophie tome 8: Le XXe siècle* (Paris: Hachette, 1972), pp. 299-335. See Deleuze (2002), *L'île Déserte*, Paris: Les Éditions de Minuit. Pp. 238-269, (DI 170-192).

[12] Deleuze has already set himself against Lacan, in his article on structuralism. He disagrees with the prominent role attributed by Lacan to the image of the phallus. This image cannot be the sole object responsible for the synthesis of various series. See Deleuze (LID 267), (DI 190).

[13] The episteme is, according to Foucault, a systematic manner to organise knowledge. An episteme expresses itself in the philosophical systems, in scientific knowledge, in art and in social practices. See Foucault (1966: 13), *Les mots et les choses*, Paris: Gallimard.

[14] This way of synthesising is, to a certain degree, applied to *The Logic of Sense* itself. The book does not produce a finished and systematic representation of the working of the structures of sense but consists rather of various separate series that continually refer to one another. It is ultimately the task of the reader to conduct the disjunctive synthesis and arrive at a partial structure. It must nevertheless be noted that I have developed a merely schematic analysis of the metaphysical surface here. A systematic analysis is developed in Chapters five and six.

The dynamic genesis is not the only kind of genesis discussed in *The Logic of Sense*, and is complemented by the analysis of the static genesis.[15] Deleuze defines the latter as the process by means of which an event brings forth changes both on the level of thought and bodies. An event alters both the bodies and their expression in thoughts and propositions. To illustrate the nature of the static genesis, we may analyse an example of a socio-political event, such as the Occupy-movement or uprisings in the Arab world. An uprising is an event. Its arrival cannot be predicted. It suddenly disrupts the organisation of a world that is organised by an actual structure. An event poses a challenge and changes this very structure. The static genesis allows for the expression of this event on the level both of thought and of the body. The uprising leads to a direct increase in the degree of political engagement of the inhabitants of a state, or for example, of the Arab world. The people find themselves suddenly on the streets, confronting the policies of their rulers. Their physical state changes. This event also expresses itself on the level of thought: people start to think differently and begin to make use of concepts that have not been applied to their situation before. They suddenly think of themselves in new terms. Egypt's citizens for example, suddenly referred to themselves as citizens with particular rights or as a revolutionary group engaged in the construction of a new common world. Suddenly the system of representation changes. An event such as the Arab spring or the Occupy movement, expresses itself both on the level of bodies and thought.[16]

The static genesis differs from the dynamic one because, in case of the former, the existence of the division between bodies (things) and thought, is directly presupposed. In the case of the static genesis, language directly refers to things by means of propositions. The dynamic genesis, on the other hand,

---

[15] Deleuze analyses the distinction between the two kinds of genesis in the following passage in the 'Twenty-Seventh Series of Orality': '*Il ne s'agit plus d'une genèse statique qui irait de l'événement supposé à son effectuation dans des états de choses et à son expression dans des propositions. Il s'agit d'une genèse dynamique qui va directement des états de choses aux événements, des mélanges aux lignes pures, de la profondeur à la production des surfaces, et qui ne doit rien impliquer de l'autre genèse. Car, du point de vue de l'autre genèse, nous nous donnions en droit manger et parler comme deux séries déjà séparées à la surface, séparées et articulées par l'événement qui résultait de l'une et s'y rapportait comme attribut noématique, et qui rendait l'autre possible et s'y rapportait comme sens exprimable.*' (LdS 217), (LoS 186).

[16] I will return to the analysis of event in Chapters five and six. See also 'Sixteenth Series of the Static Ontological Genesis' where Deleuze analyses the ideas of Leibniz and his statements about the incompossible worlds (LdS 138, LoS 118). An extensive analysis of the static genesis lies outside of the scope of this book. It would require a thorough analysis of the work of Leibniz and Husserl. For such an analysis, see for example, Bowden (2011: 64).

is the process of separation between both. It analyses the condition in terms of which an event may become possible in the first place.[17] As we will discover, the dynamic genesis of sense is also an analysis of the conditions under which we may speak of a full, univocal, use of language.[18] It reveals that the dualist distinctions, such as nature-convention, nature-custom and nature-artifice, are not ontologically primary. They are always preceded by a more fundamental distinction between the depths and the surface.[19] The dualist oppositions are a product of a process during which depths express themselves on the surface. Language and words emerge from matter, while the physical surface plays the role of an intermediary. The organisation of the bodily sensations, brought about on the physical surface of the body, contributes to the emergence of a language.[20]

3. The dynamism of the paranoid-schizoid position according to Melanie Klein[21]

Given these first schematic remarks about the fundamental concepts, such as the depths and the surface, we may now proceed to the analysis of the first position distinguished by Deleuze. In most other analyses of the emergence of an organism, Deleuze usually cites the example of an egg or an

---

[17] I refer here to the following passage: '*Il s'agit d'une genèse dynamique qui va directement des états de choses aux événements, des mélanges aux lignes pures, de la profondeur à la production des surfaces, et qui ne doit rien impliquer de l'autre genèse.*' (LdS 217, LoS 186).

[18] I here refer to the following passage: '*Mais comment parler se dégage effectivement de manger, ou comment la surface elle-même est produite, comment l'événement incorporel résulte des états de corps, est une tout autre question. Quand on dit que le son devient indépendant, on veut dire qu'il cesse d'être une qualité spécifique attenant aux corps, bruit ou cri, pour désigner maintenant des qualités, manifester des corps, signifier des sujets et prédicats. Justement, le son ne prend une valeur conventionnelle dans la désignation – et une valeur coutumière dans la manifestation, une valeur artificielle dans la signification – que parce qu'il tire son indépendance à la surface d'une plus haute instance: l'expressivité. A tous égards la distinction profondeur-surface est première par rapport à nature-convention, nature-coutume, nature-artifice.*' (LdS 217), (LoS 187).

[19] Here I am referring to the following passage: '*A tous égards la distinction profondeur-surface est première par rapport à nature-convention, nature-coutume, nature-artifice.*' (LdS 217), (LoS 187).

[20] Deleuze analyses the relation between both surfaces among others in 'Thirty-First Series of Thought'. He writes: '*Aussi bien, c'est toute la surface sexuelle qui est intermédiaire entre la profondeur physique et la surface metaphysique.*' (LdS 258), (LoS 221).

[21] In his analysis, Deleuze uses the term paranoid-schizoid position only when he refers to its original Kleinian sense. The term schizoid position is reserved for the analysis of his own understanding of its characteristics. In the rest of this text I will also follow this distinction.

embryo.[22] An embryo carries the first signs of an organism that is yet to be developed. The liquid mass gradually gains form. Various cells start to differentiate. This formation passes through several phases.[23] Every organ forms itself around a singular point, proper to a particular zone of an organism. At the moment when the tension between the various parts of an organism or between the emerging organism and its environment has reached a required level, further development becomes possible. A low concentration of some of the hormones inside the body of the mother may, for example, prevent the implanting of the embryo in her womb. A singular point, which would have led to the formation of the organism, is not passed through. The tension between various elements in the external and internal environment must be continually correct. The fragile individual organism can be destroyed or entirely changed at each moment. A road along a variety of singular points that must be passed is full of risks and possibilities. An embryo is what Deleuze calls a larval subject. It is not an entirely predetermined entity that expresses an existing structure. The skin, brain, heart and other organs emerge in the process of genesis.[24] The organism emerges in a particular environment and is, in the first instance, the result of the processes of individuation. A structured organism emerges out of the specific interactions of the larval subject with its environment.

In his account of the dynamic genesis of sense and of the schizoid position, Deleuze is not directly concerned with the physiological development of the human embryo, but rather with the emergence of a human psyche connected

---

[22] See Difference and Repetition (DR: 214-217), (DRE: 276-280). Deleuze states: 'Les embryologistes montrent bien que la division d'un œuf en parties reste secondaire par rapport à des mouvements morphogénétiques autrement significatifs, augmentation des surfaces libres, étirement des couches cellulaires, invagination par plissement, déplacements régionaux des groupes. Toute une cinématique de l'œuf apparaît, qui implique une dynamique. Encore cette dynamique exprime-t-elle quelque chose d'idéel. Le transport est dionysiaque et divin, il est délire, avant d'être transfert local (...) Les prouesses et le destin de l'embryon, c'est de vivre l'inviable comme tel, et l'ampleur de mouvement forcés qui briseraient tout squelette ou rompraient les ligaments. Il est bien vrai que la différenciation est progressive, cascadant. (...) Et avant l'embryon comme support général de qualités et parties, il y a l'embryon comme sujet individuel et patient de dynamismes spatio-temporels, le sujet larvaire.' (DR 278), (DRE 215). A thorough analysis of the relation between these statements about, on the one hand, the ideal synthesis or the larval subject and the dynamic genesis in The Logic of Sense on the other, lies outside of this book's scope.

[23] Deleuze derives this theory about the singular points from the mathematician Lautman. See i.a.. Difference and Repetition. For an analysis of this topic in relation to The Logic of Sense see Williams (2008: 91) and Bowden (2011: 95).

[24] In Difference and Repetition, Deleuze remarks: 'Et avant l'embryon comme support général de qualités et parties, il y a l'embryon comme sujet individuel et patient de dynamismes spatio-temporels, le sujet larvaire' (DR 278), (DRE 215).

to the first physical interactions of a newborn child with its surroundings. It is unsurprising that Deleuze is interested in Melanie Klein's theories. She was the first psychoanalytic theoretician to have analysed the psychic impact of the first interactions of the infant with its surroundings.[25] The first experiences of a newborn child, of the highest importance for the forming psyche, are similar to the states of tension endured by the embryo. The child experiences pleasant excitations. It enjoys them but also experiences stress and anxiety.[26] The experience of a little child is quite limited. The child must learn to tolerate either the overabundance or the lack of food. It must learn to control both the yearning accompanying its reception of food and the stress accompanying its lack. The child also experiences its first contacts with other bodies. It already smells, hears and sees. The received stimuli are nevertheless limited. The child perceives only parts of the objects in its environment and never the objects in their totality. It is surrounded by what Klein terms the partial objects. From the perspective of the child, the objects are not submitted to any law. The child lives in a world of disorganised impressions. It lives in permanent insecurity. The temporary states of pleasure quickly change into either over-excitation or into tension and subsequently anxiety.[27] The tensions are uncontrollable. The feelings of satisfaction and pleasure, caused by the presence and warmth of the body of a parent, are quickly overshadowed by the states of fear, generated by their absence.

For Melanie Klein, these experiences are accompanied by the first psychic representations.[28] The child starts to mentally differentiate between what she terms good and bad partial objects. The good partial object accompanies the

---

[25] See Klein, (1947), 'Notes on some Schizoid Mechanisms?' in Mitchel, J., (ed.), *The Selected Melanie Klein*, (1986), New York: The Free Press.

[26] Klein analyses the characteristics of this position in 'Notes on some Schizoid Mechanisms?', (Klein 1947).

[27] Klein writes: 'We are, I think, justified in assuming that some of the functions which we know from the later ego are there at the beginning. Prominent amongst these functions is that of dealing with anxiety. I hold that anxiety arises from the operation of the death instinct within the organism, is felt as fear of annihilation (death) and takes the form of fear of persecution. The fear of the destructive impulse seems to attach itself at once to an object – or rather it is experienced as the fear of an uncontrollable overpowering object. Other important sources of primary anxiety are the trauma of birth (separation anxiety) and frustration of bodily needs; and these experiences too are from the beginning felt as being caused by objects. Even if these objects are felt to be external, they become through introjections internal persecutors and thus reinforce the fear of the destructive impulse within.' (Klein 1947, in 1986: 180).

[28] For an outstanding analysis of the primary psychic experiences of a child see Susan Isaacs (1952). 'The Nature and Function of Phantasy', in *Developments in Psycho-Analysis*, Klein, Heiman *et al.*, (eds.), pp. 67-121. A description of the character of these inner representations can be found below in Section 2.4.

experiences of pleasure while the bad partial object does those of tension and fear. Melanie Klein speaks of the good and bad breast as the first internal representations.[29] The good breast accompanies the state of pleasure produced by the pleasurable excitation of the oral zone. The mouth absorbs milk and the hunger is alleviated. The child feels secure and is convinced it will not die of hunger. Other parts of the parent's body generate similar experiences. A hand is represented as a good partial object when it cuddles the body of the child. The child feels caressed and taken care of. The same body parts can nevertheless also be experienced as bad partial objects when they produce unpleasant excitations. The absence of the breast leads to hunger. The child starts to fear for its own survival. It cannot suckle the now missing breast. The warm object that produced the state of pleasure is absent. The breast is hence experienced as a threatening object. It can disappear any moment and leave the child in a state of fright. In addition, the warm body of the mother can become a bad partial object when it suddenly disappears. The child feels cold and misses her scent. It experiences the tension due to the absence of pleasurable stimulations and the overabundance of negative ones.[30]

The main focus of Klein's analysis of the paranoid-schizoid position is placed not only on the presence of negative stimuli but also on the strong impact of the death drive or aggression that accompanies those stimulations.[31] Just like Freud, Klein shows how disruptive aggression or the death drive can be when they continually intensify the negative experiences.[32] Aggression aggravates the states of tension and fear. The child screams and is frequently infuriated. It wants to bite and control the breast or the rest of its environment. It wants to keep the body of the mother as close as possible. The aggression does not

---

[29] In 'Notes on some Schizoid Mechanisms?' Klein declares: 'I hold that the introjected good breast forms a vital part of the ego, exerts from the beginning a fundamental influence on the process of the ego development and affects both ego structure and object relations.' (1986: 197). See also Klein (1935), 'A contribution to the psychogenesis of manic-depressive states', in Mitchel, J., (ed.), (1986).

[30] In this description I follow Isaacs (1952: 91).

[31] Klein builds upon the work of Freud, from 'Beyond the Pleasure Principle' (1920) onward. Aggression or the death drive is, according to both Klein and Freud, the most powerful drive. They are the root cause of the continual disruptions in the life of the child. The analysis of the role of the death drive in life of a child can be found, among others, in Tomas Geyskens and Philippe van Haute (2007), *From death instinct to attachment theory: the primacy of the child in Freud, Klein, and Harmann*, New York: Other Press.

[32] As Klein asserts: 'I hold that anxiety arises from the operation of the death instinct within the organism, is felt as fear of annihilation (death) and takes the form of fear of persecution.' (1947 in 1986: 180). Deleuze refers to the work of Melanie Klein in the following way: '*Le sien et tout le corps de la mère ne sont pas seulement clivés en un bon et un mauvais objet, mais vidés agressivement, déchiquetés, mis en miettes, en morceaux alimentaires.*' (LdS: 218), (LoS: 187).

disappear upon the return of the state of pleasure. The breast is treated with aggression after its return also. The child drinks fast and without limitations. It wants more and more, even after alleviating its hunger. It wants to break the breast into pieces. It also clutches the body of the mother. It wants to make her a part of its own world, using violence if necessary. Klein notices also that from the very beginning the child starts to develop an awareness of its own aggression. It is scared of the destruction of the body of the mother which it thinks it is causing. It also fears that it will be treated with equal aggression, and also for its own existence. This fear can be alleviated again only by the new introjection of a good partial object. The child lives, in fact, in a vicious circle.[33] The compulsive pursuits of pleasure and striving to fulfil the demands of the self-preservation drive necessarily awaken aggression and fear. Those experiences can be subsequently temporarily alleviated only by new experiences of pleasure. The paranoid-schizoid position generates a mixture of the states of pleasure, aggression and fears for self-preservation. The libido, self-preservation drive and the death drive are combined into one.[34]

Introjection and projection are the first psychic mechanisms facilitating the relationship with partial objects.[35] When the partial objects are introjected, they become part of the psychic reality and the child's imagination constitutes

[33] See Klein (1935: 119). 'Besides, he finds himself constantly impelled to repeat the incorporation of a good object, partly because he dreads that he has forfeited it by his cannibalism – i.e. the repetition of the act is designed to test the reality of his fears and disprove them – and partly because he fears internalized persecutors against whom he requires a good object to help him'. The passage analyses the beginnings of the manic-depressive position, but the dynamism described is also valid for the paranoid-schizoid position relation towards partial objects. Deleuze concurs with this analysis: 'D'où la nécessité d'une ré-introjection perpétuelle.' (LdS 218), (LoS 187).

[34] Deleuze states: 'Et l'oralité se prolonge naturellement dans un cannibalisme et une analité où les objets partiels sont des excréments capables de faire sauter aussi bien le corps de la mère que le cops de l'enfant, les morceaux de l'un étant toujours persécuteurs de l'autre, er le persécuter toujours persécuté dans ce mélange abominable qui constitue la Passion de nourrisson.' (LdS 218), (LoS 187). The mixture (intrication) of the drives in the depths of the schizoid position is analysed further in the 'Twenty-Eight Series of Sexuality'. Deleuze argues there: 'Mais l'important est de savoir quel était l'état de leur mélange (in the depths – PS), d'une part avec les pulsions de conservation, d'autre part avec les pulsions de mort' (LdS 230), (LoS 198). In Chapter four I will return to this topic.

[35] See Klein (1935: 116). Deleuze discusses the dynamic of the Kleinian paranoid-schizoid positions as follows: 'L'introjection de ces objets partiels dans le corps du nourrisson s'accompagne d'une projection d'agressivité sur ces objets internes, et d'une re-projection de ces objets dans le corps maternel: ainsi les morceaux introjetés sont aussi comme des substances vénéneuses et persécutrices, explosives et toxiques, qui menacent du dedans le corps de l'enfant en ne cessent de se reconstituer dans le corps de la mère. D'où la nécessité d'une ré-introjection perpétuelle. Tout le système de l'introjection et de la projection est une communication des corps en profondeur, par la profondeur.' (LdS 218), (LoS 187).

itself around these objects. The good breast is present in the child's mind and reassures it. This mechanism is accompanied by the mechanism of projection. The introjected objects generate not only the states of pleasure, but also lead to aggression. A child strengthens the experience of hunger by subsequent projection of aggression on a missing object. The child imagines that the milk and the breast of the mother is threatening. It imagines milk containing poisonous parts. The breast attacks it. The child subsequently gets rid of these bad partial objects from its inside. It re-projects these objects back into the body of the mother.[36] The outside object is now experienced as attacking the child. For Klein those experiences of aggression do not entirely determine the dynamic of the schizoid position. The re-projection may be less aggressive in nature and an expression of the first attempts to restore the damage caused by own acts of aggression. The child engages in attempts at reparation.[37] Not only the bad objects, but also the good ones, are able to be projected onto the outside world. The food that is thrown up may also be experienced as a gift to the mother. It is supposed to restore the damage caused. The paranoid-schizoid position nevertheless does not allow for a successful attempt at restoration. There is no principle present yet than enables it to determine which attempt is successful. A complete and undivided object, a condition for successful restoration, does not exist yet. A person with a dominant paranoid-schizoid position must, for example, continuously offer presents to others in order to ameliorate the damage he thinks he has caused. An uninterrupted flow of ever new gifts appears to be necessary. The other can be only experienced as a partial and not a complete object. A person with a dominant paranoid-schizoid position – a perfect member of contemporary consumer society – is equally unable to exercise a profound control over his own desire. He is persecuted and persecutes others. His body is continually torn apart and requires continuous new experiences. He is caught in a vicious

---

[36] Deleuze states this as follows: '*ainsi les morceaux introjetés sont aussi comme des substances vénéneuses et persécutrices, explosives et toxiques, qui menacent du dedans le corps de l'enfant en ne cessent de se reconstituer dans le corps de la mère. D'où la nécessité d'une ré-introjection perpétuelle.*' (LdS 218), (LoS 187).

[37] In her earlier work Klein connects the emergence of the reparative tendencies to the identification with complete objects: 'In certain of my earlier works I discussed in detail the concept of restoration and showed that it is far more than a mere reaction formation. The ego feels impelled (and I can now add, impelled by its identification with the good object) to make restitution for all the sadistic attacks that it has launched on that object. When a well-marked cleavage between good and bad objects has been attained, the subject attempts to restore the former, making good in the restoration every detail of his sadistic attacks. But the ego cannot as yet believe enough in the benevolence of the object and in its own capacity to make restitution.' (1935 in 1986: 120).

circle and is doomed to continuous introjections of ever new partial objects, ever new consumer goods.[38]

We should still nuance our understanding of the status of the first experiences of the child, as they have been described by Klein. To understand their nature, she chooses to use the term phantasy, written with a ph instead of fantasy, as used by Freud.[39] Klein reserves the term fantasy to describe the status of daydreams or fictions produced by any individual. A writer might for example engage in day-dreams about a text and the positive response it will receive from the readers. Phantasy is different in nature. It is not a form of escape for a person unable to bear reality. Phantasy is an unconscious mental content and not a form of denial of reality. The psychic reality has its own objectivity and is characterized by mental facts, which are equally important to the events in the external world.[40] Phantasy is a representation of a drive (an instinct).[41]

Klein's student, Susan Isaacs, analyses a number of formulations that are able to clarify the content of such primitive phantasies. Those formulations must be expressed in full sentences of a language despite the fact that they distort the non-signifying nature of those phantasies.[42] When a child feels the urge to drink milk, it experiences this desire by means of a phantasy, 'I want to suck the nipple'. At the moment when this desire is particularly intense, it

---

[38] Deleuze describes this state in the following words: '*Les corps éclatent et font éclater, dans ce système de la bouche-anus ou de l'aliment-excrément, universel cloaque.*' (LdS 218), (LoS 187).

[39] Isaacs writes: 'The psycho-analytical term "phantasy" essentially connotes unconscious mental content, which may or may not become conscious. (...) Again, the word "phantasy" has often been used to mark a contrast to "reality", the latter word being taken as identical with "external" or "material" or "objective" facts. But when external reality is thus called "objective" reality this makes an implicit assumption which denies to psychical reality its own objectivity as a mental fact.' (Isaacs 1952: 81).

[40] According to Isaacs, phantasy is present both in so-called normal people and neurotics. As she argues: 'The difference between normal and abnormal lies in the way in which the unconscious phantasies are dealt with, the particular mental processes by means of which they are worked over and modified; and the degree of direct or indirect gratification in the real World and adaptation to it, which these favoured mechanisms allow.' (Isaacs 1952: 82).

[41] Isaacs provides the following explanation: 'Phantasy is (in the first instance) the mental corollary, the psychic representative, of instinct. There is no impulse, no instinctual urge or response which is not experienced as unconscious phantasy' (See Isaacs 1952: 83).

[42] Isaacs emphasises: 'In attempting to give such examples of specific phantasies we are naturally obliged to put them into words; we cannot describe or discuss them without doing so. This is clearly not their original character and inevitably introduces a foreign element, one belonging to later phases of development, and the pre-conscious mind.' (1952: 84). It must be stressed that Deleuze in his collaboration with Guattari criticises the manner in which the unconscious phantasms are being verbalised. Deleuze and Guattari are most critical of the oedipal terminology used in those verbalisations. See i.a. Deleuze (2003), 'Quatre propositions sur la psychanalyse', in *Deux Régimes de fous*, Paris: Les Éditions de Minuit. (TRM 79).

experiences it as 'I want to eat her all up'. At the moment when the mother leaves the child alone his experience can be characterized as 'I want to keep her inside me'. At the moment when this tension rises up, he becomes aggressive. His experience at this moment can be characterized by the sentence: 'I want to bite the breast; I want to tear it to bits.'[43] When the phantasy is experienced during a phase when the tensions experienced in the anal zone are most intense, it can be described with the sentence: 'I want to drown and burn her.' Susan Isaacs underscores the importance of the fear of retaliation for the acts of the infant's own aggression. It may develop a phantasy: 'I myself shall be cut or bitten up by the mother'. The child may also experience anxiety regarding the objects that have already been internalized. This leads to the wish to eliminate these objects from the inside. The child also develops the first means of protecting itself against the attacks and a phantasy that allows for the restoration of damage caused. The fear generated by mother's absence is negated by its sucking at its finger. The corresponding phantasy is: 'If I suck my thumb, I feel she *is* back here as part of me, belonging to me and giving me pleasure.'[44]

4. *The simulacrum and Plato*

To understand the nature of the phantasy proper to the schizoid position, Deleuze introduces the concept of a *simulacrum*.[45] There is a clear philosophical reason for this choice. It allows Deleuze to criticise the Platonic philosophy and the image of thought it produces. What kind of an image of thought and the world is produced by Plato, according to Deleuze? For Plato, the material world that surrounds us is presented as merely a reflection of a higher, ideal world. Each entity we encounter is merely an imperfect copy of a perfect Idea. No actual human being can be conceived of as perfect. Every man, woman, doctor, politician, carpenter or academic by definition fails in all attempts to

---

[43] Isaacs puts this as follows: 'At other times, when he is frustrated or provoked, his impulses may be of an aggressive character; he will experience these as e.g.: "I want to bite the breast, I want to tear her to bits".' (Isaacs 1952: 84).

[44] *Cf.* Isaacs 1952: 85. She also discusses the expression corresponding to the reparative tendencies: 'he may feel he wants to restore his mother and will than phantasy: "I want to put the bits together again," "I want to make her better," "I want to feed her as she has fed me";' (Isaacs 1952: 85).

[45] As Deleuze writes: '*Ce monde des objets partiels internes, inrojetés et projetés, alimentaires et excrémentiels, nous l'appelons monde des* simulacres.' (LdS 218), (LoS 187). As we will observe later, Deleuze reserves the concept of the phantasm to experiences emerging on the metaphysical surfaces only. This issue will be discussed in Chapters five and six.

realize the Idea he or she must express. These people remain an inadequate and deficient copy. Deleuze criticizes this image of the world and thought. The overturning of Platonism does not mean that the Ideas must be replaced with copies.[46] Philosophy that wants to deny the existence of Ideas, and preach the primacy of copies, is not critical enough.[47] The world cannot be given back to the sophists. People, such as those mentioned above, do not play roles in a theatre. They do not participate in an unengaged masquerade. A philosopher pleading for a simple destruction of Ideas remains captured by the conceptual parameters of an image of thought that in the end, has to presuppose the existence of transcendent Ideas. For Deleuze, such a philosophy is a sophistry that has been justly contested by Plato.

The concept of the simulacrum, which was initially characterised by Plato in merely negative terms, must prevent us from taking such a deficient point of view.[48] For Plato, a simulacrum is a deficient copy. It is a copy that is incapable of representing the original or the Idea, in a meaningful way. In the *Sophist* Plato discusses briefly the example of the statues of Greek Gods. The statues are meant to represent their original perfect bodies. The products of his contemporaries are nevertheless not even worthy of the name copy. Plato points to the fact that they do not even maintain the exact mathematical proportions of the bodies they are meant to portray. The perspective of the viewers, unable to make a judgement upon the correct and just proportions, is the primary concern of their builders. The viewers must be impressed. A statue of a god always has a larger upper body and an even larger head. This allows the viewer, who perceives it from the ground, to appreciate it as beautiful. Adaptation to a human perspective is nevertheless an impermissible distortion. The opportunity to perceive the true proportions of a body of a god is taken away from the public. The perspective of an individual destroys the

---

[46] This argument is used by Heidegger in his monumental analysis of Nietzsche's work (Heidegger 2008). Such a overturning would only lead to plain relativism. It would lead to statements about the non-existence of truth and the predominance of appearances.

[47] Deleuze devotes a whole appendix to the concept of a simulacrum, remarking: '*Bien plus, une telle formule du renversement a l'inconvénient d'être abstraite; elle laisse dans l'ombre la motivation du platonisme. Renverser le platonisme doit signifier au contraire mettre au jour cette motivation, « traquer » cette motivation – comme Platon traquer le sophiste.*' (LdS 292), (LoS 253).

[48] See Plato (1989), *Sophist* i.a.236 a. 'STRANGER: Not always; in works either of sculpture or of painting, which are of any magnitude, there is a certain degree of deception; for if artists were to give the true proportions of their fair works, the upper part, which is farther off, would appear to be out of proportion in comparison to the lower, which is nearer; and so they give up the truth in their images and make only the proportions which appear to be beautiful, disregarding the real ones. THEAETETUS: Quite true.' Deleuze discusses it in the appendix (LdS 295-296), (LoS 256).

truth. Plato wishes to limit the impact of such mad constructions and searches for a transcendent order that will impose a limit upon the proliferation of such distorted individual perspectives.[49]

Deleuze, on the other hand, is interested exactly in the perspectivism presupposed in the analysis of the simulacra. An observer who perceives a simulacrum embodies a point of view before which everything can be transforming itself.[50] The statue cannot exist without this perspective. A Greek god can appear as perfect only to a human. Sculpting according to the exact mathematical proportions makes little sense. It would merely distort the proportions of the statue that is to be appreciated from the human perspective. The order Plato speaks about does not exist in advance, unrelated to the humans. It emerges together with the simulacra, out of the original dispersion and differences. The concept of a simulacrum allows Deleuze to deny the primacy of the opposition between the copy and original.[51] Nothing is being copied here. The simulacrum allows for the emergence of two series – two ways of organizing parts of reality – the series of imperfect humans and perfect gods. None of the series can be conceived of as more original. The perfect body of a god emerges only in relation to a series of imperfect human bodies. It emerges as a reflection of the one who wants to be perfect. A human can only pursue perfection given a relation with a perfect god. Deleuze understands a simulacrum as a sign that emerges out of a field of tensions. The defective human and a perfect god are an expression of simulating forces. The defective human emerges together with the idea of perfection.[52] This simulacrum allows for the emergence of a specific kind of a human, one that

---

[49] Deleuze writes: '*Bref, il y a dans le simulacre un devenir-fou, un devenir illimité comme celui du Philèbe (…). Imposer une limite à ce devenir, l'ordonner au même, le rendre semblable – et, pour la part qui resterait rebelle, la refouler le plus profond possible, l'enfermer dans une caverne au fond de l'Océan: tel est le but du platonisme dans sa volonté de faire triompher les icônes sur les simulacres.*' (LdS 298), (LoS 259).

[50] As Deleuze puts this: '*Le simulacre est construit sur une disparité, sur une différence, il intériorise une dissimilitude.*' (…). '*Le simulacre inclut en soi le point de vue différentiel; l'observateur fait partie du simulacre lui-même, qui se transforme et se déforme avec son point de vue.*' (LdS 298), (LoS 258).

[51] I comment here upon the following sentence: '*Le simulacre n'est pas une copie dégradée, il recèle une puissance positive qui nie et l'original et le copie, et le modèle et la reproduction. Des deux séries divergentes au moins intériorisées dans le simulacre* (the series of perfect gods and imperfect humans – PS), *aucune ne peut être assignée comme l'original, aucune comme la copie… Il n'y a pas plus de point de vue privilégié que d'objet commun a tous les points de vue.*' (LdS 303), (LoS 262).

[52] Deleuze expresses this as follows in Appendix 1 of *The Logic of Sense*: '*Que le Même et le Semblable soient simulés ne signifié pas qu'ils soient des apparences ou des illusions. La simulation désigne la puissance de produire un effet. Mais ce n'est pas seulement au sens causal, … C'est au sens de 'signe', issu d'un processus de signalisation.*' (LdS 304), (LoS 263).

perceives itself as imperfect. A simulacrum simulates and produces effects. It is an expression of a force. From the perspective of Deleuze, a statue of a Greek god is not a copy, imperfectly representing the pre-established transcendent godly perfection. A statue itself allows for the emergence of both the idea of godly perfection and the idea of human deficiency. The two emerge out of the initial mutual relation.

Given this explanation, we are now capable of understanding why the concept of a simulacrum is used to describe the phantasmatic life of the paranoid-schizoid or schizoid position. A child in the paranoid-schizoid position is not aware of the existence of an external order. It does not yet realise that it will be submitted to external laws of the world dominated by fundamental differences and oppositions.[53] The child is not yet aware of the existence of a mother, a father, brothers or sisters and the laws governing their behaviour. It is neither aware of the fact that humans communicate by means of a language nor that they live in a society which functions according to a number of fixed rules. The psychic representations of his initial experience – the simulacra – arise irrespective of any external order. The child experiences only various excitations which are experienced to different degrees of intensity. Hence the words it hears are not experienced as carriers of pre-established meaning. They are a noise that varies only in intensity. The individual experience of the world commences with independent construction of simulacra. For Deleuze, each person is capable of developing their perspective upon the world. He or she possesses a capacity to construct his or her own world. Nevertheless, this capacity is not lost with the emergence of the later awareness of the existence of external order. Each person is capable of living in a world devoid of transcendence, a world without judgement over the immanence. Our experiences are not a reflection of the experiences of somebody else. They are to a high degree independent of the shared order of signifiers.[54] The connection with an external structure only emerges given the

---

[53] Deleuze states: '*Il apparaît d'abord que la position paranoïde-schizoïde se confond avec le développement d'une profondeur orale-anale, profondeur sans fond. Tout commence par l'abîme.*' (LdS 219), (LoS 188).

[54] Employing this argument, Deleuze opposes Lacan's structuralist psychoanalysis, developed in the fifties and sixties. For Lacan, each experience must be guided by language and the symbolic order. The child must accept its existence and internalise its implicit norms in order to understand and master their own behaviour. The lack of this acknowledgement will lead to psychosis. Lacan's theoretical framework does not allow one to speak of simulacra in a positive sense, as Deleuze does. The physical and singular experiences of an individual in the end are only able to enjoy the status of a copy. For an excellent introduction to Lacan and this topic, refer to Fink (1997: 79), '*Lacanian Psychoanalysis, theory and technique*', Cambridge: HUP.

development of subsequent levels of organisation of the psyche. The concept of the simulacrum therefore forms the core of Deleuze's critique of Platonism. A simulacrum simulates. Shared meaning always emerges out of a primary individual experience. It is always dependent upon the singular manner in which everyone constructs her own world.[55]

5. The schizoid position

I have here attempted to clarify why Deleuze uses the concept of the simulacrum to characterise the imagination appropriate to the paranoid-schizoid position. Is Deleuze nevertheless cautious enough in his description of those experiences? Is he not writing an unacceptable plea in support of schizophrenia?[56] This is not the case. Deleuze fully embraces the analysis by Melanie Klein. The paranoid-schizoid position is characterized by a high degree of suffering that cannot be glorified in any manner. Pleasure and security only temporarily suspend fear and tension. Deleuze distances himself from the Kleinian analysis in a minor way only. According to him, it is not necessary to progress towards the manic-depressive position in order to gain control over the schizoid suffering.[57] The new position will generate an equal degree of fear and frustration.[58] The schizoid fears can be controlled from within the schizoid position itself. So far we have analysed one solution to the schizoid fears. The negative tension may be diminished by the continuous introjections of good partial objects that temporarily suspend the states of tension and fear appearing after the effect of the introjection is worn out. A schizophrenic lives in a vicious circle. A different possibility nevertheless exists. A child, or a person who regresses to the schizoid position, in not only willing to annihilate all tension. This person can resist the impact of continuous stimuli

---

[55] The relation between the simulacra and the phantasms that is proper to the metaphysical surface is discussed in Chapter six. (See appendix 1 'Simulacre et philosophie Antique', in The Logic of Sense). For an analysis of the concept of the simulacrum, see also: Brian Massumi, (1987), 'Realer than real, The Simulacrum According to Deleuze and Guattari', in Copyright no.1.

[56] For an interesting discussion on the role of schizophrenia in Deleuze's work, refer to: Evelyne Grossman and Jacob Rogozinski (2008). Rogozinski, particularly, criticises Deleuze, for underestimating the degree of psychic suffering in the case of schizophrenia.

[57] Klein expresses this as follows: 'The very experience of depressive feelings in turn has the effect of further integrating the ego, because it makes for an increased understanding of psychic reality and better perception of the external world, as well as for a greater synthesis between inner and external situations.' (Klein 1947: 189).

[58] The new forms of frustration and fear, proper to the manic-depressive position, are discussed in Chapter three.

by establishing a sense of unity. This experience of unity, evident for example in the retreat from the world described by terms such as autism, catatonia, is accompanied by a specific simulacrum. This simulacrum is called by Deleuze the body without organs, a term borrowed from the famous French poet and artist Antoine Artaud.[59]

To properly understand the working of the simulacrum of the body without organs, Deleuze slightly amends the description of the paranoid-schizoid position. According to him, the good partial object must be differently conceptualised.[60] It cannot be introjected in the same manner as the bad partial object, he states. The pleasure caused by the introjections of various objects will always have a drawback. A child always expects that the pleasurable stimuli will directly change into unpleasant tension. The negative tension is permanently present and cannot be overcome by introjections of objects. The insertion of even more food or enforcing of the continual presence of another person will not wipe out uncertainty. Every object that produces pleasure and provides certainty axiomatically contains threatening parts.[61] Organic food, consumed by a paranoid consumer, will always be threatening. It will never be fully trusted as it might possess some threatening parts, such as cancerous chemicals. The partial good object is always contaminated, consequently leading to a feeling of persecution.[62] According to Deleuze, the primitive thinking processes characterising the schizoid position lead to a perception of everything that is fragmented as a bad object. The bad object is an object in pieces.[63] Objects necessarily fall apart and strengthen the feelings

---

[59] Here, I discuss only the characteristics of the body without organs that are described in *The Logic of Sense* and abstracted from the later development of the concept in the work carried out with Guattari.

[60] Deleuze comments: '*Mais, à cet égard, dans ce domaine des objets partiels et des morceaux qui peuplent la profondeur orale-anale, nous ne sommes pas sûrs que le «bon objet» (le bon sein) puisse être considère comme introjeté au même titre que le mauvais.*' (LdS 219), (LoS 188).

[61] I refer here to the following passage: '*Mélanie Klein montre elle-même que le clivage de l'objet en bon en mauvais dans l'introjection se double d'un morcellement auquel le bon objet ne résiste pas, puisqu'on n'est jamais sûr qu'il ne cache pas un mauvais morceau.*' (LdS 219), (LoS 188).

[62] As Deleuze notes: '*Bien plus, est mauvais par principe (c'est-à-dire à persécuter et persécuteur) tout ce qui est morceau; seul l'intègre, le complet est bon; mais, précisément, l'introjection ne laisse pas subsister l'intègre.*' (LdS 219), (LoS 188).

[63] In the following words Deleuze expresses this: '*Bien plus, est mauvais par principe (c'est-à-dire à persécuter et persécuteur) tout ce qui est morceau.*' (LdS 219), (LoS 188). Klein suggests a similar conclusion in her analysis of the good breast and observes: 'Therefore in addition to the divorce between a good and a bad breast in the young infant's phantasy, the frustrating breast – attacked in oral-sadistic phantasies – is felt to be in fragments; the gratifying breast, taken in under the dominance of the sucking libido, is felt to be complete. This first internal good object acts as a focal point in the ego. It counteracts the processes of splitting and dispersal, makes for cohesiveness and integration, and is instrumental in building up the ego' (Klein 1947: 181).

of persecution. The good object must be radically different. It cannot contain any separate parts.[64] It must be complete. Nevertheless, according to him, no object can be absorbed as complete. The nature of the process of introjection does not allow for absorption in a complete state. The physical absorption necessarily leads to a splintering.[65]

The dynamic of the schizoid position cannot be understood by opposing the good and bad partial objects but rather by means of a different opposition.[66] According to Deleuze, the ego of the schizoid position oscillates between two depths or two forms of the id.[67] It oscillates, on the one hand, between a body without organs and, on the other, the partial objects.[68] An example mentioned by Deleuze that may clarify the distinction between the two kinds of depths, is jaw-grinding. This activity testifies to the existence of the first depth, of a struggle against the internal bad partial objects.[69] By means of the jaw-grinding the body makes an attempt to destroy the attacking objects. This first depth is hollow. It is full of whirling and exploding bits and pieces. It is a mixture of hard and solid elements, a mixture of scraps.[70] The second depth is different in nature. The body without organs is a complete and uncorrupted body. It is a body without a mouth and without an anus, a body that has given up all introjections and projections.[71] Only this resistance to interactions, and the

---

[64] In Deleuze's words: '*seul l'intègre, le complet est bon.*' (LdS 219), (LoS 188).

[65] As Deleuze remarks: '*mais, précisément, l'introjection ne laisse pas subsister l'intègre.*' (LdS 219), (LoS 188).

[66] I am referring to the following passage: '*C'est pourquoi d'une part l'équilibre propre à la position schizoïde, d'autre part son rapport avec la position dépressive ultérieure, ne semblent pas pouvoir résulter de l'introjection d'un bon objet comme tel, et doivent être révisés Ce que la position schizoïde oppose aux mauvais objets partiels introjetés et projetés, toxiques et excrémentiels, oraux et anaux, ce n'est pas un bon objet même partiel, c'est plutôt un organisme sans parties, un corps sans organes, sans bouche et sans anus, ayant renoncé à toute introjection ou projection, et complet à ce prix.*' (LdS 220), (LoS 188).

[67] I refer here to the following sentence: '*C'est la que se forme la tension du Ça et du moi.*' (LdS 220), (LoS 188).

[68] I am referencing the following passage: '*Ce qui s'oppose, ce sont deux profondeurs, la profondeur creuse où tournoient et explosent des morceaux, et la profondeur plein – deux mélanges, l'un de fragments durs et solides, qui altère; l'autre liquide, fluide et parfait, sans parties ni altération, parce qu'il a la propriété de fondre et de souder (tous les os dans un bloc de sang).*' (LdS 220), (LoS 189).

[69] Here I have in mind the following passage: '*La même dualité de pôles complémentaires se retrouve dans la schizophrénie entre les réitérations et les persévérations, par exemple entre les crissements de mâchoire et les catatonies, les unes témoignant des objets internes et du corps qu'ils morcellent et qui les morcellent à la fois, les autres manifestant pour le corps sans organes.*' (LdS 221), (LoS 189).

[70] I refer here to the following sentence: '*l'un de fragments durs et solides, qui altère*' (LdS 220), (LoS 189).

[71] As Deleuze states: '*un organisme sans parties, un corps sans organes, sans bouche et sans anus, ayant renoncé à toute introjection ou projection, et complet à ce prix.*' (LdS 220), (LoS 188).

state of emptiness it makes possible, allows for an experience of completeness. A body without organs is not in a state of tormenting tension. It is a body that stops eating and closes itself off from the world. Only by means of this activity is it able to make the negative tensions vanish. It experiences an emptiness that is an alternative to the vicious circle of continuous introjections. A simulacrum of the body without organs can therefore become an alternative for the consumer of biological food, who no longer bears the uncertainty proper to the consumption of any kind of food. Only the lack of consumption will allow it to reach a state of peace. This simulacrum may be equally present in case of anorexia that, viewed from this perspective, should be understood as a way of controlling the schizoid tensions. Anorexia may be considered to be an act of resistance to the continuous flows of products enforced upon the body, a choice that allows control over a particular kind of suffering.[72] Seen from Deleuzian perspective, anorexia is to be treated as a choice. It leads to a life at a great risk of disappearing entirely in the empty unity offered to the body by the simulacrum. It requires a search for an equilibrium in order to prevent such annihilation.

Nevertheless, according to Deleuze, the unity established by the body without organs does not only emerge through the reaching of a state of emptiness. It cannot be made equal to a state of complete rest reached by a separation from the world, to a state of catatonia.[73] The body without organs might also lead to a different experience. The various tensions can be soldered into a unity. The second depth may also correspond to the experience of fullness.[74] It could correspond to the experience of a fluid mixture. In this case the body without organs contains no morsels. It is not submitted to any change. It is complete. It solders the various parts into a whole.[75] The strongly separated elements, the bones, the pieces of food and various other experiences of the body become a unity. The tormented depths reach a state of perfection. The various negative tensions, the continuous states of threat are neutralised. The separate parts dissolve within an all-encompassing entity. The physical origin of this simulacrum can be found in the experiences of

---

[72] Anorexia is also analysed in the introduction to *Anti-Oedipus* (AE: 1, 325) in *Dialogues* (D: 90) and *A Thousand Plateaus*. MP (185-204), (ATP: 149-166).

[73] It must be stressed that catatonia in this form does not occur frequently in contemporary mental institutions as it is prevented by medication.

[74] I refer here to: '*l'autre liquide, fluide et parfait, sans parties ni altération, parce qu'il a la propriété de fondre et de souder (tous les os dans un bloc de sang).*' (LdS 220), (LoS 189).

[75] I have in mind: '*qu'il a la propriété de fondre et de souder (tous les os dans un bloc de sang).*' (LdS 220). (LoS 189).

fluidity, occurring during urinating.[76] It differs greatly from the experiences proper to the anal zone. This distinction is not to be found in Melanie Klein's work.[77] According to Deleuze the excrements are hard and similar to the separate organs and scraps of experience. They are threatening because they can contain toxic substances. They are being used as weapons against other threatening scraps and pieces. Urinating, on the other hand, testifies to the existence of what Deleuze calls the liquid principle.[78] Urine does not consist of broken morsels and cannot be used as a weapon against the environment. It is not charged with aggression that can be projected only on the partial objects. Fluid joins the separate pieces into a unity. It generates a full depth.

To understand these rather extravagant statements, we can connect the analysis of the principle of liquidity to different experiences generated in art. One of the most beautiful images that illustrates this principle can be found at the end of the movie *Kaos* – part *Colloquio con la madre* – made by the brothers Taviani. *Kaos* ends with an image of children running down from a dune towards the sea. The sea brings reconciliation. It generates a state of rest by abolishing all tension. Water provides a way out of the tormented experiences of life.[79] The principle of liquidity plays an equally fundamental role in the work of other film directors. Tarkovsky continually uses images of water and rain in his films to generate a sense of relief and peace. Water soothes the spirit that is on fire. It plays a crucial role in one of the most beautiful scenes of Tarkovsky's work, a crucial moment in the film 'Andrej Roebljow', when a woman flees into an immense Russian river. The woman escapes from

---

[76] I attempt to clarify the following sentence: '*Il ne semble pas en ce sens que le thème urethral puisse être mis sur le même plan que le thème anal; car, si les excréments sont toujours des organes et des morceaux, tantôt redoutés comme substances toxiques, tantôt utilisés comme armes pour émietter encore d'autres morceaux, l'urine au contraire témoigne d'un principe mouillé capable de lier tous les morceaux ensemble, et de surmonter l'émiettement dans la profondeur pleine d'un corps devenu sans organes.*' (LdS 220), (LoS 189).

[77] In a footnote, Deleuze notes that Klein herself does not differentiate between the anal and urethral sadism. This is one of the reasons why psychoanalysis has not been able to understand the concept of the body without organs. As Deleuze puts this: '*Mélanie Klein n'établit pas de différence de nature entre le sadisme anal et le sadisme urethral, et s'en tient à son principe d'après lequel « l'inconscient n'établit pas de distinction entre les diverses substances des corps ». Plus généralement, il nous a semblé que la théorie psychanalytique de la schizophrénie avait tendance à négliger l'importance et le dynamisme du thème corps sans organes.*' (LdS 220). (LoS 351).

[78] I refer to: '*l'urine au contraire témoigne d'un principe mouillé capable de lier tous les morceaux ensemble, et de surmonter l'émiettement dans la profondeur pleine d'un corps devenu sans organes.*' (LdS 220), (LoS 189).

[79] The murder of the peasants is the reason why Roebljow stops to paint religious themes. Similar images can also be found in other films, such as at the end of Żuławski's *Mes nuits sont plus belles que vos jours*.

49

the soldiers, who chase her for participating, along with her whole village, in forbidden pagan rituals – the midsummer night. She escapes a certain death. Her husband and other pagan farmers have already been killed for celebrating this heathen feast of fertility. The big river is literally her salvation. It absorbs her and places her out of the soldiers' reach.

6. Artaud, language and schizophrenia

Deleuze borrowed the idea of the body without organs from Antoine Artaud, who spoke about a body that does not know any tension and that constitutes a fluid unity. Deleuze discusses this point further in 'Thirteenth Series of the Schizophrenic and the Little Girl.'[80] Artaud has also made a distinction between two depths: between the dangerous morsels and the principle of liquidity. The ego confronted with the first depth is always passive. It offers no resistance to the states imposed by the threatening partial objects. This passivity can be broken by the experience of fluidity.[81] A victory over the suffering of the body is possible. According to Deleuze Artaud's poetry and performances testify to the power of the principle of liquidity over the dangerous morsels. His howls and screams particularly express a striving towards unity. The scream, full of the consonants, integrates the separate shouts. It is the body without organs at work. This striving towards unity out of depths is unknown to Carroll, an author greatly admired and extensively analysed in *The Logic of Sense*.[82] In *Alice in Wonderland*, Carroll merely plays with the meaning of the words. This is a highly artificial endeavour that remains on the surface of sense. His language games are unable to reveal the suffering, proper to the depths. Carroll's games

---

[80] To clarify his position he points to the difference between Artaud's and Lewis Carroll's work. Carroll, famous for his book *Alice in Wonderland*, is interested in depths, but is unable to reach them in the end. Deleuze makes the following point: '*Une petite fille peut chanter 'Pimpanicaille', un artiste écrire 'frumieux', un schizophrène' dire 'perspendicace': nous avons aucune raison de croire que le problème soit le même, pour des résultats grossièrement analogues. Il n'est pas sérieux de confondre la chanson de Babar et les cris-souffles d'Artaud, « Ratara ratara ratara Atara tatara rana Otara otara katara …'* (LdS 102). (LoS 83).

[81] Here I have in mind the following passage: '*Il y a dans la schizophrénie une manière de vivre la distinction stoïcienne entre deux mélanges corporels, le mélange partiel et qui altère, le mélange total et liquide qui laisse le corps intact. Il y a, dans l'élément fluide ou liquide insufflé, le secret non écrit d'une mélange actif qui est comme le « principe de la Mer », par opposition avec les mélanges passifs des parties emboîtées.*' (LdS 109). (LoS 89).

[82] In 'The Thirteenth Series of the Schizophrenic' Deleuze comments: '*Pour tout Carroll, nous ne donnerions pas une page d'Antonin Artaud; Artaud est le seul à avoir été profondeur absolue dans la littérature, et découvert un corps vital et le langage prodigieux de ce corps, à force de souffrance, comme il dit. I l explorait l'infra-sens, aujourd'hui encore inconnu.*' (LdS 114), (LoS 93).

directly presuppose a distinction between body and speech. They play with meaning and are a game unknown and useless for a schizophrenic who experiences each word as an expression of a direct physical state and never as a vehicle to convey meaning. Carroll is blind to schizophrenic suffering and he is unable to point towards a way out of it. Artaud, on the other hand, is fully in touch with the depths. The words and howls of his poetry are charged with the forces of the depths and express the physical schizoid suffering. Artaud's shouts (*cris-souffles*) establish a unity and heal the shattered experience of the depths.

A French philosopher, Jacob Rogozinski,[83] has criticised Deleuze's reading of Artaud. According to him, we cannot just claim that Artaud was able to affirm his own suffering. He might not have been able to express an affirmative, vital force. Artaud's screams are merely an expression of fears and suffering. They are by no means an example of a victory.[84] Artaud's work and life do not really fit within the vitalism characterising Deleuze's philosophy. Sad passions and mental suffering are inescapable and must be continually expressed. He opines that Deleuze's attempts to provide us with a way out of these experiences are just too easy. Nevertheless, this critique does little justice to the claims of Deleuze. Schizophrenia is not glorified here. The degree of Artaud's mental suffering is not underestimated. The simulacrum of the body without organs is a construction emerging within such a tormented world. The simulacrum allows Artaud to resist. It is not an easy way out but rather an expression of continuous attempts to gain control over his life. With all the force he possesses, he continually tries to become a vital, unified body. Unlike many others, Artaud succeeds in soldering the words and his experience into a unity. He discovers the principle of water or fire.[85]

Deleuze substantiates his reading of Artaud's work in his analysis of the language proper to the schizoid position.[86] In this position there is not yet any distinction between words and the body. In the schizoid experience everything

---

[83] See Evelyne Grossman & Jacob Rogozinski, (2008).

[84] Monique David-Ménard (2005: 150) arrives at the same conclusion. Mastery over one's own suffering is an option hardly achievable from the clinical perspective. Psychoanalytic practice consists of a confrontation with one's own weakness. The Spinozist sad passions remain dominant. The suffering can only be limited to a certain extent.

[85] Deleuze states this as follows: '*Et, si l'on suppose que le schizophrène, avec tout le langage acquis, régresse jusqu'à cette position schizoïde, on ne s'étonnera pas de retrouver dans le langage schizophrénique la dualité et la complémentarité des mots-passions, blocs soudés par un principe d'eau ou de feu.*' (LdS 220), (LoS 189).

[86] I refer here to the following passage: '*Et si l'on suppose que le schizophrène, avec tout le langage acquis, régresse jusqu'à cette position schizoïde, on ne s'étonnera pas de retrouver dans le langage schizophrénique la dualité et la complémentarité des mots-passions, morceaux excrémentiels éclatés, et des mots-actions, blocs soudés par un principe d'eau ou de feu.*' (LdS 220), (LoS 189).

is a body. The separation between things and words is not yet established. There exist only depths. The direct interactions between bodies are unmediated.[87] A schizophrenic is incapable of producing words as separate entities. This will happen only on the surface of sense. In the depths, a word refers merely to emptiness. It renders something present that is of no importance to the one uttering the word. The words lack meaning.[88] They cannot be distinguished from the body and the direct experience. Speech is a physical activity.[89] The schizophrenic use of words does not refer to the future, a major condition for functioning of a language. The words do neither refer to ideal events and do not express the unknown, asserts Deleuze. The schizoid speech lacks a certain kind of freedom. It does not allow for a free play of meaning. Every word is treated as a separate entity that is not a part of a broader structure. Meaning disintegrates into little pieces. It consists of syllables, letters and sounds that directly affect and attack the body.

According to Deleuze, the schizoid language is characterised by two kinds of words. First there are the word-passions (*mots-passions*) that characterise the disintegrated character of this language. Those words are separate. They are experienced as exploding parts that attack the body. Nevertheless, Deleuze also distinguishes the words-actions (*mots-actions*). Those words do not convey a special kind of meaning, but are, rather, capable of soldering the words-passions into a unity. Those words are guided by the principle of water or fire. The screams of Artaud that were mentioned above belong to this second category. They allow the schizophrenic to defend himself against the attacks of the words-passions.[90] Artaud struggles against the disintegration characterising

---

[87] I here have in mind the following passage from 'The Thirteenth Series of the Schizophrenic': '*La première évidence schizophrénique, c'est que la surface est crevée. Il n'y a plus de frontière entre les choses et les propositions, précisément parce qu'il n'y a plus de surface des corps. Le premier aspect du corps schizophrénique, c'est une sorte de corps-passoire: Freud soulignait cette aptitude du schizophrène à saisir la surface et la peau comme percée d'une infinité de petits trous. La conséquence en est que le corps tout entier n'est plus que profondeur, et emporte, happe toutes choses dans cette profondeur béante qui représente une involution fondamentale. Tout est corps et corporel. Tout est mélange de corps et dans le corps, emboîtement, pénétration. Tout est de la physique, comme dit Artaud; «nous avons dans le dos des vertèbres pleines, transpercées par le clou de la douleur et qui, par la marche, l'effort des poids à soulever, la résistance au laisser-aller, font en s'emboîtant l'une sur l'autre des boîtes».*' (LdS 106), (LoS 87).

[88] I refer here to the following sentence: '*Dans cette faillite de la surface, le mot tout entier perd son sens.*' (LdS 107), (LoS 87).

[89] As Deleuze states: '*Mais il perd en tous cas son sens, c'est-à-dire sa puissance à recueillir ou à exprimer un effet incorporel distinct des actions et des passions du corps, un événement idéel distinct de sa propre effectuation présente.*' (LdS 107), (LoS 87).

[90] I refer to the following passage here: '*Et de même que le blessant, tout à l'heure, était dans les éléments phonétiques affectant les parties du corps emboîte ou déboîte, le triomphe ne peut être obtenu maintenant que par l'instauration de mots-souffles de mots-cris où toutes les valeurs*

the schizoid position without the knowledge of the surface. He does not need words that convey particular meaning. He is capable of undoing the fragmentation by means of the howl-words and breath-words. In those words all literal, syllabic and phonetic values are replaced by tonic ones (*valeurs toniques*). Artaud's body starts to sing. The modulation replaces the literal and syllabic values. A word-action expresses the struggle against the shattered experience. The words-actions cannot be divided. They cannot disintegrate. Artaud's language of words-actions lacks articulation. It establishes a unity and arrives in the vicinity of a fluidity, close to the principle of the sea that eliminates all tension.[91] It prevents the words from attacking the weak ego.

Artaud's and Deleuze's work have also exerted a major influence on other artistic practices, such as our contemporary theatre and dance. The simulacrum of the body without organs is, for example, occasionally generated in contemporary modern dance. A choreographer working in the Netherlands – Bruno Listopad – uses it to guide his work. His choreographies are far removed from the classical ballet that provides the dancers and the public with the security of a limited set of moves and with a pleasurable organised aesthetic experience. The dancers of Listopad do not dance according to limited patterns of movement. Their dance is spastic and full of suffering. It is shattered. At various moments the dancers nevertheless seem to be capable of overcoming this experience and produce the equivalents of Artaud's words-actions. Reconciliation, but also unification of the shattered experience becomes possible. Psychic suffering is temporarily defeated also in dance.

A similar simulacrum may also be found at work in literature. The behaviour of Bartleby, the main hero of a short story by Melville, expresses a similar tendency. In the beginning of the story the scrivener exercises his work with great precision and devotion. He nevertheless starts to malfunction and slowly regresses into what we can call the schizoid position. He refuses to speak and ceases to complete the assigned tasks. He starts to fall asleep in the office. At the end of the story he dies. His only response to all the requests is to utter the strange sounding formula '*I would prefer not to*'. It would be wrong

---

littérales, syllabiques et phonétiques sont remplacées par des valeurs exclusivement toniques et non écrites, auxquelles correspond un corps glorieux comme nouvelle dimension du corps schizophrénique, un organisme sans parties qui fait tout par insufflation, inspiration, évaporation, transmission fluidique (le corps supérieur ou corps sans organes d'Antonin Artaud).' (LdS 108), (LoS 88).

[91] Deleuze writes: '*Il y a dans la schizophrénie une manière de vivre la distinction stoïcienne entre deux mélanges corporels, le mélange partiel et qui altère, le mélange total et liquide qui laisse le corps intact. Il y a, dans l'élément fluide ou liquide insufflé, le secret non écrit d'une mélange actif qui est comme le « principe de la Mer », par opposition avec les mélanges passifs des parties emboîtées.*' (LdS 109), (LoS 89).

to state that the story of Bartleby is one of mental deterioration. Bartleby does not strive towards death, towards nothingness. The use of the formula implies a bond with the world. Bartleby does not refuse to live. The formula allows him to discover a new way of being. It allows him to neutralise the language and the rules of conduct proper to his society. The formula cannot be understood by a reference to a shared system of meaning. It does not carry a hidden but, instead, a decipherable message. It is part of a schizoid language. It allows Bartleby to refuse or negate the will to act enforced upon him by the capitalist society; the formula allows him to remain motionless, as Deleuze contends in a later essay.[92] His regression allows him to serve a higher goal. For Deleuze, Bartleby is a clinician of the capitalist society. Bartleby is capable of constructing a different schizoid response.[93]

7. Conclusion

The account of the dynamic genesis of sense is analysed here from three perspectives. It is treated as a psychoanalytic theory, as a philosophical account about the emergence of sense and as a specific period in Deleuze's thought about desire. This chapter has provided us with an analysis of the experience of the world out of the schizoid position. The said experience appeared to be characterised in terms of pleasure and negative tensions. In the schizoid position the death drive, aggression and a self-preservation drive are mixed with the libido and strengthen the person's fears and distrust of the surroundings. The partial objects attack the body and threaten to tear it apart. It was evident that the schizoid position can be referred to as a vicious circle. Continuous absorption of new good partial objects is the first way out of the misery of schizoid experience. In the second part of the chapter we noticed that Deleuze redefines the architecture of the paranoid-schizoid position that was developed by Klein. The conflict between good and bad partial objects is in no sense primary and is preceded by an opposition between the partial objects and the complete body without organs. Hence the second option for

---

[92] In the text 'Bartleby; or the Formula' Deleuze avers: '*La formule anéantit « copier », la seule référence par rapport à laquelle quelque chose pourrait être ou non préféré. Je préférais rien plutôt que quelque chose: non pas une volonté de néant, mais la croissance d'un néant de volonté. Bartleby a gagné le droit de survivre, c'est-à-dire de se tenir immobile et debout face à un mur aveugle. (…) Il ne peut survivre qu'en tournoyant dans un suspens qui tient tout le monde à distance.*' (CeC 92), (ECC: 71).

[93] Deleuze notes: '*Vocation schizophrénique: même catatonique en anorexique, Bartleby n'est pas le malade, mais le médecine d'une Amérique malade, le Medicine-man, le nouveau Christ ou notre frère à tous.*' (CeC 114), (ECC: 90).

overcoming the schizoid suffering is found in either a withdrawal from the continuous absorption of objects or in an attempt to generate an experience of unity. A schizophrenic does not only have the option to turn away from the world, closing himself off in his own secret universe. His 'no' is also a solution. The simulacrum of the body without organs allows him to strive towards fullness or emptiness as a manner of defeating tensions and conflicts. The no of an anorectic sufferer, of Artaud, modern dance or of Bartleby, may well be an affirmation. It is a search for a body that unites all experience and that solders all the fragments into a unity. This analysis allows one also to partially understand the nature of Deleuze's critique of a structuralist psychoanalysis. Psychosis and schizophrenia are not a pathology generated by a negation of the world, by the lack of acceptance of the symbolic order. Schizophrenia is an independent construction, generating a peculiar relation towards the world.

One is now also able to understand why Deleuze is so interested in Klein's work during this period of his writing. Life commences with a phase in which simulacra play a fundamental role. A child constructs its own free relationship to its surroundings, without any awareness of the existence of an order that attaches meaning to actions. The schizoid position expresses our capacity to relate to our environment without the mediation of a pre-given external structure. Noticeable here is an analysis that will be returning in Deleuze's collaboration with Guattari. Schizophrenic experience of a world, one unmediated by an external structure, is universal and must be cherished as such. Some limiting remarks must nevertheless be made here. This experience is always very fragile. Moreover, the schizoid position, by itself, does not allow for a proper construction of sense. Only the completion of all the steps of the dynamic genesis opens up the full possibility for the latter. The schizoid position will be overcome by the development of the depressive position and subsequent developments. The child has to recognise the existence of an external order and, even temporarily, fully submit itself to its demands. The characteristics of this position are analysed in the next chapter.

CHAPTER 3

Depressive position

1. Introduction

The previous chapter was devoted to the analysis of the characteristics of the schizoid position. I have emphasised that in this position individual desire is not organised by an external structure of sense. The schizoid experience consists of states of tension and fear. A child experiences pleasure while absorbing objects and is threatened by their absence or by states of over-excitation. Experiences of aggression and persecution dominate. It became evident that defence against these threats may be found either in a continuous introjection of new, good partial objects or in the experience of emptiness or completeness of the body without organs. In both cases the experiences of fear and tension will continuously and inevitably reappear. For this reason Melanie Klein, in her account of the paranoid-schizoid position, points to the unquestionable importance of a progression towards what she calls the manic-depressive position. According to her, only in this way may a more complete and trustful relationship with the world be developed.

In this chapter I first discuss the characteristics of the manic-depressive position as described by Melanie Klein. I pay attention, for instance, to the characteristics of the psychopathology proper to this position; that is, to depression and mania and their differences from paranoia and schizophrenia. Subsequently, I discuss the amendments to her theory that are developed by Deleuze in 'The Twenty-Seventh Series of Orality'. The reader will perceive how the discovery of the body without organs leads to a change of the characteristics of the complete good object that plays a key role within this position. In this chapter I also discuss the characteristics of an idol, the central object of the depressive position and simulacra proper to the schizoid position. At the end of the chapter, I draw attention to the philosophical implications of Deleuze's analysis of this position by discussing its contribution to the development of language. As in the previous chapter, the analysis focuses both on the psychoanalytic and philosophical aspects of the theory. In several instances, I moreover try to point to similarities and differences between *The Logic of Sense* and Deleuze's other work on desire.

2. The manic-depressive position of Melanie Klein

According to Melanie Klein, the various positions develop during the different developmental phases of a child's life. The paranoid-schizoid position fully determines the experience during the first half year of life, but its influence diminishes when new cognitive developments occur. With time, the child develops the capacity to see objects from a greater distance and is quickly able to differentiate between them. It starts by differentiating between familiar and unfamiliar faces. It also starts to perceive complete objects, instead of just partial ones. For example, the separate parts of a body, such as the breast, hand or face become part of a complete object, such as the mother. The sense of hearing develops equally fast. The noise it hears is progressively organised into separate sounds and subsequently into voices. The increased cognitive capacities also allow the child to start anticipating events in its environment. It now expects food at the moments when the mother approaches.[1] According to Klein, these new cognitive capacities are of tremendous importance for its emotional life. The child who relates to complete objects starts to realise that the parents are taking care of it.[2] The dominant experiences of fear and tension slowly fade away into the background and give place to new ones. The libidinal fixation changes its object. The partial object, such as the breast, is replaced by a complete object, such as the mother.[3] The child starts to identify with these persons. It wants to be similar to the complete objects. It wants to move, laugh and speak in a manner similar to the mother or other caretakers.

This identification leads directly to a state of dependence. The child becomes aware of its own limitations and lack of power. The complete good object exceeds it in all respects. The parents are larger and possess a tremendous amount of knowledge and power. They make all the fundamental decisions. They decide when the child eats, when it is being cleaned, when it goes to

---

[1] For the description of the relationship towards objects from the manic-depressive position see i. a. Paula Heimann (1952: 126), 'Certain functions of introjection and projection in early infancy', in Klein *et al.* (1952) *Developments in Psychoanalysis*, London: Hogarth Press. For the analysis of the role of the death instinct in Klein refer also to van Haute & Geyskens (2007).

[2] Klein expresses this as follows: 'The dread of persecution, which was at first felt on the ego's account, now relates to the good object as well and from now on preservation of the good object is regarded as synonymous with the survival of the ego. Hand in hand with this development goes a change of the highest importance, namely, from a partial object relation to the relation to a complete object. Through this step, the ego arrives at a new position, which forms the foundation of that situation called the loss of the loved object. Not until the object is lived as a whole can its loss be felt as a whole.' (Klein 1935: 118).

[3] Klein 1935: 141.

sleep and when and how it can play. The child needs its parents for its survival. In the analysis of this relation, Klein points not only to the limits imposed by the parents upon a child as Freud does in texts such as *The Ego and the Id*. They are not only imposing restrictions upon the developing sexuality of a child but also fulfil a different role. They take care of the child and protect it. They caress and support. Only the identification with the parents allows for the overcoming of the paranoid-schizoid fears. Only the protection of the good object can defend the ego of a child against the attacks of the bad partial object and guarantee its survival.[4] The interaction with the complete objects in the outside world changes the structure of the psyche. The complete object now becomes part of the internal world. It is incorporated in order to protect the ego against the attacks of bad partial objects.[5] This introjection strengthens the ego that may become less anxious in its interactions with the external objects. The relation between the external and internal objects is nevertheless not lost. The ego continually needs a confirmation of the existence of the good internal object. This is reached by the re-projection of the internal object onto an object in the outside world. The external object serves as the proof of the existence of the internal good object. First, the parents, but later in life a loved one, a boss or a political leader, receive the characteristics of the internal complete good object. These figures secure the existence of the internal good object and help to protect the ego against hostile attacks.[6]

The emergence of the manic-depressive position leads to the predominance of other psychic mechanisms than those in the paranoid-schizoid position. The ego ceases to project as much aggression on its environment. This allows for an increased idealisation of the good object.[7] A mechanism that gains more importance is introjection. The good object must be continually absorbed. Child's phantasmatic life is increasingly directed at its parents, while at a later age objects such as God, a loved one, a political leader or national identity come to the fore. Only the continual introjection of these objects may secure the existence of the internal object. The emergence of the manic-depressive

---

[4] I refer to: '…from now on preservation of the good object is regarded as synonymous with the survival of the ego.' (Klein 1935: 118).

[5] Klein makes the following statement: 'In this stage the ego is more than ever driven both by love and by need to introject the object. Another stimulus for an increase of introjections is the phantasy that the loved object may be preserved in safety inside oneself.' (Klein 1935: 119).

[6] The introjection of the complete object into the psyche during the manic-depressive position is less physical in nature than in the paranoid-schizoid position. The introjection is made possible by extended interactions with the complete objects in the outside world. See Klein (1935: 119).

[7] See: Klein (1935: 120).

position also leads to the strengthening of the psychic mechanism of reparation. According to Klein, the ego not only wants to protect the internal and external objects against the sadistic and aggressive attacks. It also wants to undo the supposed effects of these attacks. The good object must be restored. The ego must prevent its disintegration and disappearance. The child wants to perceive its parents as complete, good objects and puts a lot of psychic effort into forgetting about all the tensions. It frequently blames itself and tries to restore the damage. Klein nevertheless considers these early attempts at restoration as doomed to fail.[8] The ego of the manic-depressive position is not fully capable of trusting in the good intentions of the complete objects because it is still partially subservient to the power of the paranoid-schizoid mechanisms. When parents are perceived as bad partial objects, the attempts at restoration will cease to exist. More importantly, the ego of this position is also weak. The protection or restoration of the good object might be entirely out of its reach.

The manic-depressive position must hence inevitably lead to the emergence of new problems and fears. According to Klein, in the paranoid-schizoid position it is still relatively easy to differentiate between a good and a bad partial object. The bad and good breasts, for example, accompany two very different physical states. This situation alters once the ego relates to complete objects. The sharp distinction between a good and a bad object blurs. Parents can be both a good object and a bad one.[9] They are a source of both pleasure and frustration. They generate a large number of positive experiences but inevitably prohibit many. This ambiguous experience is strengthened by the mechanism of projection which initially still exists. The sadistic and aggressive impulses do not disappear directly and may still be projected onto the complete objects. The parents may be experienced as threatening. The uncertainty and fear do not evaporate. If the sadistic impulses remain equally strong, as in the previous position, they may undermine the belief in the complete good object and prevent the full development of the manic-depressive position.

The most important cause of psychic suffering proper to the fully developed manic-depressive position is nevertheless, not the lack of trust in the good nature of the complete good object as such but rather the fear of losing it. For the ego, this internal object is its only source of protection against the attacks of the bad partial objects. The internal object is its only defence against surrounding aggression and disintegration. The ego struggles first of all to protect it against the attacks of the external bad partial objects. Any possible

---

[8] See: Klein (1935: 120).
[9] See Klein (1935: 141).

attack on the good object is warded off. The parents, political and religious leaders, or the boss- figures that secure the existence of the internal object, cannot contain any bad parts. Hence they are continually idealised while any critique uttered by others against them is directly forgotten or aggressively contested. The existence of the internal good object is nevertheless not only threatened by the external objects. The bad partial objects are also found inside the psyche. The mental struggle proper to this position is also directed against the ego itself.[10] The ego distrusts itself. It struggles against own aggression and other unwanted behaviour. The environment contributes greatly to this sense of distrust. An aggressive or misbehaving child is reprimanded; the punishment leads to a new awareness – the love that guarantees the existence of the internal good object is not unconditional. Only a continuous struggle against the internal bad objects is able to secure this love and protect the ego against the loss of the good object.

The fear of losing the protection of the internal good object due to the attacks of the internal and external bad partial objects is thus permanently present.[11] The ego is continually anxious about a regression to the paranoid-schizoid position and about being delivered to the attacks of the bad objects. Klein speaks of two strategies that could minimise these fears. The first one is the development of the awareness that the external objects – for example the real parents – are always ambivalent in their relation towards the ego. It must come to realise that the loved and hated object can be united in one person. A mother is not only a source of pleasure but also of frustration. A child must learn that the mother is not turning away when she is not fulfilling its wishes. It must therefore develop a clear sense of the difference between the psychic and external realities. It must understand that the real objects and the introjected objects are intertwined but also separated. The temporarily frustrating behaviour of the mother should not lead to a direct fear of losing the internal good object.[12]

---

[10] I base my remarks here on the following passage: 'In my experience there is, furthermore, a deep anxiety as to the dangers which await the object inside the ego. It could not be safely maintained there, as the inside is felt to be a dangerous and poisonous place in which the loved object would perish. Here we see one of the situations which I have described as being fundamental for 'the loss of the loved object', the situation, namely, when the ego becomes fully identified with its good, internalized objects, and at the same time becomes aware of its own incapacity to protect and preserve them against the internalized, persecuting objects and the id.' (Klein 1935: 119).

[11] Klein discusses this in the following words: 'A little child which believes, when his mother disappears, that it has eaten her up and destroyed her (whether from motives of love or hate), is tormented by anxiety both for her and for the good mother which it has absorbed into itself.' (Klein 1935: 121).

[12] See: Klein (1935: 143).

The second strategy that may allow for the overcoming of the fear of losing the good internal object is that of becoming less dependent on one external object for the confirmation of the existence of the internal one. According to Klein, this strategy might help in cases of depression, a state in which the ego actually perceives the internal complete good object as already lost.[13] A depressive person attempts to mask this sense of loss by an excessive orientation towards external objects. Klein discusses an example of an excessive orientation towards a real mother. Severe problems may occur when she is the only external object that masks the lack of the internal good object. Such exclusive identification may for example lead to extreme fears. Every situation that might indicate the mother's death – for example, when she does not pick up the phone – appears to be highly traumatic.[14] The ego continually fears that the loss of the external good object will directly reveal the absence of the internal one. Such fears can be contained in cases where the ego becomes less dependent on one external object. Not only dealing with the fear generated by the absence of a simple telephone conversation, but also coping with the true loss of an external object, could become possible.

Another example of the depressive relationship to objects that can be countered by the strategies mentioned, are the inhibitions at work. In this case, the ego ceases to defend the good object against the hostile attacks. The said object falls to pieces and cannot be restored any more. The attempts to restore this object are perceived as doomed to fail. Attempts at production of a perfect external object that can guarantee the existence of the internal are suspended. Depression unmasks the disintegration and lack of the good internal object. Such inhibitions are frequently present during writing. A book must be welded into a unity and receive the characteristics of the perfect object of the heights.[15] Such attempts will inevitably fail. A depressive person is continually confronted with their own incapacities; merely seeing their own lack of power. They fail to produce an object that can meet the standards of a complete object. The yet unwritten book is in a state of perpetual

---

[13] See: Klein (1935: 121).

[14] I here consider the following passage: 'Both cases signify to it that it has lost its loved mother and I would particularly draw attention to the fact that dread of the loss of the "good", internalized object becomes a perpetual source of anxiety lest the real mother should die. On the other hand, every experience which suggests the loss of the real loved object stimulates the dread of losing the internalized one too.' (Klein 1935: 121). See also Klein (1940), 'Mourning and its relation to manic-depressive states', in Mitchel, J., (ed.) 1986, pp. 146-174.

[15] For Klein, the desire of perfection is unmistakably connected to the depressive fear of disintegration: 'It appears that the desire for perfection is rooted in the depressive anxiety of disintegration, which is thus of great importance in all sublimations'. (Klein 1935: 125).

disintegration.[16] Another example of an activity that may be an expression of depressive tendencies is extreme nationalism. A nation can become the sole object that guarantees the existence of the internal good object. Additionally, in this case significant problems arise: the nation must be protected at all costs. It is in danger of disintegration if anybody is critical of this external object. He or she must therefore be silenced at all costs. Any possible critique is experienced as a direct attack, a threat to the weak ego that is entirely dependent on this object. A substantial amount of stress and conflict with the environment is evoked and the absence of the complete good object must be masked at all costs.

According to Klein, the development of good relations with a variety of external objects, and especially with the analyst, is also crucial for a successful psychoanalytic therapy.[17] It was the key to her successful treatment of the aforementioned patient of hers, known as little Dick. The almost autistic boy was enabled to open himself towards his environment and progressed from the paranoid-schizoid position to the manic-depressive one. Klein was successful in limiting his sadism and aggression by means of strengthening their mutual relation. As an analyst she successfully fulfilled the role of the good object. The parents, good friends or a therapist are indispensable for the development of a strong internal complete good object. They contribute to a trustful and non-violent relation with other objects.[18]

The emergence of the manic-depressive position may be considered to be a liberation for the ego from the paranoid-schizoid position. The most severe anxieties and tensions are able to simply start to fade away. As we have seen, the established liberation is still problematic. The new position introduces new forms of suffering, making the progress towards it far from obvious. What are the reasons for resisting the development of the manic-depressive position? According to Klein, the development of a complete good object can

---

[16] We must point here that depression can lead to very productive results. Many writers have suffered from depression for long periods of time; Andersen, Baudelaire, Dostoyevsky and Foucault furnish some examples.

[17] See for example Klein (1930: 110), 'Symbol formation in the Ego Development', in Mitchel, J., (ed.) (1986).

[18] Klein describes this as follows: 'But as the adaptation to the external world increases, this splitting is carried out on planes, which gradually become increasingly nearer and nearer to reality. This goes on until love for the real and the internalized objects and trust in them are well established. Then ambivalence, which is partly a safeguard against one's own hate and against the hated and terrifying objects, will in normal development again diminish in varying degrees.' (Klein 1935: 144).

be inhibited when the fears of persecution remain strong.[19] In that case, the good object is prevented from becoming a part of the psychic life because the paranoid person is unable to conceive of an object that does not contain any bad parts. The relationships of such people with others are always accompanied by fears of being persecuted by objects that are present in the inside of others. Stable and loving relations are in fact prevented from developing. Another reason preventing the development of the manic-depressive position is the person's incapacity to deal with the new emotions. The intensity of the feeling of guilt, generated by the incapacity to protect the good object, may frequently be experie4nced as unbearable.[20] We are able to observe it in cases of resistance to the strong commandments of the super-ego. A person driven to take up a certain career might begin to resist this commandment due to the incapacity to cope with the stress generated by the high expectations. A monogamous romantic love relationship might be abandoned due to the persistence of the feeling of guilt and submission. Regression to the paranoid-schizoid position and giving up of the relationship to the good object follows.

One may be tempted to regard the complete good object as the origin of morality. For Klein, this is nevertheless not the case. The complete good object is not equal to the Freudian super-ego.[21] Klein disagrees with Freud who claims that the super-ego develops when the oedipal sexuality is repressed, just before the latency phase. According to her, the super-ego already emerges during the early introjections and projections, for example, when the child is afraid of losing a good partial object or the mother, due to its own actions. According to both Klein and her followers, the first introjections contribute both to the development of the ego and the super-ego. Learning a certain activity contributes to the development of the ego, while being confronted with the ethical attributes of the same activity develops the super-ego. A child

---

[19] I have the following passage in mind: 'The paranoiac, I should say, has also introjected a whole and real object, but has not been able to achieve a full identification with it, or if he has got as far as this, he has not been able to maintain it'. (Klein 1935: 126).

[20] Klein expresses it thus: 'Another important reason why the paranoiac cannot maintain his whole-object relation is that while the persecution anxieties and the anxiety for himself are still so strongly in operation he cannot endure the additional burden of anxieties for a loved object and, besides, the feelings of guilt and remorse which accompany this depressive position.' (Klein 1935: 126).

[21] See among others, Heimann: 'There is a genetic continuity between the persecutory fears of the infant, roused initially by his cannibalistic impulses, the anxiety of the latency child in connection with the disapproving internal voice of his parents, and the sense of guilt, mortification and remorse of the adult who has failed to act in accordance with his ideals.' (Heimann, in Klein et al. 1952: 135).

that is washed by its parents develops in both instances. It first of all learns a task. In the future it will be able to wash itself. The capacities of the ego are strengthened. Being washed nevertheless does also carry an unmistakeable moral dimension. The child learns that being dirty is unpleasant and not accepted by others. It is confronted with initial limitations. Such limitations are nevertheless not the only moral lesson. Being washed can also allow for the development of reparative tendencies. The disintegrated and dirty object can become unified and clean due to the simple activity of washing. The child learns to undo the state of disintegration found in its environment.[22]

The internal necessity to develop a strong super-ego is not dismissed. Klein agrees with Freud's later work, where, in *Civilisation and its Discontents,* he emphasised the necessity of repression of the aggression proper to the id.[23] The social existence of human beings is dependent on the strong super-ego that restrains the lawlessness of the id. A strong super-ego protects the ego against the attacks of the id. A parent, who prohibits certain behaviour, in fact allows the child to respond to its excessive desires and allows it to develop a good relation with others. The submission to the super-ego's demands actually prevents the loss of the internal good object. The high degree of anxiety about the loss of the good object frequently leads to a higher degree of submission to the rules of others. In that case the ego becomes fully dependent on the rules imposed upon it by the super-ego.[24] As will be evident below, in *The Logic of Sense* Deleuze distances himself from Klein on a number of points. In the following part of this chapter, I analyse the changes he suggests.

---

[22] Heimann makes the following statement: 'In unconscious phantasy, however, washing may have a moral meaning, like restoring an object harmed by soiling, and this meaning may be actually of predominant significance. In this case, the introjections of the mother, whilst she washes the child would also strongly add to the super-ego system.' (Heimann, in Klein *et al.* 1952: 137). As we will observe below, Deleuze is more interested in the Freudian analysis of morality's the emergence of morality.

[23] Freud states this as follows in *Civilisation and its Discontents*: 'Civilisation has to use its utmost efforts in order to set limits to man's aggressive instincts and to hold the manifestations of them in check by psychical reaction-formations' (1962: 59). See also the remarks on super-ego and Klein in the same text (Freud 1962: 77).

[24] Heimann avers: 'These strict demands serve the purpose of supporting the ego in its fight against its uncontrollable hatred and its bad attacking objects, with whom the ego is partly identified. The stronger the anxiety is of losing the loved objects, the more the ego strives to save them, and the harder the task of restoration becomes the stricter will grow the demands which are associated with the super-ego.' (Klein 1935: 123).

3. The depressive position according to Deleuze: the object of the heights[25]

In the previous chapter we have seen that Deleuze distances himself from Klein's analysis of the paranoid-schizoid position at an important point. The activity of the psyche within the schizoid position is not determined by the opposition between the good and bad partial objects. The ego is capable of dealing with the negative tensions not only by means of the continuous introjection of good partial objects. Every partial object inevitably contains a bad part and awakens aggression and sadism. The simulacrum of an internal good object, the body without organs, already develops in the schizoid position. This object corresponds to an experience of no tension. The separate pieces of the shattered experience are fused into a unity. This precise simulacrum is of fundamental importance for the subsequent development of the depressive position.[26] It contributes to the development of the new topological dimension, not distinguished by Klein: the height. It nevertheless does not belong to this dimension and remains proper to the depths only.[27] The height is not opposed to the depths.[28] It is an entirely separate topological dimension that emerges suddenly from the depths. It differentiates itself from them by means of a new object that occupies it, as Deleuze states.[29] This object possesses similar characteristics to the body without organs. It is complete and not shattered. In the depths the body without organs already allows for the development of a distance towards the partial objects. When this distance is strengthened, the dimension of the height emerges. Deleuze points directly

---

[25] Deleuze changes the name of the position to depressive position (see LdS: 221, LoS 190). I will use this term when referring to Deleuze's version. By the term 'object of the heights' I translate the French term *objet des hauteurs*.

[26] I refer here to the following passage: '*Si le bon objet n'est pas comme tel introjeté, nous semble-t-il, c'est parce que dès le début il appartient à une autre dimension. C'est lui qui a un autre 'position'. Le bon objet est en hauteur, il se tient en hauteur, et ne se laisse pas tomber, sans changer de nature. Par hauteur, il ne faut pas entendre une profondeur inversée, mais une dimension originale qui se distingue par la nature de l'objet qui l'occupe comme de l'instance qui la parcourt.*' (LdS 221), (LoS 189).

[27] Just like the ego, the body without organs finds itself in the middle between the depths and the heights. For Deleuze: '*Il* (object of the heights – PS) *entretient donc des rapports complexes avec le Ça comme réservoir d'objets partiels (…) et avec le moi (comme corps complet sans organes).* (LdS 221), (LoS 189).

[28] I am here referring to the following sentence: '*Par hauteur, il ne faut pas entendre une profondeur inversée, mais une dimension originale qui se distingue par la nature de l'objet qui l'occupe comme de l'instance qui la parcourt.*' (LdS 221), (LoS 189).

[29] I allude here to this passage: '*se distingue par la nature de l'objet qui l'occupe*' (LdS 221), (LoS 189).

to the simultaneous emergence of the super-ego that does not begin with the first introjections of the good and bad object, as stressed by Melanie Klein.[30] In order to be moral, the ego must first acknowledge the existence of the good object of the height.[31] I return to this topic, below.

We first have to be more precise about the process of emergence of the new dimension. When are we able to speak of the strengthening of the distance towards partial objects?[32] The first contribution to this process must originate from the increased capacity to perceive. The child starts to differentiate between different human figures and between them and itself. The child is incredibly small compared to the parents and the environment. It starts to understand that it has a very limited influence on its own surroundings. It starts to realise how dependent it is. This has a tremendous impact on the psyche. Child's experience ceases to consist of the constant exchange of the states of hunger and satisfaction, or of tension and pleasure. The experience cannot be determined by dynamic categories such as container-contained, empty-full or massive-meagre. For Deleuze, the experience of the depressive position is determined by the vertical nature of the good object of the heights. The ego looks up towards the heights. The importance of the relation towards the partial objects diminishes.[33] The environment is less frequently perceived as aggressive. The complete good object of the heights protects and cherishes the ego.[34] It strengthens its power. The good object is nevertheless not only a source of protection but is also cruel towards the ego. The parents not only fulfil child's wishes but also impose prohibitions and punish. The child

---

[30] I here discuss the following sentence: '*Le surmoi ne commence pas avec les premiers objets introjetés, comme dit Mélanie Klein, mais avec ce bon objet qui reste en hauteur.*' (LdS 221), (LoS 189).

[31] Deleuze stresses here that Freud also recognises the importance of the topological characteristics of the super-ego in *The Ego and the Id*. Deleuze writes: '*Freud a souvent insisté sur l'importance de cette translation du profond en haut, qui marque entre le Ça et le surmoi tout un changement d'orientation et une réorganisation cardinale de la vie psychique.*' (LdS 221), (LoS 189).

[32] I comment here on the following passage: '*Alors que la profondeur a une tension interne déterminée par les catégories dynamiques de contenant-contenu, vide-plein, gros-maigre, etc., la tension propre à la hauteur est celle de la verticalité, de la différence des tailles, du grand et du petit.*' (LdS 221), (LoS 190).

[33] Here I have the following passage in mind: '*Par opposition aux objets partiels introjetés, qui n'expriment pas l'agressivité de l'enfant sans exprimer aussi une agressivité contre lui, et qui sont mauvais, dangereux par là même, le bon objet comme tel est un objet complet. S'il manifeste la plus vive cruauté aussi bien qu'amour et protection, ce n'est pas sous un aspect partiel et divisé, mais en tant qu'objet bon et complet dont toutes les manifestations émanent d'une haute unité supérieure.*' (LdS 221), (LoS 190).

[34] See: '*S'il manifeste la plus vive cruauté aussi bien qu'amour*' (LdS 221), (LoS 190).

frequently experiences frustration. It does not understand why it is being punished. It is frustrated by its own state of powerlessness. The parents belong to an unreachable realm. They represent the superior unity of the heights that is out of the ego's reach.[35] The relationship to the heights is almost unbearable. A person with dominant schizoid tendencies may thus resist the subjection to the object of the heights. He or she can unconsciously refuse to accept its authority and, instead, cultivate schizoid tendencies.[36] In that case, no real object will be associated with the emerging dimension. The frustration, generated by the relationship to the new object, becomes unbearable.[37]

In a case where the tension is bearable, the new dimension emerges out of the depths of the schizoid position. The object of the heights emerges and starts to derive its characteristics from the object of the depths.[38] From the partial objects, it extracts their force.[39] The good object of the heights loves and punishes in a manner corresponding to the states of pleasure and tension generated by the partial objects. The love of the parents corresponds with the feeling of lust generated by the absorption of the good partial objects. Frustration, on the other hand, corresponds to the states of tension and fear caused by the bad partial objects. The object of the heights also derives its characteristics from the body without organs. It gains its form. It is just as complete and uncorrupted as this perfect full or empty body. The external objects may therefore be idealised, only because in the depths the ego has already experienced a state of perfection, represented by this simulacrum.

The new dimension directly changes the relation between the ego and the id.[40] Both develop a different relation to the object of the heights. Deleuze

---

[35] See: '*mais en tant qu'objet bon et complet dont toutes les manifestations émanent d'une haute unité supérieure.*' (LdS 221), (LoS 190).

[36] I refer here to: '*A la limite, sans doute, le schizoïde peut renforcer la tension de sa propre position pour se fermer aux révélations de la hauteur ou de la verticalité.*' (LdS 222). (LoS 190).

[37] The topological structure of the psyche in a case of schizophrenia consists merely of the id and the ego. As Freud, Klein and Heimann point out, the ego fulfils the role of a surface that can reject or filter out some of the experiences while accepting others. (*Cf.* Heimann 1952: 127).

[38] I here refer to the following passage: '*En vérité, le bon objet a pris sur soi les deux pôles schizoïdes, celui des objets partiels dont il extrait la force et celui de corps sans organes dont il extrait la forme, c'est-à-dire la complétude ou l'intégrité. Il entretient donc des rapports complexes avec le Ça comme réservoir d'objets partiels (…) et avec le moi (comme corps complet sans organes).*' (LdS 221). (LoS 190).

[39] See: '*des objets partiels dont il extrait la force*' (LdS 221), (LoS 190)

[40] It must be noted that in the series of orality, Deleuze does not yet fully discuss the characteristics of the ego. The analysis of the properties of the ego will play a more fundamental role in the description of what he calls the sexual position, the topic of Chapter four.

stresses that the id struggles against this object.[41] It rejects it completely. The reason is the topological dimension to which it belongs. The object of the heights exceeds them. It withdraws itself from the depths. The importance of the states of pleasure, generated by the partial objects, diminishes. The id cannot accept the relative lack of concern or sometimes even the complete disappearance of such states. It must consequently resist the power of the heights over the ego. The good object is equally hostile towards the id.[42] From the perspective of the heights, the id may only be perceived as a reservoir of aggression. The id is perceived as full of threatening parts that continually challenge its authority. As such, it must be suppressed at all costs.

The ego is now caught between two conflicting dimensions.[43] On the one hand, it identifies with the good object.[44] It loves this object and is impressed by its power. It is also convinced that some of this power is able to be appropriated. It wishes to liberate itself from the depths. It rejects its chaos and tensions. It detests the id because it can only provide a temporary release of tension, only very brief states of pleasure. The heights on the other hand hold the promise of order and the disappearance of all tensions. They hold out a promise of an infinite state of pleasure. This identification with the object of the heights leads to a mutual struggle against the id. The ego is strengthened by the power of the heights. It feels stronger when, for example, in the name of a religious belief or social norms, it distances itself from the bodily pleasures. The ego is suddenly strong enough to aim at other goals. It can now live a decent, moral life or work exceptionally hard towards a high position in society. The partial objects attacking the object of the heights are now perceived as directly attacking the ego.[45] We have already analysed the example of a nationalist who is not able to endure any criticism of his country.

---

[41] I comment here on the following extract: '*Mais de toute façon le bon objet de la hauteur entretient une lutte avec les objets partiels, dont l'enjeu est la force dans un affrontement violent des deux dimensions. Le corps de l'enfant est comme une fosse pleine de bêtes sauvages introjetées qui s'efforcent de happer en l'air le bon objet, lequel à son tour se comporte vis-à-vis d'eux comme un oiseau de proie sans pitié.*' (LdS 222), (LoS 190).

[42] See: '*lequel à son tour se comporte vis-à-vis d'eux comme un oiseau de proie sans pitié.*' (LdS 222), (LoS 190).

[43] I refer to: '*Dans cette situation le moi s'identifie d'une part au bon objet lui-même, se modèle sur lui dans un modèle d'amour, participe à la fois de sa puissance et de sa haine contre les objets internes, mais aussi de ses blessures, de sa souffrance sous le coup de ces mauvais objets.*' (LdS 222), (LoS 190).

[44] I am referring to: '*le moi s'identifie d'une part au bon objet lui-même, se modèle sur lui dans un modèle d'amour, participe à la fois de sa puissance et de sa haine contre les objets internes.*' (LdS 222), (LoS 190).

[45] I comment on: '*aussi de ses blessures, de sa souffrance sous le coup de ces mauvais objets.*' (LdS 222), (LoS 190).

The critique of the idealised object is directly perceived as a personal attack. We can also think of the reactions of followers of monotheistic religions towards atheism. The denial of God's existence is perceived to be a direct threat to the ego. The ego of the depressive position suffers together with the good object, states Deleuze.

This does not mean that the identification with the good object of the heights is complete. The ego is still secretly identifying with the partial objects.[46] It frequently supports them and suffers during their struggle against the commandments coming from the heights. The ego cannot distance itself completely from the id. It can never fully orient itself to the heights. The lust and pleasure generated by the id are too important. A child will never perfectly exercise the given commands. It cannot and does not want to become one with its parents. An excessive external pressure to make a successful career or to restrain bodily pleasures, might lead to a break with the environment. Even the most ambitious person will at moments distance himself from a social career. The demands of the object of the heights will always be too excessive. The ego will always want to experience pleasure and in order to obtain it, it will at times confront the power and demands of the object of the heights. This object has to resolve such resistance.[47] It will offer guidance to the ego in order to strengthen the identification.[48] Climbing the ladder of the social hierarchy will, for example, need to be accompanied by temporary states of pleasure that are able to make up for the sacrifices. Strengthening the identification with the object of the heights may only be achieved through knowing there will be pleasure at the end of the experience. The ego's position towards the id must be made stronger. The abandonment of temporary pleasures must eventually pay off.

---

[46] I here have the following passage in mind: '*Et d'autre part il s'identifie à ces mauvais objets partiels qui s'efforcent d'attraper le bon objet, il leur donne aide, alliance et même pitié.*' (LdS 222), (LoS 190).

[47] I refer here to this passage: '*Tel est le tourbillon Ça-moi-surmoi, où chacun reçoit autant de coups qu'il en distribue, et qui détermine la position maniaque-dépressive. Par rapport au moi, le bon objet comme surmoi exerce toute sa haine pour autant que le moi a partie liée avec les objets introjetés. Mais il lui donne aide et amour, pour autant que le moi passe de son côté et tente de s'identifier à lui.*' (LdS 222), (LoS 190).

[48] I am referring to the following sentence: '*Mais il lui donne aide et amour, pour autant que le moi passe de son côté et tente de s'identifier à lui.*' (LdS 222), (LoS 190).

4. Good object as lost object

Experience generated by the various positions is always accompanied by unconscious representations. In Kleinian psychoanalysis, those representations are called phantasms.[49] Deleuze differentiates between different kinds of phantasms. In the case of the schizoid position, he speaks of simulacra. The depressive is characterised by the Idol that represents the object of the heights. What characteristics of the Idol are absent from Klein's analysis? The first difference has already been noted and is topological in nature: the good object belongs to the heights. As has been seen, the development of the depressive position leads to the emergence of new emotions.[50] Pleasure and tensions are complemented by love and hate. According to Deleuze, these emotions are not caused by the relationship with the complete objects, as Klein argues. A child does not love its parents because they are experienced as complete good objects. According to him, love and hate are caused by the topological position of the good object. They arise because the good complete object transcends the ego. When perceived from the depressive position, the parents and the loved ones of later adult life are experienced as perfect and complete. They belong to this yet unreachable dimension. They belong to the heights.

The second difference between these two views is that according to Deleuze, the good object is unreachable and withdrawn in the heights.[51] Klein does not go as far in this respect. A person with a dominant manic-depressive position is afraid of losing an object that it in fact has already been internalised. She is afraid that the aggressive attacks will alter it into a bad object and lead to its loss. The chances of losing the object may nevertheless be minimised. The good object can always be safeguarded on the inside. For Deleuze, on the other hand, the good object is always already lost. It is directly withdrawn in the heights. It is structurally unreachable.[52] Moreover, it appears for the first time

---

[49] I comment here upon this passage: '*La position maniaque-dépressive déterminée par le bon objet présente donc toutes sortes de caractères nouveaux, en même temps qu'elle s'insère dans la position paranoïd-schizoïde. Ce n'est plus le monde profond des simulacres, mais celui de l'idole en hauteur. Ce ne sont plus les mécanismes de l'introjection et de la projection, mais celui de l'identification. Ce n'est plus la même* Spaltung *ou division du moi.*' (LdS 224), (LoS 192).

[50] Deleuze writes: '*Que l'amour et la haine ne renvoient pas à des objets partiels, mais expriment l'unité du bon objet complet, cela doit se comprendre en vertu de la « position » de cet objet, de sa transcendance en hauteur.*' (LdS 222), (LoS 191).

[51] I refer here to the following: '*Au-delà d'aimer ou haïr, aider ou battre, il y a 'se dérober', 'se retirer' dans la hauteur. Le bon objet est par nature un objet perdu: c'est-à-dire qu'il ne se montre en n'apparaît dès la première fois que come déjà perdu, ayant été perdu. C'est là son éminente unité.*' (LdS 222), (LoS 191).

[52] Deleuze remarks: '*Au-delà d'aimer ou haïr, aider ou battre, il y a 'se dérober', 'se retirer' dans la hauteur,*' (LdS 222), (LoS 191).

as already lost, as if it has been lost. Its appearance is its rediscovery.[53] How can we understand the genesis of this object? The body without organs, the instance that contributes to the emergence of the object of the heights, is not yet unreachable. It does not appear as a lost object. Its fullness or emptiness is a direct physical experience. A child can always experience emptiness when it refuses to eat. It can experience fullness in situations of unification. The emergence of the heights alters the situation. The object ceases to correspond to direct physical states. The determination of the internal experience by means of the opposition large and small further contributes to the experience of the good object as a lost object. An unbridgeable gap between the ego and the object is unambiguously present. The ego relates to a transcendent object: the height is principally unattainable. The ego will never reach the good object's state of completeness or perfection. It will always be imperfect.

The object of the heights appears moreover as already lost, as found again. Why is this the case? Deleuze refers here indirectly to Plato, who considers that the Ideas appear as having been lost. In his metaphysical theory we are capable of returning to the Ideas by the sheer force of memory. But to what kind of experiences of the child must Deleuze be referring here? The emergence of the object of the heights as a lost and withdrawn object must be thought by means of a genetic argument, not a metaphysical detour. Its emergence is not only a structural given. The first experiences of complete persons, emerging inside the dynamic of the schizoid position, are related to their presence and absence. The parents withdraw and the child fears that they will abandon it. It is increasingly aware of the fact that they are outside of its control. The child experiences itself as infinitely small and entirely dependent on the parents. Exactly at this moment of separation the child must learn to deal with such loss. They cannot always be there. It must learn to accept that it cannot see, feel and smell them all the time. It comes to realise that primordial unity with the environment does not exist. Children's games testify to the existence of this experience. This was signalled by Freud in his analysis of the game of *fort-da*.[54] In this game with an appearing and disappearing object a child learns to accept the existence of the separation. By means of the game it makes a first attempt again to find something that appears to have been temporarily

---

[53] Here, I refer to the following passage: '*c'est-à-dire qu'il ne se montre ne n'apparaît dès la première fois que come déjà perdu, ayant été perdu. C'est en tant que perdu qu'il donne son amour à celui qui ne peut le trouver la première fois que comme 'retrouvé' (le moi qui s'identifie à lui)*' (LdS 222), (LoS 191).

[54] For the analysis of the *fort-da* game see: Freud (1961), *Beyond Pleasure Principle*, New York: Norton & Company.

lost.[55] The unity with the mother and the environment is constructed as found again. The child is aiming at an impossible experience. It constructs an idea of unity, but can do so only at the moment when it becomes fully aware of the unbridgeable separation from the mother and the environment.

The characterisation of the good object of the heights as a lost one is of fundamental importance for Deleuze and is visible in his analysis of the different relationships of the ego with this object. The object of the heights gives its love only to the ego that experiences it as found again, he states. The ego must learn to consider the good object as lost and rediscovered.[56] Only such a relation towards this object does liberates the ego from aggressive attitude towards this object. Under this condition alone, the ego ceases to act with the intention of dominating the good object; in this case, solely, it maintains a respectable distance.[57] This relation to the good object of the heights is different when the object is not treated as rediscovered but rather as discovered for the first time. In that case the object is considered to be ready at hand. It is considered to be an entity that cannot be lost.[58] In this second case the ego is guided by a will to dominate, by aggression. The object of the heights perceives the ego as a dangerous internal object. It turns itself against the ego and dismisses its incapacity to accept its withdrawal.

The love and hate expressed by the good object of the heights towards the ego is hence intrinsically connected to its withdrawal.[59] The love given

---

[55] I here have the following passage in mind: 'The interpretation of the game then became obvious. It was related to the child's great cultural achievement – the instinctual renunciation (that is, the renunciation of instinctual satisfaction) which he had made in allowing his mother to go away without protesting. He compensated himself for this, as it were, by himself staging the disappearance and return of the objects within his reach'. (Freud 1961: 9).

[56] I refer here to this extract: '*C'est en tant que perdu qu'il donne son amour à celui qui ne peut le trouver la première fois que comme 'retrouvé' (le moi qui s'identifie à lui), et sa haine à celui qui l'agresse comme quelque chose de 'découvert', mais en tant que déjà là – le moi prenant le parti des objets internes.*' (LdS 222), (LoS 190).

[57] I am referring here to: '*C'est en tant que perdu qu'il donne son amour à celui qui ne peut le trouver la première fois que comme 'retrouvé' (le moi qui s'identifie à lui),*' (LdS 222), (LoS 191).

[58] Here I refer to: '*et sa haine à celui qui l'agresse comme quelque chose de 'découvert', mais en tant que déjà là – le moi prenant le parti des objets internes.*' (LdS 222), (LoS 191).

[59] I refer here to the following passage: '*C'est pourquoi, plus haut que le mouvement par lequel il donne de l'amour et des coups, il y a l'essence par laquelle, dans laquelle il se retire et nous frustre. Il se retire sous ses blessures, mais aussi dans son amour et dans sa haine. Il ne donne son amour que comme redonné, comme pardonnant, il ne donne sa haine que comme rappelant des menaces et des avertissements qui n'auront pas lieu. C'est donc à partir de la frustration que le bon objet, comme objet perdu, distribue l'amour et la haine. S'il hait, c'est en tant que bon objet, non moins qu'il aime. S'il aime le moi qui s'identifie à lui, s'il hait le moi qui s'identifie aux objets partiels, plus encore il se retire, frustre le moi qui hésite entre les deux et qu'il soupçonne d'un double jeu.*' (LdS 223), (LoS 191).

by the ego is experienced as already having been given in the past. It is a love
that has been lost and is now found as regained. This love is intertwined with
a peculiar feeling of guilt. It is a love that forgives. The ego feels that it is
forgiven for the aggression that it has supposedly expressed towards the good
object in the past. The object of the heights makes it believe that an experience
of unity has existed in the past but has been destroyed by the ego in its acts
of aggression. The feeling of love experienced from the depressive position is
therefore intrinsically connected with the experience of guilt. Deleuze argues
moreover that hate of the super-ego towards the ego has a similar structure
and is related to the memory of the threats uttered by the ego towards the
good object.[60] The hate expressed by the super-ego is related to a constructed
memory of threats that in fact have never been uttered. The ego blames itself
for a constructed aggression.

The lost-and-found-again good object plays a fundamental role in daily
life. It is central for a perfectionist or a career maker. The striving for perfection
allows one to give up many pleasures. The ego can only be satisfied when a
higher goal is reached. In this case alone it is able to obtain the feeling of being
loved by the good object. But the good object may also punish. The ego, in
its own perception, fails frequently; it does not attain the goals at which it
aims. It experiences these failures as a punishment for its own mediocrity.
The failure is perceived as caused by an orientation to bad partial objects and
a lack of orientation to the object of the heights. In this case the ego simply
wants to possess perfection and aims at discovering it. It cannot realise that
perfection can only be 'rediscovered'. It is doomed to experience frustration.
The ego of the depressive position fails to realise that perfection can never be
discovered or be possessed. Deleuze states that the object of the heights loves
only the one who feels guilty. 'Finding again' or 'rediscovering' is only possible
once the subject acknowledges the existence of own aggression and once he
considers itself capable of renouncing it. The same analysis may be given for
love that is experienced out of the depressive position. In this instance, there
are no precise reasons for loving the other.[61] The voice, smell, character are
not sufficient to clarify love's origin. The precise reasons of attraction for the
other cannot be grasped. The other transcends the depressive lover. The object

---

[60] I am commenting on this passage: '*il ne donne sa haine que comme rappelant des menaces et
des avertissements qui n'auront pas lieu*'. (LdS 223), (LoS 191).

[61] I base my analysis on the following passage: '*La frustration, d'après laquelle la première fois
ne peut être qu'une seconde fois, est la source commune de l'amour et de la haine. Le bon objet
est cruel (cruauté du surmoi) pour autant qu'il réunit tous ces moments d'un amour et d'une
haine donnés d'en haut, avec une instance qui se détourne et qui ne présente ses dons que comme
redonnés.*' (LdS 223). (LoS 191).

of love is a withdrawn good object of the heights. Love reminds the ego of the experience of unity that must have existed in the past. In love, the depressive lover rediscovers something that should have been lost forever. When love appears for the first time it is experienced as if it has already existed in the past, argues Deleuze. Just as in the case of perfection, here too, guilt plays a fundamental role. Love can be experience as rediscovered, only because of the sense of guilt for the acts of aggression that must have been committed in the past.[62] The ego hopes it can be forgiven.

5. Lack and affirmation in the depressive position

The depressive position is dominated by the experience of lack.[63] The desired good object is withdrawn in the heights. It is unreachable. Lack causes frustration that cannot be overcome. No single existing object can soothe it. In his books written in collaboration with Guattari, Deleuze has always been very critical of the importance assigned to this experience in Jacques Lacan's structuralist psychoanalysis. According to the former authors, lack can never be the starting point for the analysis of desire.[64] Desire is first of all productive and does not need this notion to operate. Deleuze holds a similar position in *The Logic of Sense*. Desire is directed at various internal objects while lack characterises only the depressive relationships with objects and is virtually unknown in other positions. Secondly, even in the depressive position, lack is productive. The analysis of a person with strong depressive tendencies cannot lead to the cognitive recognition of the unfulfillable nature of desire, but should lead to a specific kind of relation towards this object. Just as with the schizoid, so also the depressive position does not have to lead to resignation. Lack and frustration can accompany particular practices and experiences. A creative and affirmative stance towards the problems characterising the depressive position can be developed.

---

[62] In the next chapter it will, nevertheless, be argued that love can also be experienced from the other positions.

[63] Here I am commenting on the passage which follows: '*Il n'y a pas de place pour la privation, pour la situation frustrante* (in the schizoid position - PS). *Celle-ci apparaît au cours de la position schizoïde mais émane de l'autre position. C'est pourquoi la position dépressive nous prépare à quelque chose qui n'est ni action ni passion, mais l'impassible retirement. C'est pourquoi aussi la position maniaque-dépressive nous a paru avoir une cruauté qui se distingue de l'agressivité paranoïd-schizoïde.*' (LdS 224), (LoS 192).

[64] In *Anti-Oedipus*, Deleuze and Guattari assert: '*Le désir ne manque de rien, il ne manque pas de son objet.*' (LAO 34), (AO 26).

One of the examples mentioned in *The Logic of Sense* is masochism. The differentiation between the schizoid and depressive position allows Deleuze to differentiate between sadism and masochism.[65] Here, Deleuze builds upon the arguments developed earlier in *Coldness and Cruelty*, where he stresses that sadism and masochism are two unrelated kinds of sexual perversion. His book is a partial critique of Freud, who understands masochism to be a form of sadism directed against the ego. For Freud, masochism is made possible by the reversal of the drives.[66] For Deleuze, on the other hand, both perversions are characterised by entirely different physical experiences and entirely different kinds of imagination. He makes a similar point in *The Logic of Sense*, where he stresses that sadism is experienced out of the schizoid position.[67] A sadist expresses the schizoid aggression. His experience is characterised by interchanging states of pleasure and pain. In his offences, a sadist releases all the accumulated tension. He fully expresses his aggression and enjoys the pain inflicted upon the others and upon himself.[68] This is visible in the behaviour of the characters described by de Sade. They cold-bloodedly humiliate both others and themselves. They torture and are tortured. Everybody is treated as a partial object. No idealised object of the heights ever emerges.

The world of a masochist is entirely different and originates in the depressive position.[69] A masochist subjects himself to a mistress who represents the unreachable object of the heights. According to Deleuze the pain is less

---

[65] I here refer to the following sentence: '*La masochisme appartient à la position dépressive non seulement dans les souffrances qu'il suit, mais dans celles qu'il aime à donner par identification à la cruauté du bon objet comme tel.*' (LdS 224), (LoS 192). Deleuze continues his reflection on masochism and sadism that has been developed first in *Coldness and Cruelty*. In that book he stressed the differences between these two forms of perversion. Nevertheless, he was not yet using the Kleinian differentiation between the schizoid and depressive positions.

[66] Freud develops this point both in *Instincts and their Vicissitudes* (Freud 1915) and slightly nuanced – by stressing the role of repression – in his essay *A Child is Being Beaten*: 'To begin with, there seems to be a confirmation of the view that masochism is not the manifestation of a primary instinct, but originates from sadism which has been turned round upon the self – that is to say, by means of regression from an object to the ego. (…) But passivity is not the whole of masochism. The characteristic of unpleasure belongs to it as well,– a bewildering accompaniment to the satisfaction of an instinct. The transformation of sadism into masochism appears to be due to the influence of the sense of guilt which takes part in the act of repression.' (Freud 1919 in 1955:194).

[67] I refer here to this passage: '*tandis que le sadisme dépend de la position schizoïde, non seulement dans les souffrances qu'il inflige, mais dans celles qu'il se fait infliger par projection en intériorisation d'agressivité*' (LdS 224), (LoS 193).

[68] I am referring to the following sentence: '*mais dans celles qu'il se fait infliger par projection en intériorisation d'agressivité*'. (LdS 224), (LoS 192).

[69] I here have the following sentence in mind: '*La masochisme appartient à la position dépressive non seulement dans les souffrances qu'il suit, mais dans celles qu'il aime à donner par identification à la cruauté du bon objet comme tel.*' (LdS 224), (LoS 193).

physical in nature than in the case of sadism. It is already highly spiritual. The identification with the object of the heights allows the ego to be cruel towards the id. The ego strengthens its identification with the object of the heights by punishing the id. The mistress must be cruel and inflict suffering upon the masochist. She can nevertheless rule over him only because, as an unreachable object, she keeps him at a distance. The strict separation between the masochist and the mistress is of fundamental importance. This point is also made in *Coldness and Cruelty*. The masochist signs a contract with his mistress and she subjects her behaviour to a number of very strict rules.[70] One of them is exactly the maintaining of distance between both parties. The mistress must be unreachable and cold in order to prove that she belongs to the heights. The breaching of the distance, the disappearance of the heights, directly leads to the end of the masochistic relationship. The physical pain can be endured only when inflicted within this narrow framework. In *Coldness and Cruelty*, Deleuze stresses that the masochist does not care about the physical punishment as such. What is more important is the suspense, the waiting for the punishment.[71] A masochist enjoys the uncertainty. The object of the heights must be unpredictable. He does not want to know what his mistress will do. In order to incarnate an unreachable ideal she must be outside of his reach.[72] The masochist elevates the suspense to a form of art. He especially enjoys the images in which the actions are temporarily frozen.

Another clinical and literary example that is proper to the depressive position is alcoholism.[73] In *The Logic of Sense*, Deleuze analyses the time structure proper to this experience. An alcoholic lives in a past perfect, a structure of time that replaces the tragic present of schizophrenia. The object of

---

[70] See i.a. (PSM 20, 80). (CC 21, 92).

[71] I comment here on this passage: '*Il ne s'agit donc pas de nier le monde ou de le détruire, mais pas davantage de l'idéaliser; il s'agit de le dénier, de le suspendre en le déniant, pour s'ouvrir à un idéal lui-même suspendu dans le phantasme. … Dans les romans de Masoch, tout culmine dans le suspens. Il n'est pas exagéré de dire que c'est Masoch qui introduit dans le roman l'art du suspens comme ressort romanesque `a l'état pur: non seulement parce que les rites masochistes de supplice et de souffrance impliquent de véritables suspension physiques (le héros est accroché, crucifié, suspendu). Mais parce que le femme-bourreau prend des poses figées qui l'identifient à une statue, à un portrait ou à un3e photo. Parce qu'elle suspend le geste d'abattre le fouet ou d'entrouvrir ses fourrures.*' (PSM 31), (CC 33).

[72] The image of the masochist discussed by Deleuze in *Coldness and Cruelty* is far more complicated than the sketch given here. I do not have space at this point to analyse all the differences between the analysis developed in *The Logic of Sense* and *Coldness and Cruelty*.

[73] I refer here to the following passage: '*D'une autre point de vue, nous avons vu comment l'alcoolisme convenait à la position dépressive, jouant le rôle à la fois du plus haut objet, de sa perte et de la loi de cette perte au passé composé, remplaçant enfin principe mouillé de la schizophrénie dans ses présent tragiques.*' (LdS 224), (LoS 193).

the heights replaces the schizophrenic principle of liquidity (*principe mouillé*). The orientation towards the heights allows him to overcome the hegemony of the unbreakable present. An alcoholic lives in a world in which two separate moments, the present and the past, are intertwined.[74] He experiences the present always in relation to the past. This is visible in the way he, for example, speaks about a love relationship. An alcoholic does not say 'I love her' but 'I have loved'. He lives the two moments at once. He remembers the not yet alcoholic past and is at the same time caught in a terrible present. It is exactly this mutual relation of both moments that allows him to keep on living. He identifies with the objects from the past and engages in a negative relationship with the objects of the present.[75] According to Deleuze, he does not enjoy the harshness of the present as such. An alcoholic is interested rather in something that emerges in the relation of the present to the past. The alcoholic denigrates the present only in order to glorify the past – the more unbearable the present, the more glorious the past.

The same depressive relation to the world is found in the case of Gatsby, the main character of the book *The Great Gatsby* by F. Scott Fitzgerald.[76] In his love life, Gatsby behaves similar to an alcoholic. He is in love with Daisy, a rich woman whom he meets again after five years of forced separation. She still loves Gatsby. Despite being married she expresses a desire to return to him. Her love is sincere and not motivated by the wealth Gatsby has gathered in the five years of absence. Gatsby nevertheless rejects her love; he does not want to believe that Daisy still loves him. He does not wish to believe that she is willing to divorce her husband and leave her child in order to be able to live with him. Gatsby lives in the idealised past. He only desires to experience the old love in all its glory. This directly paralyses his activity. The present must in fact become infinitely harsher than the past. An agreeable present would only disturb the image of the past; it would disavow its perfection. Gatsby's behaviour leads to disaster. The love of his life disappears from his life and returns to her husband while Gatsby is unjustly shot for a crime

---

[74] Deleuze discusses the problematic of alcoholism in one of the most famous passages of *The Logic of Sense*, in 'Twenty-Second series – Porcelain and volcano', (LdS 186), (LoS 158).

[75] As Deleuze states: '*On vit deux temps à la fois, on vit deux moments à la fois, maar pas du tout à la manière proustienne. … En ce centre mou de l'autre moment, l'alcoolique peut donc s'identifier aux objets de son amour, 'de son horreur et de sa compassion', tandis que la dureté vécue et voulue du moment présent lui permet de tenir à distance la réalité.*' (LdS 185), (LoS 158).

[76] Deleuze writes: '*Soit la grande scène amoureuse de Gatsby: au moment où il aime et est aimé, Gatsby dans son 'effarante sentimentalité' se conduit comme un homme ivre. Il durcit ce présent de toutes ses forces, et veut luit faire enrerrer la plus tendre identification, celle à un passé composé où il aurait été aimé par la même femme, absolument, exclusivement et sans partage (les cinq ans d'absence comme les dix and d'ivresse).*' (LdS 187), (LoS 160).

he did not commit.[77] Just like an alcoholic, so Gatsby also lives in a perfect past. He constructs an imaginary one that is valuable only when the present is unbearable. The unification of these two moments is nevertheless difficult to endure. Both the present and the past have to slip away. An alcoholic is doomed to lose everything.[78] The continuous flight, caused by the orientation to an unreachable object of the heights, is unsustainable. Being able to bear this process of continuous destruction requires an extreme force, a power that cannot be found inside the depressive position only, asserts Deleuze. Alcoholism may lead to a deeper spiritual health but only when controlled by another instance.[79] Only an orientation to an event can transform this suffering into something productive. Only the development of the metaphysical surface, and of the proper form of the phantasm, will allow for a true transformation of an alcoholic. To be bearable, alcoholism needs a counter-effectuation. It needs a phantasm that will allow for an affirmation of an unknown future.[80]

The analysis of the dynamic genesis and of the psychopathology it implies, allows Deleuze to look at the philosophical tradition from a humorous perspective. The body and its suffering speak through the words of the philosophers, even though it does not fully determine their speech. Deleuze compares the schizoid position to pre-Socratic philosophy.[81] This does not yet know any transcendence. The pre-Socratics live in the world of simulacra.

---

[77] Deleuze writes: '*C'est à ce sommet d'identification — dont Fitzgerald disait: il équivaut « à la mort de toute réalisation » — que Gatsby se brise comme verre, perd tout, et son amour proche et son ancien amour et son amour fantastique. Ce qui donne à l'alcoolisme une valeur exemplaire pourtant, parmi tous ces événements du même type, c'est que l'alcool est à la fois l'amour et la perte d'amour, l'argent et la perte d'argent, le pays natal et sa perte. Il est à la fois l'objet, la perte d'objet et la loi de cette perte dans un processus concerté de démolition (« bien entendu »).*' (LdS 188). (LoS 160).

[78] As Deleuze comments: '*Tout culmine en un* has been. *Cet effet de fuite du passé, cette perte de l'objet en tous sens, constitue l'aspect dépressif de l'alcoolisme. Et cet effet de fuite, c'est peut-être ce qui fait la plus grande force de l'œuvre de Fitzgerald, ce qu'il a le plus profondément exprimé.*' (LdS 186), (LoS 159).

[79] Deleuze says the following about this deeper spiritual power: '*On ne peut pas dire d'avance, il faut risquer en durant le plus de temps possible, ne pas perdre de vue la grande santé. On ne saisit la vérité éternelle de l'événement que si l'événement s'inscrit aussi dans la chair; mais chaque fois nous devons doubler cette effectuation douloureuse par une contre-effectuation qui la limite, la joue, la transfigure.*' (LdS 188), (LoS 161).

[80] The concepts of counter-effectuation and phantasm are discussed extensively in Chapter six.

[81] I comment here upon the following passage: '*Après la présocratisme schizophrénique vient donc le platonisme dépressif: le Bien n'est saisi que comme l'objet d'une réminiscence, découvert comme essentiellement voilé; l'Un ne donne que ce qu'il n'a pas parce qu'il est supérieur à ce qu'il donne, retiré dans sa hauteur; et de l'Idée, Platon dit: 'elle fuit ou elle périt'- elle périt sous le coup des objets internes, mais elle fuit par rapport au moi, puisqu'elle le précède, se retirant à mesure qu'il avance et ne lui laissant qu'un peu d'amour ou de haine. Tels sont, nous l'avons vu, tous les caractères du passé-composé dépressif.*' (LdS 223). (LoS 191).

Platonism emerges in the middle of this universe. Its central concepts carry all the characteristics of the object of the heights. The concept of the Good is an example. It transcends humans. They do not have any direct access to it. The knowledge of it has been lost at the moment of their birth. The good as such is never present. It reveals itself only through the veils that cover it.[82] The Good can be accessed only by means of memory. In addition, the gap between humans and the One is unbridgeable.[83] The One is superior in all respects. It is responsible for the emergence of the world and of the humans, but is at the same time fully separated from them. The One transcends the world. It is withdrawn in the heights. Furthermore, the ideas belong to the heights and withdraw within them.[84] They cannot be destroyed by the attacks of the bad internal objects. This is, for example, the situation as regards the idea of a perfect and just society. Justice is a notion worth striving for. It must nevertheless also remain transcendent. Every claim, of having realised it, leads to its destruction. The concept can be realised only in such a way that it only suits particular interests. This directly leads to the loss of its essence.[85] The notion must always escape the present and the particular interests. Only in that case can one aim at realising it. The idea can only give a glimpse

---

[82] Deleuze puts this as follows: '*le Bien n'est saisi que comme l'objet d'une réminiscence, découvert comme essentiellement voilé;*' (LdS 223), (LoS 191). The notion of the veil is frequently used by Derrida in his analysis of difference (see Derrida, J., (1982), *Margins of philosophy*, Brighton: The Harvest Press). We immediately become aware of a significant dissimilarity between the approaches of Deleuze and Derrida. Deleuze stresses that the relationship to the lost object is characteristic only of the depressive position. Derrida, on the other hand, is less interested in the tendencies that are proper to what Deleuze calls the schizoid position. He, Derrida, has an interest in psychoanalysis; nevertheless, this interest has been limited to the work of Lacan. See a.o. Derrida (1987), *The Post card. From Socrates to Freud and beyond*. Chicago: UCP. An interesting analysis of the relationship between the work of Deleuze and Derrida may be found in P. Patton and J. Protevi (eds), (2003), '*Between Deleuze & Derrida,*' London: Continuum. Lack of space prevents a fuller discussion of this topic.

[83] I here consider the following passage: '*l'Un ne donne que ce qu'il n'a pas parce qu'il est supérieur à ce qu'il donne, retiré dans sa hauteur*' (LdS 223), (LoS 191).

[84] I refer here to: '*de l'Idée, Platon dit: 'elle fuit ou elle périt'- elle périt sous le coup des objets internes, mais elle fuit par rapport au moi, puisqu'elle le précède, se retirant à mesure qu'il avance et ne lui laissant qu'un peu d'amour ou de haine.*'(LdS 223), (LoS 192).

[85] The concept of a perfect society may be found in the work of Derrida and his idea of democracy to-come (*a-venir*), or in the idea of justice that transcends the law. Democracy to-come is according to him a quasi-condition of the possibility of contemporary democracy, while justice is a quasi-condition of possibility of the law. A democracy must always be oriented towards a future perfect democracy and law towards justice. Both must make an attempt to realise what is to-come, despite the structural incapacity to succeed. The transcendent horizon is necessary for a properly functioning democracy and law. See Derrida (1990), 'Force of law', in *Cardozo Law Review*, vol 11: 919, pp. 943.

of love and hate but can never be revealed as such.[86] When a just society is being striven for, some signs of success and development must become visible. Without those signs the pursuit loses sense. Constant setbacks will in that case lead to depressive resignation. A similar relation to the object in the heights is also found in monotheistic religions. God is feared, but along with the glimpses of hate God must also send love and hope. God must not only be held responsible for disasters, but also for prosperity. In the experience of the depressive believers God must always perform miracles.[87]

6. Body, language and the depressive position

The dynamic genesis is not only a psychoanalytic theory about the nature of desire but also a philosophical one concerning the emergence of sense and the relation between body and the structures of language or a society. For Deleuze, both language and the structures of a society do not inscribe themselves onto an empty physical surface, as Lacan claims, but become possible, given the bodies active role. The body is not passive when it enters an already existing language. It actively re-constructs it. In the previous chapter it has been indicted that the domination of the schizoid position is characterised by a large distance towards language. A little child hears separate noises, but is at the same time not aware of the existence of any structure of language.[88] Language and speech are not separated from the direct physical experience. The noises and words are not yet carriers of meaning. They produce intensities. The nature of the schizoid language is probably most vividly evident in the shouts uttered by patients in the older mental institutions or in the screams of drug addicts,

---

[86] I here have in mind: '*se retirant à mesure qu'il avance et ne lui laissant qu'un peu d'amour ou de haine.*' (LdS 223), (LoS 192).

[87] The difference between pre-Socratic philosophy and Platonism may also be understood by referring to the economic base, analysed by Deleuze and Guattari in 'Anti-Oedipus'. Both writers employ the Marxist theory about the different modes of production to analyse corresponding systems of representation. A society governed by what they call a 'primitive mode of production', one governed by kinship relations, must necessarily worship ancestors and speak of many gods. This situation changes with the rise of the despotic mode of production or the feudal society. The corresponding system of representation makes use of the concept of transcendence to ground the idea of the law and justify the existence of a unified power structure with a king at the top of the hierarchy (see i.a. Chapter three).

[88] I am discussing this passage: '*La profondeur est bruyante: les claquements, craquements, crissements, crépitements, explosions, les bruits éclatés des objets internes, mais aussi les cris-soufflés inarticulés du corps sans organes qui leur répondent, tout cela forme un système sonore témoignant de la voracité orale-anale.*' (LdS 225), (LoS 193).

during psychotic episodes. Deleuze's favourite example is Artaud's work.[89] The howls and screams uttered during his performances express the suffering of his body. They are explosions of agony and distress. They reveal his suffering but sometimes also express hope.[90] For Deleuze, such schizoid howls are in fact, to be found in daily speech. Words that express the feelings of love or anxiety and even words conveying an abstract meaning are intertwined with the schizoid tendencies. Each speech is an outlet of aggression and pleasure.[91] It is an outlet of what he calls an oral-anal voracity.

The depressive position must be considered to be the first raw sketch of language that is able to communicate an abstract meaning.[92] The first reason of this ascendance may be found in the higher capacities of the body, as noted in Klein's analysis. The child is increasingly capable of recognising voices and sounds in the midst of the noise. The separate sounds are connected to persons. The child eventually recognises the voice of its mother. Nevertheless Deleuze does also point to other reasons. According to him, the child is capable of distinguishing between noises and a voice only due to the emergence of the heights.[93] The voice is distinguished only because it is perceived as being uttered from the heights.[94] The separate sounds become a voice only when a child starts to realise that the complete objects transcend it. It connects a sound to a particular person and starts to realise at that moment that it cannot understand the utterance. The awareness of this incapacity is child's first contact with language. It marks an important change with respect to

---

[89] For further discussion of this topic see chapter two.

[90] I refer here to: '*mais aussi les cris-souffles inarticulés du corps sans organes qui leur répondent, tout cela forme un système sonore témoignant de la voracité orale-anale.*' (LdS 225), (LoS 193).

[91] Deleuze stresses that he is influenced here by Artaud. I discuss the following sentence: '*Et ce système schizoïde est inséparable de la terrible prédiction: parler sera taillé dans manger et dans chier, le langage sera taillé dans la merde, le langage et son univocité … (Artaud parle du 'caca de l'être et de son langage').*' (LdS 225), (LoS 193).

[92] I refer here to the following passage: '*Mais, précisément, ce qui assure la première ébauche de cette sculpture, la première étape d'une formation du langage, c'est le bon objet de la position dépressive en hauteur. Car c'est lui qui, de tous les bruits de la profondeur, extrait une Voix. Si l'on considère les caractères du bon objet, de ne pouvoir être saisi que comme perdu, d'apparaître la première fois comme déjà là, etc., il semble que ces caractères se réunissent nécessairement en une voix qui parle et qui vient d'en haut.*' (LdS 225), (LoS 193).

[93] See: '*il semble que ces caractères se réunissent nécessairement en une voix qui parle et qui vient d'en haut.*' (LdS 225), (LoS 193).

[94] My commentary here concerns the following extract: '*Freud insistait sur l'origine acoustique du surmoi. Pour l'enfant, la première approche du langage consiste bien à saisir celui-ci comme le modèle de ce qui se pose comme préexistant, comme renvoyant à tout le domaine de ce qui est déjà là, voix familiale qui charrie la tradition, où il doit s'insérer avant même de comprendre.*' (LdS 225), (LoS 193).

the schizoid position. A child begins to realise that the sounds uttered by others are organised. It discovers that the voices are part of a larger system. It discovers the existence of an external order. The child starts for example to realise that some of the sounds refer to him. He comes to realise that he has a name and that he will have to make use of it in the future. He starts to realise that he has to subject himself to the external order without yet grasping its nature.[95] Thus the voice marks the moment of access to language.

Deleuze stresses that the voice already possesses all the dimensions of language.[96] It denotes (*désigne*) the good object and the partial internal objects. The child is now able to realise that the words uttered by others are connected to its internal experience. It hears similar sounds when people denote similar objects or states. It concludes that the voice has a capacity of denoting these objects. The child also discovers that the voice allows the act of signification to take place (*signifié*).[97] It begins to realise that everything that exists must be structured in concepts and classes. This also happens when the child hears that similar sounds refer to various objects. It starts to realise that the different objects must have something in common. When it hears similar, reassuring words at moments when it is angry, it begins to realise that these separate states must somehow be connected to one another. It starts to understand that the various emotional states overflowing inside it might belong to the same categories. According to Deleuze, the voice is in the third instance, a manner of manifesting something.[98] It also manifests emotional variations of the complete persons. A child now begins to realise that the person before it has its own inner life and its own emotions. It discovers that the other person can be aggressive or full of love. It hears a voice that manifests tenderness or aggression.

The discovery of the existence of language and its functions does not mean that the child is directly capable of grasping the meaning and the principles

---

[95] See: '*voix familiale qui charrie la tradition, où il doit s'insérer avant même de comprendre.*' (LdS 225), (LoS 193).

[96] I comment here upon the following sentence: '*D'une certaine façon cette voix dispose même de toutes les dimensions du langage organisé: car elle désigne le bon objet comme tel, ou au contraire les objets introjetés; elle signifie quelque chose, à savoir tous les concepts et classes qui structurent le domaine de la préexistence; et elle manifeste les variations émotionnelles de la personne complète (voix qui aime et rassure, qui attaque t qui gronde, qui se plaint elle-même d'être blessée, ou qui se retire et se tait).*' (LdS 225), (LoS 194).

[97] See: '*elle signifie quelque chose, à savoir tous les concepts et classes qui structurent le domaine de la préexistence.*' (LdS 225), (LoS 194).

[98] See: '*et elle manifeste les variations émotionnelles de la personne complète (voix qui aime et rassure, qui attaque et qui gronde, qui se plaint elle-même d'être blessée, ou qui se retire et se tait).*' (LdS 225), (LoS 194).

of organisation of language.[99] It is still far removed from sense. It leaves the world of non-sense, characterising the schizoid position, behind and enters into the realm of pre-sense (*pré-sens*). Nevertheless, the child does not yet possess the univocity of language (*univocité*).[100] It does not yet possess the language itself. The child is unable to express itself fully in the language. It does not yet control what it says. It still has doubts about the use of language. The voice transcends the child. It is not yet fully grasping what the parents say, it guesses the meaning of their words. Sometimes, it can already trust its own understanding, but this fragile confidence is frequently undermined. The child is constantly confronted with its own limitations. It guesses wrongly and frequently faces the consequences of its own mistakes. Deleuze stresses here that the voice is thus caught in the equivocity (*équivocité*) of its designations (*désignations*), in the analogy of its significations (*significations*) and in the ambivalence of its manifestations.[101] The state of pre-sense (*pré-sens*) characterises various experiences arising from the depressive position. A person with strong depressive tendencies, who learns a foreign language is overwhelmed by the strange sounds she hears. She cannot fully discover their meaning. The order of the language is hidden. It escapes and transcends her and feelings of inferiority dominate. She is continually afraid of expressing herself incorrectly. The mastery of the foreign words and sentences appears to be unreachable. No univocity is present here. The language keeps its equivocal character. Each word might be referring to different objects, convey different meanings and manifest ambivalent feelings. The uttering of each word and sentence is accompanied by doubts and insecurity.

According to Deleuze, the inability to use language in a univocal manner emerges because the voice refers to a lost object.[102] In the depressive position,

---

[99] I here have this sentence in mind: '*Mais la voix présente ainsi les dimensions d'un langage organisé sans pouvoir rendre saisissable encore le principe d'organisation d'après lequel elle serait elle-même un langage. Aussi restons-nous en dehors du sens, et loin de lui, cette fois dans un pré-sens des hauteurs: et n'ayant d'unité que par son éminence reste empêtré dans l'équivocité de ses désignations, l'analogie de ses significations, l'ambivalence de ses manifestations.*' (LdS 226), (LoS 194).

[100] See: '*la voix ne dispose pas encore de l'univocité qui en ferait un langage.*' (LdS 225), (LoS 194).

[101] See: '*et n'ayant d'unité que par son éminence reste empêtré dans l'équivocité de ses désignations, l'analogie de ses significations, l'ambivalence de ses manifestations.*' (LdS 226), (LoS 194).

[102] I comment here upon the following passage: '*Car, en vérité, comme elle* (the voice – PS) *désigne l'objet perdu, on ne sait pas ce qu'elle désigne; on ne sait pas ce qu'elle signifie, puisqu'elle signifie l'ordre des préexistences; on ne sait pas ce qu'elle manifeste puisqu'elle manifeste le retirement dans son principe ou le silence. Elle est à la fois l'objet, la loi de la perte et la perte. Elle est bien la voix de Dieu comme surmoi, celle qui interdit sans qu'on sache ce qui est interdit, puisqu'on ne l'apprendra que par la sanction. Tel est le paradoxe de la voix (..): elle a les dimensions d'un langage sans en avoir la condition, elle attend l'événement que en fera un langage.*' (LdS 226), (LoS 194).

the gap between the language and things is not breached. The child does not realise what the voice is referring to; it cannot understand what is being signified (*signifie*).[103] The direct, self-constructed, experience is not related to this transcendent order. The objects and their names are still unknown. They are still far removed from the direct experience. The child does not understand what the voice is manifesting.[104] The voice is a manifestation of a withdrawal. It is an expression of a structurally inaccessible instance. The child is uncertain about the manifested emotions of, for example, its parents: 'Do they love me?', 'Are they really angry now or are they pretending?' The voice manifests only its withdrawal in the heights. It remains a secret and establishes the feeling of lack. The voice is at the same time the object, the law of the lack and the lack itself, contends Deleuze.[105] The voice heard in the depressive position is like the God's voice.[106] It supports but also punishes. It dictates the rules to be followed without clarifying why these rules are in place. The child begins to realise that some behaviour is forbidden, without yet understanding why. It learns by means of sanctions, asserts Deleuze.[107] The child learns about the nature of the objects and about the differentiations of the language by means of sanctions. The sentences 'This object is dangerous', 'You can play here the whole day', 'Biting and hitting is bad' are the most basic examples of prohibitions that allow the children to learn in the depressive position.

One immediately perceives the difference between the schizoid and depressive positions here.[108] In the schizoid position, the child is not fully affected by the imposed prohibitions. It constructs its own world. The objects carry a meaning only because they have a certain value in child's direct experience. Meaning emerges out of the unmediated interactions with environment. The child simply wants to avoid punishment. The depressive position introduces a large shift. The ego submits itself to an external order. It does not consider itself able to learn and act by itself. The world is too large and too overwhelming. The others are too powerful. It does not understand why

---

[103] See: '*on ne sait pas ce qu'elle désigne; on ne sait pas ce qu'elle signifie, puisqu'elle signifie l'ordre des préexistences.*' (LdS 226), (LoS 194).

[104] See: '*on ne sait pas ce qu'elle manifeste puisqu'elle manifeste le retirement dans son principe ou le silence*' (LdS 226), (LoS 194).

[105] See: '*Elle* (de stem – PS) *est à la fois l'objet, la loi de la perte et la perte.*' (LdS 226), (LoS 194).

[106] See: '*Elle est bien la voix de Dieu comme surmoi, celle qui interdit sans qu'on sache ce qui est interdit, puisqu'on ne l'apprendra que par la sanction.*' (LdS 226), (LoS 194).

[107] See: '*on ne l'apprendra que par la sanction.*' (LdS 226), (LoS 194).

[108] I am referring to the passage which follows: '*Il ne faut pas se demander si les échos, contraintes et vols sont premiers, ou seulement seconds par rapport à des phénomènes automatiques. C'est un faux problème car, ce qui est volé au schizophrène, ce n'est pas la voix, c'est au contraire, par la voix d'en haut, tout le système sonore* prévocal *dont il avait su faire son « automate spirituel ».*' (LdS 227). (LoS 194).

certain things are being prohibited, but presupposes that there must be good reasons behind each prohibition. It does not choose to avoid punishment, but rather accepts the existence of abstract principles that lead to punishment. It resigns itself to this situation.

The depressive position is characterised by a paradox of the voice, according to Deleuze.[109] The voice has all the dimensions of language at its disposal but lacks a necessary condition for being a language. It lacks univocity. It lacks what Deleuze calls a relation to an event. The univocal use of language is only possible once the inferior relation towards the heights is broken. The ego must seize control over the language. The words must be truly connected to the internal experience. For Deleuze, the existence of the paradox of the voice marks the insufficiency of the theories pronouncing the language's necessary equivocal nature.[110] Those theories presuppose an irreducible inequality between bodies on the one hand and thought and overarching order on the other. A body must resign itself. It must accept the rules of the external order. According to Deleuze, such a relationship with language may be proper to the depressive position only. It is possible to reach a full command over language, but only after an event that changes the way a body relates to its environment. It will be only possible once the ego becomes stronger, once the physical surface of the body emerges in its unified state. This will be the topic of the next chapter. Deleuze closes his analysis of the relationship between the schizoid and depressive position with an example derived from Bergson.[111] On a daily basis we experience the steps from the schizoid to the depressive position and subsequently to the new, yet to be discussed, sexual position. This occurs at moments when we are woken up by someone. Our relation to the environment in our dreams is limited. We only hear noises and live completely inside our own imagination. When we start to wake up, we first hear clear sounds that infiltrate our dreams. At a certain moment a

---

[109] I comment here upon the following passage: '*Tel est le paradoxe de la voix (qui marque en même temps l'insuffisance de toutes les théories de l'analogie et de l'équivocité): elle a les dimensions d'un langage sans en avoir la condition, elle attend l'événement qui en fera un langage. Elle a cessé d'être un bruit, mais n'est pas encore langage.*' (LdS 226). (LoS 194).

[110] Deleuze seems to be referring here to the theory of Lacan for whom the entry into language implies an insertion of an inferior object – the child – into an overarching transcendent order. The inferior object acquires meaning and sense only by means of this order. The body as such is meaningless. For Lacan, schizophrenia does not mark an original relationship with the world, but is caused by regression or a loss of language. See Lacan (1966) 'Subversion du sujet et dialectique du désir dans l'inconscient freudien', in *Ecrits I*. For a commentary on this text see van Haute (2001).

[111] See Bergson (1919), '*L'Energie spirituelle*', pp. 101-102. Deleuze states: '*Nous sommes schizophrènes en dormant, mais maniaques-dépressifs en approchant du réveil.*' (LdS 226), (LoS 194).

qualitative change occurs. Noise's intensity increases and reaches a point when it transforms into a voice. We start to truly wake up but cannot yet grasp the meaning of the words uttered by others in our vicinity. The depths of the sleep are left behind, but we are not yet fully awake. The reality gains access to our mind, but slowly. The full meaning of the shout 'Wake up!' will be accessed only once a state of full consciousness is reached. Deleuze postulates that we are schizophrenic in our sleep and manic-depressive once we begin to wake up.

7. Conclusion

The depressive position in this chapter has been analysed from three perspectives. It has first of all been treated as part of a psychoanalytic theory concerning the nature of desire. It was postulated that it is characterised by the emergence of a new topological dimension, the heights, that emerge in the middle of the depths. The unreachable object that occupies it brings with it a new dynamic. The ego that desires this object is confronted with an unbridgeable lack. It wants to obtain an unreachable object and is frustrated by its incapacity to meet its demands. The depressive position of the dynamic genesis has also been analysed as part of a philosophical theory about the emergence of language and of the structures of sense. It was evident that this position changes the individual's relationship towards language. The existence of an external order is discovered. This analysis allows Deleuze to formulate his critique of philosophical theories that take the equivocal relationship of a body with language for granted. The unbridgeable gap between a body and a structure is only temporary and is able to be overcome. Language can be used univocally but not out of the depressive position, where the ego is still too weak and too dependent on the protection of a higher instance.

The third perspective that has made a brief appearance at various moments in this chapter concerns these instances: Deleuze points to the insufficiency of any theory that takes the equivocal use of language as the point of departure and claims that the schizoid position fully contributes to the emergence of language. The limitations imposed upon the internal automatic schizoid life by the external order, are in no sense primary.[112] The order of language is at best,

---

[112] I refer here once again to the following passage: '*Il ne faut pas se demander si les échos, contraintes et vols sont premiers, ou seulement seconds par rapport à des phénomènes automatiques. C'est un faux problème car, ce qui est volé au schizophrène, ce n'est pas la voix, c'est au contraire, par la voix d'en haut, tout le système sonore prévocal dont il avait su faire son « automate spirituel ».*' (LdS 227), (LoS 195).

of equal importance to that of the schizoid phantasmatic life of the depths. Schizophrenia is not caused by regression. It is not a state of disintegration in which one has been deprived of a meaningful voice. Schizophrenia cannot be understood by means of the notion of lack. The schizophrenic lives in a world that does not yet know the object of the heights and does not lose this voice. He loses something else instead. The voice of the heights deprives him rather of an entire, pre-vocal sonorous system. The voice takes away the possibility of constructing a spiritual automaton and a self-constructed language. Just as in the work with Guattari, Deleuze stresses that the schizoid position therefore marks an original relationship with the environment. The depressive position merely builds upon those experiences; it allows for a further development and organisation of the schizoid experiences but does not lead to their complete destruction. Each ego continues to relate to the environment by means of the schizoid position. It maintains its own singular experiences that are often incommunicable to others. Those experiences remain primary with respect to the external order.

CHAPTER 4

Sexual-perverse position

1. Introduction

The previous two chapters have been devoted to the analysis of the schizoid and depressive positions, the characteristics of their topology and the nature of their internal objects. I have pointed out how the depths and partial objects were supplemented by the dimension of the heights and an idol – the complete and withdrawn object of the heights. Schizoid tensions and fears were replaced by depressive frustration arising due to unfulfilled demands. The present chapter is devoted to the analysis of the sexual or sexual-perverse position that is developed in the 'Twenty-Eight Series of Sexuality.'[1] As we will see, Deleuze considers the ego to be strengthened by the triumph of the libido over the destructive drives and by the emergence of the surface of the body as an independent topological dimension. As in the previous chapters, I will argue that Deleuze builds here upon the work of Melanie Klein and separates himself from the understanding of sexuality developed by both Freud and Lacan. We will for example, observe how genital sexuality allows the ego to believe in its reparative capacities and to confront the disintegration found in its environment. The sexual-perverse position as such does not lead to an unconscious conflict with the father and to a corresponding feeling of guilt.[2] Finally, I describe the change in the relationship of the ego to the structures of sense. It will become clear that the ego increasingly considers itself capable of producing and changing those very structures. This analysis will be complemented by a discussion of the nature of two syntheses proper to this sexual-perverse position: the connective and conjunctive syntheses.

The first part of the chapter is devoted to the analysis of the characteristics of the first phase of the position: pre-genital sexuality. It will start with the discussion of the difference between a zone and a phase. This distinction will allow one to understand the different roles played by the surface of the body both in earlier positions and in the sexual-perverse position. I will subsequently describe the genesis of the new position arising from the previous ones. I will pay attention to the role of the process of the defusion of the drives and to the

---

[1] As Deleuze does, I will use both terms interchangeably and consider them to be synonymous.

[2] The nature of such conflict plays a crucial role in the work of Freud and particularly in the work after the case study of Little Hans. See Freud, S., (1909), 'Analysis of a phobia in a five-year-old boy,' in Freud (1955).

differences between Deleuze's and Laplanche's understanding of this process. The second part of the chapter is devoted to the analysis of genital sexuality and particularly to its contribution to the emergence of a coherent experience of the ego. The discussion of the characteristics of the image of the phallus will lead to an analysis of Deleuze's version of the Oedipus complex. The chapter closes with an analysis of the implications of this position for the individual in relation to language and structures of sense.

2. Pre-genital phase of the sexual-perverse position: surface of the body

The sexual-perverse position is directly dependent on the emergence of a new topological instance added to the already existing depths and heights: the surface of the body.[3] The previous chapter showed how the schizoid experience of the complete object of the depths contributes to the emergence of the heights and of the depressive position. Similar steps occur during the emergence of the sexual position. As in the instance of the heights, so the surface is also already present in the depths, without yet being the separate dimension it will later become in the sexual position. In the depths it allows for the establishment of a relationship to the partial objects. The word partial refers in this case first of all to objects and drives aiming at these objects.[4] The partial object breast, for example, satisfies the oral drive. The word partial nevertheless also refers directly to a specific zone on the surface of the body.[5] According to Deleuze, who in this respect is in agreement with Freud's '*Three essays on the theory of sexuality*', this surface consists of various erotogenic zones that correspond to isolated areas of the body.[6] The zones develop in the vicinity of orifices marked by mucous membranes.[7] Each one of them

---

[3] This is my comment upon the following passage: '*Partiel a deux sens: il désigne d'abord l'état des objets introjetés et l'état correspondant des pulsions qui s'attachent à ces objets. Mais il désigne d'autre part zones électives du corps et l'état des pulsions qui y trouvent une « source ». Celles-ci ont bien un objet qui peut être lui-même partiel: le sein ou le doigt pour la zone orale, les excréments pour la zone anale.*' (LdS 228), (LoS 196).

[4] I refer here to: '*Partiel a deux sens: il désigne d'abord l'état des objets introjetés et l'état correspondant des pulsions qui s'attachent à ces objets.*' (LdS 228), (LoS 196).

[5] Here I refer to: '*Mais il désigne d'autre part zones électives du corps et l'état des pulsions qui y trouvent une « source ».*' (LdS 228), (LoS 196).

[6] I comment here upon this passage: '*Au contraire, les zones représentent un certain isolement d'un territoire, des activités qui l'investissent et des pulsions qui y trouvent maintenant une source distincte. L'objet partiel d'un stade est mis en morceaux par les activités auxquelles il est soumis; l'objet partiel d'une zone est plutôt séparé d'un ensemble par le territoire qu'il occupe et qui le limite.*' (LdS 228), (LoS 196).

[7] Deleuze expresses this as follows: '*Les zones érogènes sont découpées à la surface du corps, autour d'orifices marqués par des muqueuses.*' (LdS 229), (LoS 197).

responds only to certain kinds of stimuli. This happens with varying degrees of intensity. Each zone may also become the origin of a partial drive. In this case, the experience of sucking a breast generates pleasure when the oral zone is stimulated and is the origin of the oral drive.

The various erotogenic zones are moreover focussed on different partial objects. The skin can be pleasurably stimulated by a hand. A nose can be stimulated by the smell of, for example, the mother's body. The anal zone and the coupled digestive system can be satisfied by the activity of excretion. It is clear that a zone does not allow for a relationship with all kinds of external objects. Rather, it limits their experience.[8] When we enjoy looking at an object and exercise the scopophilic drive, the object we interact with must have visual characteristics. The oral zone on the other hand, can only relate to objects that may be physically absorbed. Such stimulations of the surface of the body are fundamental in all positions.

Before returning to an analysis of the role of the surface in the sexual position a clear distinction between bodily zones and various phases in which these zones may be playing an important role must still be made. In Freudian psychoanalytic terms, a phase refers to a particular kind of activity.[9] The oral phase is characterised by a will to absorb objects. The anal phase on the other hand is characterised by attempts of the ego to control its own body and the environment. Seizing control of the process of defecation is considered fundamental in this case.[10] The central activity of the body within a given phase dominates others.[11] The absorption of food during the anal phase is experienced differently from that in the oral phase. In the anal phase emphasis is placed on the control of the process of absorption rather than on the absorption as such. A child wishes to be able to either reject or accept the food rather than absorb it. The domination of a certain activity is directly

---

[8] As Deleuze remarks: '*l'objet partiel d'une zone est plutôt séparé d'un ensemble par le territoire qu'il occupe et qui le limite.*' (LdS 228), (LoS 196).

[9] Deleuze is referring here to the Freudian understanding of a phase that has been developed in 'Three essays on the theory of sexuality' (Freud 1905b). In this paragraph, I refer to the following passage: '*On a souvent remarqué que les deux notions psychanalytique de stade et de zone ne coïncidaient pas. Un stade se caractérise par un type d'activité, qui s'assimile d'autres activités et réalise sur tel ou tel mode un mélange des pulsions – ainsi l'absorption dans le premier stade oral, qui assimile aussi bien l'anus, ou bien l'excrétion dans le stade anal qui le prolonge, et qui récupère aussi bien la bouche.*' (LdS 228), (LoS 194)

[10] According to Freud, any disruption of this process may have pathological consequences. See for example, Freud's article on the anal personality, Freud, S. (1908), 'Character and anal erotism', in Freud (1959: 167).

[11] Deleuze writes: '*Un stade se caractérise par un type d'activité, qui s'assimile d'autres activités*' (LdS 228), (LoS 196).

intertwined with the various drives.[12] In the oral phase, for example, the drives extracting pleasure from the processes of absorption dominate others. In the anal phase, drives are satisfied by the activity of gaining of control over objects.

Deleuze is nevertheless mainly interested in the analysis of the various positions and does not follow the Freudian account of the various phases of the polymorph-perverse body's development. For him, the oral or anal phases are first of all subjected to the logic of the various positions. Seizing control of their own body – proper to the anal phase discussed by Freud – may be experienced differently within the schizoid and depressive positions. In the schizoid position, the continuous absorption of the partial object must be controlled. The child must be able to introject only the good partial objects. In the depressive position, on the other hand, the ego is mainly attempting to meet the demands of the object of the heights. This object becomes the main reason behind the attempts to gain control over the body. We could point here to the role of the parents, who may force the child to eat or to control its defecation. In the case of the prevalence of the oral drives, discussed by Freud as the oral phase, on the other hand, the role of the mechanism of introjection would be more emphasised. In the case of the depressive position, one could for example stress the importance of the mechanism of introjection, visible in the attempts to interact with the idealised good objects, such as parents.

Upon the emergence of the sexual-perverse position, the nature of the experiences generated by the various erotogenic zones is altered. An important shift is the reappearance of the mechanism of projection that was of minor importance in the depressive position but dominant in the schizoid one.[13] It has been seen that in the schizoid position, aggression has continually been projected onto the external objects. Partial objects generated not only states of comfort and pleasure; they were also attacking the ego. Due to the mechanism of projection, a finger could quickly transform into a threatening morsel. This mechanism alters in the sexual-perverse position.[14] The destructive drives cease to be projected onto the external objects and are replaced by the internal partial objects of a zone. An external object that stimulates a certain

---

[12] Deleuze notes: '*réalise sur tel ou tel mode un mélange des pulsions – ainsi l'absorption dans le premier stade oral, qui assimile aussi bien l'anus, ou bien l'excrétion dans le stade anal qui le prolonge, et qui récupère aussi bien la bouche.*' (LdS 228), (LoS 196).

[13] I am referring to the following sentence: '*On pourrait dire que l'objet d'une zone est « projeté », mais projection ne signifie plus un mécanisme des profondeurs et indique maintenant une opération de surface, sur une surface.*' (LdS 228) (LoS 197).

[14] I refer here to the passage which follows: '*mais projection ne signifie plus un mécanisme des profondeurs et indique maintenant une opération de surface, sur one surface.*'(LdS 228), (LoS 197). An analysis of the reasons why aggression ceases to be projected on the external objects will be given below in the section explicitly devoted to the process of defusion of the drives.

bodily zone produces a certain state of pleasure characterising this zone. This experience is accompanied by the development of an image of an internal partial object that always accompanies this state of satisfaction. The image is, as such, not visual in nature. The oral zone is satisfied by the very activity of sucking. The partial object of the zone has little in common with the external object that has first satisfied it. It does not serve as a substitute of such an earlier object. The internal object of a zone does not temporarily suppress the tension caused by the absence of an external object. The breast, the finger or a cigarette do not refer to the lost breast any more. They all generate similar experiences of pleasure exactly because they are accompanied by the same internal object of a zone that is projected onto them.

The ego now pursues states of pleasure that could be generated by the various zones. In the case of the oral zone, it is thus the activity of sucking, per se, that becomes fundamental. A person with a highly sensitive nasal organ, on the other hand, will now desire to interact with objects that are capable of satisfying this sense without trying to compensate for any sense of loss. Food will neither be consumed out of a necessity for survival nor as a means to refer to a lost experience. It will neither have to imitate an ideal taste nor meet the requirements of, for example, 'healthy food', as in the case of the depressive position. The experience of pleasure is now liberated. In the sexual-perverse position, food merely stimulates the gustatory and the nasal organs. Similar, carefree experiences can be found in the cases of the connoisseurs of wine, music, coffee, beer, cinema or various forms of sexual behaviour. The consumption of those objects is in all cases accompanied by the projection of internal partial objects of various zones. This projection leads to various states of pleasure that are not interrupted by any sense of tension or frustration.[15] One can briefly conclude here that for Deleuze, the sexual position is, in this sense, perverse in nature. Pleasure is able to be generated by interaction with any external object that is capable of interacting with one of the zones.[16] The external objects are of no importance for the survival of the body and do not refer to an unreachable object of the heights.

---

[15] In the interview *Abecedaire*, filmed at the end of Deleuze's life, he characterises friendship in similar terms. A friend is first of all a person who generates pleasurable affects, but nevertheless also a person with whom one can establish a working or intense assemblage. Assemblage cannot be understood as the state of pleasure described here. It also consists of elements from the social and political environment. It necessarily leads also to various states of discomfort. This topic will be addressed again in Chapter six.

[16] I refer here to the following sentence: '*Conformément a la théorie freudienne des zones érogènes et de leur rapport avec la perversion, on définit donc une troisième position, sexuelle-perverse, qui fonde son autonomie sur la dimension qui lui est propre (la perversion sexuelle comme distincte de l'ascension ou conversion dépressive et de la subversion schizophrénique).*' (LdS 229), (LoS 197).

The erotogenic zones that are central in the sexual-perverse position's pre-genital phase have five distinguishing characteristics.[17] As we have seen, every zone consists, first of all, of one or more singular points. The eye, the ear or the skin are points that can be stimulated to varying degrees of intensity. Somebody with a strongly developed tactile sense will experience physical contact with another person far more intensely than others. The second characteristic is a series that develops around a singular point.[18] The experiences generated by each erotogenic zone become directly organised. Experiences of a particular nature emerge. Hearing of sounds is organised by means of a series that develops itself around the hearing organ as an erotogenic zone. A stimulation that is too strong – for example street noise or loud screams – can be experienced as unpleasant. The stimulation incurred by another person's warm voice will be experienced as pleasurable. Culture inscribes itself into this primary bodily constellation. It privileges some of those experiences but is at the same time, dependent on the mentioned bodily predisposition.

The third characteristic of a zone is that it is inseparable from the drive that invests it.[19] Any stimulation of a zone directly leads to a state of pleasure. A strong genital drive will consequently lead to continuous attempts to generate states of pleasure by means of the genital zone.[20] The fourth characteristic of a zone is a partial object that is projected onto the zone.[21] These partial objects, different from the partial object of the schizoid position, are called images. As has already been noted, the image is not visual in nature, as it was for Lacan.[22] An image must be understood as an instance that accompanies pleasurable

---

[17] In this paragraph, I have the following passage in mind: '*Chaque zone érogène est donc inséparable: d'un ou plusieurs points singuliers; d'un développement sériel défini autour de la singularité; d'une pulsion investissant ce territoire; d'un objet partiel « projeté » sur le territoire comme objet de satisfaction (image); d'un observateur ou d'un moi lié au territoire, et éprouvant la satisfaction; d'un mode de raccordement avec les autres zones.*' (LdS 229), (LoS 197).

[18] A short definition of the concept of a series has also been given in the introduction. The notion is derived from structuralism and is extensively analysed by Deleuze in his text on structuralism: '*How do we recognise structuralism?*' (ID: 238), (DI: 170).

[19] I refer to: '*Chaque zone érogène est donc inséparable(…); d'une pulsion investissant ce territoire*' (LdS 229), (LoS 197).

[20] As will become evident in the analysis of the process of defusion of the drives characterising the sexual position, Deleuze understands the working of these drives differently from Freud and criticises the idea of a drive that is comprehended as leading to a discharge.

[21] I am referring to: '*Chaque zone érogène est donc inséparable(…) d'un objet partiel « projeté » sur le territoire comme objet de satisfaction (image)*' (LdS 229), (LoS 197).

[22] The concept of image is used by Lacan in his analysis of the Imaginary realm. The Imaginary characterises an orientation of images representing objects. A strong focus on the images, to be found in psychosis, is equal to a lack of orientation to the reality and the symbolic order structuring it. It is equal to a lack of knowledge of the meaning and role of these objects in the society. (see a.o. Lacan 1966: 11, *Écrits1*, Paris: Éditions du Seuil).

experiences of a particular zone. Sucking is hence always accompanied by an image, that is a particular state of pleasure characterising the oral zone. The image is unrelated to any external object that might have generated a state of pleasure in the past, such as the breast. The skin or its various parts produce their own images that are tactile and not visual in nature. The fifth and final characteristic of each zone is that it has its own observer.[23] It contains its own little or partial ego that experiences the state of pleasure generated by the zone. It is precisely this ego that produces the image projected onto the zone. For Deleuze, the pre-genital phase of the sexual-perverse position is therefore autoerotic in nature. The external objects are now relevant only in so far as they can generate pleasure for the egos of the various zones. The egos of this phase are not unified.[24] There exists only a variety of partial egos, investing the various zones of the body. A coherent experience is absent. The partial egos strive to fulfil their own wishes. The attempts at organisation of experience are still very weak. A zone can merely develop its own way of relating to other zones.[25] A child sucking his finger can thus relate it to the experience of the stimulation of its skin and mouth. It may also experience pleasure by the combination of the senses of hearing and smell; for example, when its mother is approaching. The emergence of a unified experience is discussed below.

Before clarifying the genesis of the physical surface as a separate dimension, we need to point to the Gilbert Simondon's influence on Deleuze's conceptualisation of the surface.[26] According to both thinkers, the surface is of fundamental importance for the regulation of the interaction between the inside and the outside of the body. The physical surface is a border that separates the inside from the outside of the body. It is precisely the surface that allows for the emergence of an organism as a separate entity. For Simondon, an organism is not an entity existing prior to its interaction with the

---

[23] I have in mind: '*d'un observateur ou d'un moi lié au territoire, et éprouvant la satisfaction*' (LdS 229), (LoS 197).

[24] I refer here to this passage: '*Mais, justement parce que l'ensemble de la surface ne préexiste pas, la sexualité sous son premier aspect (prégénital) doit être définie comme une véritable production des surfaces partielles, et l'auto-érotisme qui lui correspond doit être caractérisé par l'objet de satisfaction projeté sur la surface et par le petit moi narcissique qui le contemple en s'en repaît.*' (LdS 229), (LoS 197).

[25] I here refer to: '*Chaque zone érogène est donc inséparable (…) d'un mode de raccordement avec les autres zones. La surface dans son ensemble est le produit de ce raccordement, et nous verrons qu'elle pose des problèmes spécifiques.*' (LdS 229), (LoS 197).

[26] Simondon is known for his book '*L'Individu et sa genèse physico-biologique,*' Paris: PUF, 1964, where he criticises the ontological primacy of the opposition form - matter. For a series of articles on Simondon, see Stengers, I., (et al), in *Multitudes* 2004 (18). Simondon's influence on *The Logic of Sense* is analysed extensively by Bowden (2011: 117). For additional analysis see also Levi Bryant (2009: 372) in van Tuinen (*et al.*), (2009).

environment. It cannot be thought by means of the distinction form - matter. The organism is not a pre-given form applied to inanimate matter, but emerges out of the interactions between the inside and the outside. It arises in a given environment and is dependent on changes happening there. The organism may in fact be understood as a solution to the problems posed by a particular environment. It is a result of the continuous process of individuation, a response to continuous changes. An organism relies upon the membrane or the surface which separates it from the outside and that interweaves the inner experience with the events in the outside world.

This membrane does not form a unified whole. For Simondon, too, it consists of separate zones, forming a whole dynamic system.[27] The zones stand in direct contact with certain parts of the inside of the body. Oral or anal zones are, for instance, directly connected to the digestive organs and to the brain. The absorption of food or discharge of excrements has direct impacts on these organs.[28] The skin is connected to the brain but also, for example, to the reproductive organs. These same zones are also the place of exchange with certain parts of the outside world. The skin responds for example to temperature, and the eyes to the amount of light. To both Simondon and Deleuze, the organism does not interact with the environment as a whole. The specific organs and zones interact only with separate components of the environment. The organism is not a unity, but, rather, a complex system consisting of various interacting instances.[29] Separate events in the outside world influence only some parts of the organism. Living in a noisy environment, for example, does not influence the digestive system directly.

This reference to Simondon's understanding of the nature of organism has important consequences for our understanding of the organisation of desire in the sexual position. The physical surface is not a pre-existing entity. It is not a form that is applied to matter. The separate erotogenic zones are not parts of a pre-existing entity. The physical surface emerges in the process of genesis. It is constituted during the various interactions with the outside world. It is initially fragmented and becomes a unity only after a longer process.[30] Initially, we may only speak of continuous stimulations of various orifices. These can

---

[27] I refer here to this passage: 'Quand on remarque que les organes internes peuvent devenir aussi zones érogènes, il semble que c'est seulement sous la condition de la topologie spontanée du corps d'après laquelle, come disait Simondon à propos des membranes, « tout le contenu de l'espace intérieur est topologiquement en contact avec le contenu de l'espace extérieur sur les limites du vivant ».' (LdS 229), (LoS 197).

[28] The role of the brain, as an independent dimension of the psyche, is analysed in Chapter six.

[29] Refer for example to: Simondon 1964: 263.

[30] Deleuze puts this as follows: 'Il ne suffit même pas de dire que les zones érogènes sont découpées à la surface. Celle-ci ne leur préexiste pas.' (LdS 229), (LoS 197).

be considered to be singular points that allow for the emergence of separate zones around them. In some cases, the zone will be stretched into the vicinity of others, constituted around other singular points.[31] In such instances alone, a more unified experience occurs and a larger surface starts to emerge. Initially the surface of the sexual body can be compared only to the Harlequin's cloak.[32] The cloak of this medieval precursor of the contemporary clown, providing satirical commentary on theatre performances, is covered with a chequered pattern. It visualises his disdain of the existing order. It expresses the urge of this naughty personage to continually contest the unified experience. The cloak can only consist of separated zones. It can never become a unity.[33]

3. The physical surface and the defusion of the drives

Before analysing the emergence of a unified experience we still have to understand the nature of the transition from the schizoid and depressive positions to the sexual-perverse one.[34] What are the reasons for the emergence of the physical surface as a separate topological instance? How can the surface arise out of the previous positions? According to Deleuze, the sexual-perverse position is a particular form of response towards the schizoid tendencies present within the depressive position. In the previous chapter I showed that the ego distances itself from the depths by turning towards the object of the heights. The ego develops its own point of view with respect to the depths. It becomes capable of overseeing the pleasurable and frightening experiences of the body. It resides above the depths and undertakes initial attempts at controlling it. Distance from direct bodily impulses, and disapproval of certain kinds of behaviour, becomes possible. A paralysing fear, generated by the continuous consumption of food, may now be confronted by means of a successful identification with the object of the heights. An anorexic can start

---

[31] I am referring to the following sentence: '*En fait, chaque zone est la formation dynamique d'un espace de surface autour d'une singularité constituée par l'orifice, et prolongeable dans toutes les directions jusqu'au voisinage d'une autre zone dépendant d'une autre singularité.*' (LdS 229), (LoS 197).

[32] Deleuze states it thus: '*Notre corps sexué est d'abord un habit d'Arlequin.*' (LdS 229), (LoS 197).

[33] I discuss the emergence of the whole surface of the body later in the text. It will become clear that Deleuze distances himself from Lacan, who denies the existence of any primary fragmented experience of the body (*Cf.* Kristeva 2001: 174 and Lacan 1966: 93).

[34] I analyse this passage: '*Comment se fait cette production, comment se forme cette position sexuelle? Il faut évidement en chercher le principe dans les positions précédentes, et notamment dans la réaction de la position dépressive sur la position schizoïde. La hauteur en effet à un étrange pouvoir de réaction sur la profondeur*' (LdS 229). (LoS 198).

to follow the suggestions of others. The feeling of disgust with respect to food is able to be partially tamed. Despite their fierce resistance, the depths can be potentially controlled, asserts Deleuze.[35]

During the depressive position, the depths begin to increasingly display itself in front of the ego.[36] The ego starts to relate to the body as the source of its suffering. The depths start to appear as an extremely sensitive zone that consists of local orifices.[37] The ego is increasingly able to discover the surface amid the depths. The surface, as a separate topological dimension, begins to emerge. The heights play a crucial role here. They are the condition of possibility for the emergence of the sexual-perverse position. Without the heights, the ego would remain forever subjected to the accidental states of pleasure and tension, characterising the depths.[38] The states of fear would prevail and every zone would remain as merely the source of dangers. Without the heights the surface can only consist of countless orifices, argues Deleuze.[39] In such a state any emerging surface would be directly destroyed. In the best scenario, the surface could be perceived as a body without organs. In that case, the surface would have no limits and refer to an infinite subjectivity. The different experiences of pleasure, fear and frustration could not be separated from each other any longer. Pleasure, separated from frustrations and fear, would not emerge.

Self-evidently, the emergence of the heights does not necessarily lead to the development of a surface as a separate topological instance.[40] Deleuze

---

[35] I refer here to the passage which follows: '*Il semble que, du point de vue de la hauteur, la profondeur tourne, s'oriente d'une nouvelle manière et s'étale: vue d'en haut par l'oiseau de proie, elle n'est plus qu'un pli plus ou moins facilement dépliable, ou bien un orifice local entouré, cerne de surface.*' (LdS 230), (LoS 198).

[36] I am referring to: '*Il semble que, du point de vue de la hauteur, la profondeur tourne, s'oriente d'une nouvelle manière et s'étale*' (LdS 230), (LoS 198).

[37] I have in mind the following remark: '*vue d'en haut* (profondeur est - PS) *un orifice local entouré, cerne de surface.*' (LdS 230), (LoS 198).

[38] Deleuze remarks: '*Sans doute la fixation ou la régression à la position schizoïde implique-t-elle une résistance à la position dépressive, telle que la surface ne pourra pas se former: chaque zone est alors percée de mille orifices qui l'annulent, ou au contraire le corps sans organes se referme sur une profondeur pleine sans limites et sans extériorité.*' (LdS 230), (LoS 198).

[39] I refer to this passage: '*chaque zone est alors percée de mille orifices qui l'annulent, ou au contraire le corps sans organes se referme sur une profondeur pleine sans limites et sans extériorité.*' (LdS 230), (LoS 198).

[40] I refer here to the following passage: '*Bien plus, la position dépressive ne constitue certes pas elle-même une surface; elle précipite plutôt dans l'orifice l'imprudent qui s'y aventurerait, comme on le voit dans le cas de Nietzsche qui ne découvre la surface d'en haut, de six mille pieds de hauteur, que pour être englouti par l'orifice subsistant. (cf. les épisodes d'apparence maniaque-dépressive avant la crise de démence de Nietzsche).*' (LdS 230), (LoS 198).

refers here to the example of Nietzsche, who after the discovery of the depths and the heights, did not construct the surface of the sexual-perverse position. Such a step could have protected him, during his philosophical explorations of the depths, from the entire mental collapse. Nietzsche lost contact with his surroundings and died in a mental institution after enduring long periods of manic-depressive states.[41] The nature of the process of his mental collapse might be understood by considering the case of Gatsby, who refuses to enjoy his life as it is. He is too obsessed with the past. He remembers the pleasures of the past life with his beloved Daisy, but is unable to live it again. He removes himself too far from the once constructed surface. He does not want to degrade himself again to the level of the depths; too anxious about exposing himself again to those negative experiences. He is afraid that the fragile surface might become depths again and thus wishes to eliminate the risk of negative experiences at all costs. The identification with an unreachable object of the heights appears to be the only solution. Precisely because of these fears and excessive orientation to the unreachable object of the heights, Gatsby is destined to lose the woman of his life. As with Gatsby, so Nietzsche was unable to remain on the fragile physical surface. However, in contrast to Gatsby, he was not afraid of what was hidden directly below it. Nietzsche disappeared into the depths because he did not want to maintain the necessary distance from them. He might have despised the heights too much and therefore could not protect himself against the intensity of the experience proper to the depths. No images, proper to the sexual position, had been constructed.[42]

The emergence of the surface of the body is consequently far from necessary. Both the heights and the depths are able to have a strong hold

---

[41] For an analysis of Nietzsche's manic-depressive period of life see Klossowski (1997: 210), *Nietzsche and the vicious circle*, London: The Athlone Press. Deleuze analyses the collapse of Nietzsche in the 'Fifteenth Series of Singularities' where he points to Nietzsche's philosophical incapacity to relate to the depths by means of a surface. He claims the following: '*Mais il est vrai qu'il fut pris par une besogne plus profonde, plus grandiose, plus dangereuse aussi: dans sa découverte il vit un nouveau moyen d'explorer le fond, de porter en lui un œil distinct, de discerner en lui mille voix, de faire parler toutes ces voix, quittée à être happé par cette profondeur qu'il interprétait et peuplait comme elle n'avait jamais été.*' (LdS 131), (LoS 108). It is outside of the scope of the present analysis to determine whether these remarks imply any kind of philosophical critique of Nietzsche by Deleuze.

[42] Deleuze expresses this as follows: '*Il ne supportait pas de rester sur la surface fragile, dont il avait pourtant fait la tracé à travers les hommes et les dieux. Regagner un sans-fond qu'il renouvelait, qu'il recreusait, c'est là que Nietzsche à sa manière a péri.*' (LdS 131) (LoS 108).

over the ego.[43] The possibility of the development of the surface, due to the contribution of the heights, means, however, that the heights do not only suppress the libido. This statement can only be uttered within the Kleinian framework.[44] According to Klein, the super-ego is not only oriented to the suppression of destructive drives.[45] It also wants to assure the victory of the libido over the destructive drives. A strengthening of the libido is in fact the most important goal of Kleinian analysis. Only the power of the libido allows the ego to trust and love others and diminishes the feelings of guilt and fear. Nevertheless, according to Klein, the victory over the destructive drives will always be partial.[46] Temporary regressions to the paranoid-schizoid and manic-depressive positions will always occur; the libido is immensely fragile.

We have already clarified that the object of the heights is the main contributor to the emergence of the physical surface as a separate topological dimension. The second factor is the defusion of the drives. According to Deleuze, in the sexual position, the libido becomes independent of the destructive drives[47] as well as of the self-preservation drive. As will be seen, understanding of the nature of this process differs from the one developed by Freud and, subsequently, Laplanche and Pontalis. The sexual or libidinal

---

[43] I refer to this passage: '*Reste que la hauteur rend possible une constitution des surfaces partielles, comme les champs bariolés se déplient sous l'aile de l'avion – et que le surmoi malgré toute sa cruauté, n'est pas sans compliance à l'égard de l'organisation sexuelle des zones superficielles, pour autant qu'il peut supposer que les pulsions libidinales s'y séparent des pulsions destructrices des profondeurs.*' (LdS 230), (LoS 198).

[44] I comment on the following passage: '*C'est un thème constant dans l'ouvre de Mélanie Klein: le surmoi réserve d'abord sa répression, non pas aux pulsions libidinales, mais seulement aux pulsions destructrices qui les accompagnent (cf. par exemple La psychanalyse des enfants, pp. 148-149). C'est pourquoi l'angoisse et la culpabilité ne naissent pas des pulsions libidinales, même incestueuses, mais d'abord des pulsions destructrices et leur répression ...*' (LdS 230), (LoS 352).

[45] See for example, the Appendix of *The Psycho-Analysis of Children*. In this early book – one in which she does not yet fully develop the distinction between the two positions discussed in Chapters two and three – Klein analyses the importance of the victory over the destructive drives. These drives can still invest the super-ego: 'All the analysis can do is to relax the pre-genital fixations and diminish anxiety and thus assist the super-ego to move forward from pre-genital stages to the genital stage. Every advance in this lessening of the severity of the super-ego is a further victory for the libidinal instinctual impulses over the destructive ones and signifies that the libido has attained the genital stage in a fuller measure.' (Klein 1997: 280, 175).

[46] Klein puts this as follows: 'The view that the early anxiety-situations never cease to operate completely also demarcates the limits of psycho-analysis, for it follows that a complete cure does not exist.' Klein (1997: 281).

[47] As Deleuze did, so I use the notion of the death drive and the destructive drive as substitutes in the analysis of the schizoid and depressive position. In Chapters five and six the reader will nevertheless see that the death drive proper to the metaphysical surface – called the speculative death drive – is different from the aggression and destruction central in the earlier positions.

drives of the surface differ in nature from the ones of the depths.[48] The latter are fused with the destructive drives and with the self-preservation drive. In the depths, the sexual drive leans on the self-preservation drive.[49] Its goal is to produce objects or simulacra that will be able temporarily to soothe the self-preservation drive when the real objects it aims at, are temporarily out of reach. A hungry little child can temporarily substitute a real object for an imaginary one. A real object is replaced by a partial introjected object or a simulacrum. The sexual drive is in this case responsible for the production of the simulacra.[50] The child can release the tension caused by the emerging hunger or lack of the physical presence of another person simply by sucking a finger. The finger replaces the breast or the physical presence of another person. The breast is projected onto another object.[51] The working of simulacra is visible in the case of a person who fails to reach a position in a society that will guarantee him a carefree survival. A feeling of power and safety may be obtained only by taking hold of unnecessary luxury products. An expensive car temporarily soothes the self-preservation drive and provides an illusion of safety and power.[52] A truly rich person might be far less dependent on such objects in order to pacify their self-preservation drive.

---

[48] I here have in mind: '*Certes, les pulsions sexuelles ou libidinales étaient déjà au travail dans les profondeurs. Mais l'important est de savoir quel était l'état de leur mélange, d'une part avec les pulsions de conservation, d'autre part avec les pulsions de mort. Or, en profondeur, les pulsions de conservation qui constituent le système alimentaire (absorption en même excrétion) ont bien des objets réels et des buts mais, en raison de l'impuissance de nourrisson, ne disposent pas des moyens de se satisfaire ou de posséder l'objet réel. C'est pourquoi ce qu'on peut appeler pulsions sexuelles, ne naissent qu'à leur occasion, substituant aux objets hors d'atteinte des objets partiels introjetés et projetés: Il y a stricte complémentarité des pulsions sexuelles et des simulacres.*' (LdS 231), (LoS 198).

[49] In this respect, Deleuze still follows Laplanche who also stresses that in certain situations a libido can lean on the self-preservation drive. For an analysis of this topic *cf.* van Haute en Geyskens (2004: 109), *Confusion of tongues. The primacy of sexuality in Freud, Ferenczi and Laplanche*, New York, Other Press. The authors use the technical term 'anaclysis', replaced here by the term 'fusion'.

[50] I refer here to this passage: '*C'est pourquoi ce qu'on peut appeler pulsions sexuelles, ne naissent qu'à leur occasion, substituant aux objets hors d'atteinte des objets partiels introjetés et projetés: Il y a stricte complémentarité des pulsions sexuelles et des simulacres.*' (LdS 231), (LoS 198).

[51] Deleuze comments: '*Or, en profondeur, les pulsions de conservation qui constituent le système alimentaire (absorption en même excrétion) ont bien des objets réels et des buts mais, en raison de l'impuissance de nourrisson, ne disposent pas des moyens de se satisfaire ou de posséder l'objet réel.*' (LdS 231), (LoS 198).

[52] I presume here that the struggle for a higher position within a society is driven by the self-preservation drive and less so by an attempt to meet the demands of the object of the heights.

The fusion of the sexual drive of the depths with the destructive drives is different in nature from the fusion of the sexual drive with the self-preservation drive. The destructive drive plays a different role. Deleuze stresses that it is not emerging out of the relation towards any real object.[53] The destructive drive aims exclusively at the partial internal objects, created by the activity of the sexual drive. The schizoid position does not allow for a simple state of pleasure generated by the sucking of a finger because it is destruction that determines the relation towards the internal objects. The ego is continually attacked by objects that inevitably produce negative stimulations. Continuous discharges of tension are a necessity. The rage directed at an internal partial object must temporarily disappear. Such discharge is also necessary in case of the aforementioned schizoid careerist. He can never be simply satisfied and enjoy the acquired position and possessions. Every new product or lifestyle – new job, shoes, car or television – quickly disappoints him. Destruction leads to a continuous search for a release of tension. The depths can consequently be described as a mixture of the three drives.[54] Every drive fulfils its own function and relates to another drive. The self-preservation drive contributes to the emergence of the sexual drives. The sexual drive subsequently provides the self-preservation drive with substitutes. The destructive drives finally furnish the relation of the ego towards these substitutes.[55]

According to Deleuze, this system is not in equilibrium.[56] The destructive drives influence the self-preservation drive and generate continuous states of fear. Food – or for that matter innocent foreign workers within a nation state – become the sources of threat precisely due to the working of this drive. Such fears cannot be infinitely contained by further introjections of new objects. As noted in chapter two, the overcoming of this permanent state of chaos may be approached in an attempt at withdrawal into an empty body without

---

[53] I refer to the following sentence: '*Mais alors la destruction ne désigne pas un certain caractère du rapport avec l'objet réel formé, elle qualifie tout le mode de formation de l'objet partiel interne (les morceaux) et la totalité du rapport avec lui, puisqu'il est a la foi détruit et destructeur, et sert à détruire le moi autant que l'autre, au point que détruire – être détruit occupe toute la sensibilité interne*'. (LdS 231), (LoS 199).

[54] I analyse the following sentence here: '*C'est en ce sens que les trois pulsions se mélangent en profondeur, dans de telles conditions que la conservation fournit plutôt la pulsion, la sexualité l'objet substitutif, et la destruction la rapport entier réversible.*' (LdS 231), (LoS 199).

[55] I refer to this passage: '*dans de telles conditions que la conservation fournit plutôt la pulsion, la sexualité l'objet substitutif, et la destruction la rapport entier réversible.*' (LdS 231), (LoS 199).

[56] I have the following passage in mind: '*Mais précisément, comme la conservation est dans son fond menacée par ce système où elle entre, manger devant être mangé, on voit tout le système se déplacer; et la mort se récupère comme pulsion dans le corps sans organes, en même temps que ce corps mort se conserve et s'alimente éternellement, et se fait sexuellement naître de lui-même.*' (LdS 231), (LoS 199).

organs. At such a moment, the simulacrum of the body without organs reveals the fundamental role it plays within the depths. Death is now recovered as a death drive in the body without organs, avers Deleuze in a rather enigmatic fashion.[57] The ego now reveals that it is continually trying to obtain an object that cannot be consumed. The organism aims at a perfect state of rest or of death and not truly at yet another good partial object. In truth, it continually aims at an eventual suspension of all tensions, or at a state of complete unity. The body without organs becomes an integral part of the unconscious and is strengthened by every experience, by every unwanted state of tension. As Deleuze states, the body without organs is eternally conserved and nourished inside the body. It is sexually born out of itself (*se fait sexuellement naitre de lui même*). As we have observed, the object of the heights of the depressive position takes on some of the characteristics of the body without organs. The identification with this object is intertwined with a schizoid pursuit of rest and discharge.[58] The unreachable object of the heights holds a promise of an eventual and complete suspension of all tensions. We may therefore regard the world of the oral-anal-urethral depths as a revolving mixture.[59] It is a bottomless world, a world of perpetual subversion. The threatened organism searches for a state of rest that it will never find.

The analysed state of mixture is terminated, upon the emergence of the sexual-perverse position. The autoeroticism characterising this position is possible only given the liberation of the libido from both the destructive and self-preservation drives.[60] First of all, the libido ceases to produce substitutes for the objects that guarantee the self-preservation of the organism. The libido no longer leans on the self-preservation drive. The states of pleasure are now separated from the survival strategies of the body. The sexual drives find their source directly in the various erotogenic zones. They are oriented to external objects by means of the images that are projected onto these zones.[61] As we

---

[57] I refer to the following passage: '*et la mort se récupère comme pulsion dans le corps sans organes*' (LdS 231), (LoS 199).

[58] Deleuze does not develop this point further.

[59] Deleuze expresses this as follows: '*Le mode de la profondeur orale-anale-uréthrale est celui d'un mélange tournant, qu'on peut vraiment nommer sans-fond, et qui témoigne d'une subversion perpétuelle.*' (LdS 231), (LoS 199).

[60] I comment on this passage: '*Quand on lie la sexualité à la constitution des surfaces ou des zones, on veut donc dire que les pulsions libidinales trouvent l'occasion d'une double libération au moins apparente, qui s'exprime précisément dans l'auto-érotisme. D'une part elles se dégagent du modèle alimentaire des pulsions de conservation, puisqu'elles trouvent dans les zones érogènes de nouvelles sources, et de nouveaux objets dans les images projetées sur ces zones: ainsi le suçotement, qui se distingue de la succion.*' (LdS 231), (LoS 199).

[61] As pointed out above, an image is pre-representational and not visual in nature.

have seen above, the fingers cease to be substitutes for the breast. Sucking becomes a state of pleasure that may emerge during interactions with a variety of objects. Sexual intercourse on the other hand is now fully separated from the reproductive function. Homosexual intercourse for example becomes just one among many possibilities of reaching sexual gratification.

Secondly, the emergence of the sexual-perverse position leads to liberation of sexuality from the destructive drives or from the death drive.[62] Desire no longer aims at objects that are supposed to eliminate the continuous states of tension, such as the body without organs or the object of the heights. It no longer aims at states of discharge. The sexual drives engage in the productive work of the surface, as Deleuze states. They aim at an intensification of the experience and not at an unreachable state of rest. The drives are satisfied by states of pleasure produced in interactions with various objects. A connoisseur of wine satisfies his oral drive by experiencing the often complicated taste of wine. He experiences joy by the excitation of his oral zone and the nasal organ that are stimulated with the right amount of intensity. Sexual intercourse is in this case not aiming at a direct release of tension, nor is it an activity imposed by the demanding super-ego.[63] Sexual intercourse aims at satisfaction of various erotogenic zones and leads to experiences of intense sexual arousal, states that are not orgasmic in nature. Deleuze and Guattari make a similar point in *A Thousand Plateaus,* where they claim that orgasm should not be considered to be the most fundamental part or goal of the sexual experience. The ancient Chinese sexual practices are exemplary in this respect. For the ancient Chinese, intercourse was not intended for the release of tension but rather at generation of pleasure experienced with a particular kind of intensity. In their mutual work, Deleuze and Guattari consider sexuality to be an assemblage. Both consider it to be a machine that produces intensity, experienced at various erotogenic zones.[64] Sexual pleasure can become a particular practice that is directly linked to the environment of the body.

---

[62] I refer here to: '*D'autre part elles se libèrent de la contrainte des pulsions destructrices pour autant qu'elles s'engagent dans le travail productif des surfaces et dans de nouveaux rapports aves ces nouveaux objets pelliculaires.*' (LdS 231), (LoS 199).

[63] It must be noted here that at this point, we only analyse the pre-genital phase of the sexual position; genital sexuality does not yet dominate the other forms.

[64] See (MP 194), (ATP 157). In *A Thousand Plateaus*, a change of terminology occurs. The body without organs is characterised there as an instance allowing for the experience of 'another' kind of pleasure.

4. Sexual position – discussion with Laplanche and Pontalis

It is now obvious that according to Deleuze, the erotogenic zones play different roles within the schizoid, depressive and sexual positions.[65] He is convinced that this point nuances the psychoanalytic theory of his time and particularly Laplanche and Pontalis's understanding of autoeroticism. According to these psychoanalysts, autoeroticism emerges due to the defusion or separation of the libido from the self-preservation drive, a point adopted by Deleuze in his analysis.[66] It occurs when a division between a real object – an object of the self-preservation drive – and a fantasmatic object[67] – an object of the sexual drives – is established. The emergence of autoeroticism leads to an exclusive orientation towards fantasmatic objects. The first point of Deleuze's critique of Laplanche and Pontalis concerns the visual character of the fantasmatic object. According to both authors, a child hallucinates signs that are associated with the states of pleasure generated by the original object. A breast or a finger is consequently associated with milk, the original source of pleasure and security.[68] Laplanche and Pontalis develop a theory of the pronominal. Given the emergence of autoeroticism, the body is able to experience a state of self-enjoyment. The lips enjoy the sucking of the finger or the capacity to kiss themselves. This state is nevertheless possible only because an external object,

---

[65] I here have the following passage in mind: '*C'est pourquoi, encore une fois, il est si important de distinguer par exemple le stade orale des profondeurs et la zone orale de surface; l'objet partiel interne, introjeté et projeté (simulacre) et l'objet de surface projeté sur one zone d'après un tout autre mécanisme (image): la subversion dépendant des profondeurs et la perversion inséparable des surfaces.*' (LdS 232), (LoS 199). For an explanation of the difference between a phase and zone, see paragraph 4.2.

[66] See Laplanche and Pontalis 1967: 43, (English: 1973: 44). Deleuze states this as follows in note three: '*Le premier point – les pulsions sexuelles se libèrent des pulsions de conservation ou d'alimentation – est bien marqué par J. Laplanche en J.B. Pontalis: Vocabulaire de la psychanalyse, P.U.F., 1967, p. 43 (et « Fantasme originaire, fantasmes des origines, origine du fantasme », Temps modernes, n. 215, 1964 pp. 1866-1867). Mais il ne suffit pas de définir cette libération en disant que les pulsions de conservation ont un objet extérieur, et que les pulsions sexuelles abandonnent cet objet au profit d'une sorte de « pronominal ». En effet, les pulsions sexuelles libérées ont bien encore un objet projeté en surface: ainsi le doigt suçoté comme projection du sein (à la limite, projection d'une zone érogène sur une autre). Ce que Laplanche et Pontalis reconnaissent parfaitement.*' (LdS 232), (LoS 352).

[67] When referring to Laplanche and Pontalis I use here their own terminology and speak here of a fantasmatic object.

[68] For the description of this process, refer also to van Haute & Geyskens (2004: 109). Van Haute and Geyskens point here to the fact that the theory concerning the 'leaning on' of the drives (the anaclysis) is interpreted by Laplanche in a manner that allows them to distance themselves from the biologism of Freud's theory. Sexuality is regarded not as a purely biological activity, but as a biopsychic one instead. See Van Haute and Geyskens (2004: 110).

for example a breast, is considered to have been projected onto a bodily zone.[69] The pleasure does not arise solely due to the mere functioning of the zone.

The second point of critique concerns the inability of Laplanche and Pontalis to systematically distinguish between different positions.[70] The authors are unable to distinguish between different internal objects, between the two forms of the sexual drives and two different mechanisms of projection. The various objects – the internal object, the lost object and the object of the surface – are inappropriately united into one. According to Deleuze, psychoanalysis has developed an uncritical notion of a hallucinatory object.[71] This limited understanding of the nature of the sexual drives leads to a confused analysis of human behaviour. The connoisseur of wine, as mentioned above, is able to experience the states of pleasure proper to the sexual-perverse position's pre-genital phase, exactly because the sexual drive invests the surface of the body and because it is accompanied by a particular image. This state should not be confused with the schizoid one, where the tasted wine is first of all a source of certainty and rest. The tasting of wine would in that case be a temporary protection against the attacks of bad partial objects. This state does not refer to an original object, such as the breast. Another phenomenon that can be only partially understood by means of the notion of the hallucinatory object, is nationalism. Slavoj Žižek claims, for example, that each nationalist claims a possession of an indefinable national 'thing'.[72] Seen

---

[69] Deleuze puts it thus: '*Mais il ne suffit pas de définir cette libération en disant que les pulsions de conservation ont un objet extérieur, et que les pulsions sexuelles abandonnent cet objet au profit d'une sorte de « pronominal ». En effet, les pulsions sexuelles libérées ont bien encore un objet projeté en surface: ainsi le doigt suçoté comme projection du sein (à la limite, projection d'une zone érogène sur une autre). Ce que Laplanche et Pontalis reconnaissent parfaitement.*' (LdS 232), (LoS 352). The notion of the pronominal as developed by Laplanche and Pontalis will be more extensively critiqued in Chapter six.

[70] I refer to the following passage: '*Mais, surtout, les pulsions sexuelles, tant qu'elles épousaient les pulsions alimentaires en profondeur, avaient déjà des objets particuliers distincts de l'objet de ces pulsions: les objets partiels internes. Ce qu'il faut séparer, c'est donc deux états des pulsions sexuelles, deux sortes d'objets pour ces pulsions, deux mécanismes de projection. Et ce qui doit être critiqué, c'est une notion comme celle d'objet hallucinatoire, qui s'applique indistinctement à l'objet interne, à l'objet perdu, à l'objet de surface.*' (LdS 232), (LoS 353).

[71] Here I refer to: '*Et ce qui doit être critiqué, c'est une notion comme celle d'objet hallucinatoire, qui s'applique indistinctement à l'objet interne, à l'objet perdu, à l'objet de surface.*' (LdS 232), (LoS 353).

[72] Slavoj Žižek uses the notion of an hallucinatory object to analyse the phenomenon of nationalism. According to him, any person defining his personality in terms of a nation, is claiming that he is in possession of something proper to this nation. He is claiming the possession of some indefinable national 'thing'. Žižek expresses this as follows: 'If we apprehend this Cause as the Freudian Thing (das Ding), materialized enjoyment, it becomes clear why it is precisely "nationalism" that is the privileged domain of the eruption of enjoyment into the social field: the national Cause is ultimately the way subjects of a

from the perspective of Deleuze, Žižek's explanation unmistakeably carries depressive characteristics. 'Nationalist' is identified with an idealised object of the heights that the nationalist wants to defend at all costs. Nevertheless, nationalism may be equally experienced in the two other positions we have recognised so far. A schizophrenic, oriented towards partial objects, rather than towards an idealised one, will experience in nationalism only a temporary state of pleasure. Identifying with Dutch nationality, for instance, is in this case only possible when this identity allows for an overcoming of fears or when it is useful as a defence of the social position. A schizoid nationalist may nevertheless suddenly become a dedicated European, if this option proves to be more suitable. In the pre-genital phase of the sexual position on the other hand, nationalism could be accompanied by an object of the surface. Having a national identity would contribute to an autoerotic state of enjoyment. In that case, the critical remarks about the national identity are far from threatening; the nation would not be an idealised and threatened object any more. The ego is strong enough simply to enjoy and experience pride.[73]

The third and most important point of critique of the Freudian psychoanalysts concerns their inability to comprehend a defusion of the libido (sexual drives) from the destructive drives (death drive).[74] It is precisely this point that has been recognised by Klein as leading to a limited understanding of human sexuality. According to Deleuze, sexuality is entangled with the destructive drive only in the depths. The feeling of guilt that frequently reappears in Freudian analysis and that appears to be inevitably intertwined with human sexuality, can only occur in this position. Here, however, desire is fused with aggression and leads to excessive states of discharge. The sexual position on the other hand, is entirely liberated from such experience. The

---

given nation organize their collective enjoyment through national myths. What is at stake in ethnic tensions is always the possession of the national Thing: the "other" wants to steal our enjoyment (by ruining our "way of life") and/or it has access to some secret, perverse enjoyment.' See Žižek (1991: 165), '*Looking Awry*', Cambridge: MIT Press.

[73] The distinction between the various types of nationalism could contribute to our understanding of the various manners in which nationalism is experienced by different groups. The bad economic or social position could lead to a more schizoid or depressive relation to the phenomenon. The nation might become just another consumption product or an idealised object instead. A person with a better social or economic position is threatened less quickly and might experience his national identity merely as the source of pride and pleasure. I return to this topic in the chapters that follow.

[74] I am referring to the following sentence: '*D'ou l'importance de l'autre point – les pulsions sexuelles se dégagent des pulsions destructrices. Mélanie Klein y insiste constamment.*' (LdS 232), (LoS 353).

107

sexual experience of this position is entirely innocent.[75] According to Deleuze, the difference between these two kinds of sexuality is visible in Heimann's analysis of sexual assault.[76] Heimann rejects the idea that rape may be understood as a perverse form of sexuality. According to her, it is necessary clearly to distinguish the sexual-perverse practices from acts of violence that have a sexual component. Perverse sexuality that aims at creating various states of pleasure, by stimulation of the erotogenic zones, may be entangled with aggression in merely a limited manner. In case of violence the destructive drives fully dominate the sexual drives and may even make them completely vanish.[77] According to Deleuze, the destructive drives are able to repress the sexual ones only in the schizoid position.[78] The physical overpowering of the other, as a means of releasing overpowering tension, is possible only in this instance; perversion proper to the sexual position on the other hand, never aims at a violent release of tension. The sexual drives are strong enough to completely repress the destructive ones. They allow for a development of pure states of pleasure, per se.

The differentiation between the schizoid and perverse-sexual positions allows Deleuze to refine our understanding of regression to a pre-genital phase.[79] In the case of the domination of the oral zone, we can speak either of a regression to the oral phase of the depths or of one to the oral zone of the surface. This distinction may for example, allow for a different understanding

---

[75] I refer here to this passage: '*Il y a dans toute l'école de M. Klein une tentative justifiée de disculper la sexualité et de la dégager des pulsions destructrices auxquelles elle n'est liée qu'en profondeur. C'est en ce sens que la notion de crime sexuel est discutée par Paula Heimann: in Développements de la psychanalyse, p. 308. Il est bien vrai que la sexualité est perverse, mais la perversion se définit avant tout par le rôle des zones érogènes partielles et de surface. La « crime sexuel » appartient à un autre domaine, où la sexualité ne joue qu'en mélange de profondeur avec les pulsions destructrices (subversion plutôt que perversion).*' (LdS 232), (LoS 353).

[76] See Heimann 1952: 328.

[77] Heimann describes this as follows: 'Strangely enough, such (aggressive - PS) behaviour is usually regarded as perverse sexuality, and often such crimes are called 'sexual crimes'. It is true that sadism is a form of sexual perversion, but it is necessary to distinguish between sexual practices in which sadism (and masochism) have some share, and violent assaults in which cruelty is the predominant feature.(...) I think the hypothesis is justified that in cases of wanton cruelty a kind of instinctual disaster takes place, that for some reason the fusion between the two primary instincts is broken up, and the death instinct stirs within the self to an extreme degree without any mitigation by the life instinct' (Heimann 1952: 329).

[78] This interpretation of Heimann by Deleuze is only partially correct, as seen in the previous note. Heimann makes a clear distinction between acts of violence as such and sexuality. For her, sexuality is inevitably partially entangled with aggression.

[79] I refer here to the following passage: '*En tout cas, on ne confondra pas deux types de régression très différents sous le thème trop général d'un retour au « prégénital »: par exemple la régression à un stade oral des profondeurs, et la régression à la zone orale de surface.*' (LdS 232), (LoS 353).

of some of the Freud's case studies. A woman known as Dora, a patient of Freud's, with a strong oral fixation, repressed all pleasurable experiences in this zone and responded to its stimulation with hysterical attacks. In the standard explanation, the source of the hysterical attacks is found in the Oedipus complex. Dora repressed her sexuality because she was in love with her father. The attacks were understood as a response to the fact that her love was forbidden. A more accurate reading of the analysis of Freud also reveals a different cause.[80] The hysteria has its source in a bodily disposition and emerges due to an organic and not social repression. The experience of bodily pleasure in the case of Dora was severely impeded. The organic repression of the pleasurable stimuli occurs exactly during the stimulation of the most active oral one.[81] Such stimulation is experienced as repulsive and directly leads to episodes of hysteria.

We may use Deleuze's analysis to understand the behaviour of Dora in a different manner. In her case, two kinds of regression to a pre-genital sexuality are possible. The attacks of hysteria after being kissed can be attributed to the domination of the schizoid position. Dora interacts with bad partial objects. The threats are most strongly felt in the most active erotogenic zone – the mouth. Mr. K's kisses must directly generate the most intense states of repulsion and subsequent hysteric attacks. Another explanation could also be offered. Dora may be regressing to the oral zone of the sexual-perverse position. In that case, the source of the hysterical episodes and of the repression of bodily pleasure may be found in the social prohibitions imposed on her bodily desire. Dora desires a forbidden object. She is most likely in love with Mr. K's wife. She responds with an attack of hysteria to his kisses because her true desire has no way of being expressed.[82] Her lesbian desire is forbidden

---

[80] See van Haute and Geyskens, 2012: 45-60.

[81] Van Haute and Geyskens report: 'In the case of Dora it concerns an oral fixation expressed in the following order: in thumb sucking (until five), coughing, dyspnoea and aphonia (from eight), reacting with revulsion when confronted with sexuality (at fourteen) and finally, the fellatio-phantasy repressed during the second trauma (sixteen). Thus, although the view that the symptom is an expression of a sexual phantasy is not wrong, this view is incomplete unless one takes into account the symptom's organic basis. Dora's fellatio-phantasy is not the cause of the oral symptoms; rather it is the psychical articulation and mental representative of an oral fixation that has always determined her entire erotic corporality. The oral fixation lends direction to the sexual phantasy, and the sexual phantasy imbues the symptoms with meaning they did not have before.' Van Haute and Geyskens (2012: 53).

[82] Freud expresses this as follows: 'I believe, therefore, that I am not mistaken in supposing that Dora's supervalent train of thought, which was concerned with her father's relations with Frau K., was designed not only for the purpose of suppressing her love for Herr K., which had once been conscious, but also to conceal her love for Frau K., which was in a deeper sense, unconscious'. (Freud 1905a in 1953: 62).

and must be repressed. The return of the repressed desire, the rage at not being able to exercise her own sexuality and hence a regression to the schizoid position, occurs exactly at the moment when her most active erotogenic zone is stimulated. We may directly conclude here that only in the second scenario, in the instance when the sexual position is already well established, might her problems be more easily resolved.

We can thus infer that the emergence of a sexual-perverse position is possible, given the defusion of the drives. In this respect, the libido must be considered as the energy of the surface.[83] The liberation of the libido from the destructive drives and drives for self-preservation is nevertheless very fragile, as was demonstrated in the analysis of one of the possible causes of the state of Dora's desire. Both drives remain active in the depths and might directly threaten the state of enjoyment proper to the pre-genital phase of the sexual-perverse position. These states may quickly become sources of frustration and tension. They could suddenly become bad partial objects. The wine, coffee, music, dance, the physical presence of another person, or as is noticeable in Dora's case, the stimulation of the oral zone, might suddenly begin to threaten the weakened ego; fear and aggression may quickly reappear.

5. Pre-genital sexuality – relation towards structures

The pre-genital phase of the sexual-perverse position leads to a change in the relationship with the structures of sense. The emergence of the new position slowly leads to liberation from the depressive subjection to external structures of sense that has been analysed in the previous chapter. The slavish subjection to the incomprehensible order diminishes. Its rules are increasingly comprehended. The ego, or rather its multiple instances, wants to enjoy the relationship with the surrounding objects; it increasingly acts as a full member of this environment. It slowly starts to impose its own rules. This influence is nevertheless still highly limited. The ego remains too divided to have a lasting impact on the outside world. The various erotogenic zones and the various corresponding egos do not yet produce a unified experience, but, rather, a

---

[83] I refer here to the following passage: '*On doit donc considérer la libido doublement libérée comme une véritable énergie superficielle. On ne peut croire toutefois que les autres pulsions aient disparu et qu'elles ne continuent pas leur travail en profondeur, ou surtout qu'elles ne trouvent une position originale dans le nouveau système.*' (LdS 232), (LoS 199).

still unrelated series.[84] The ego is unable to unify them and have a lasting influence on the outside world. The only means of organising experience is the connective synthesis.[85] The ego has learned to experience pleasure in the various zones and makes extensive use of this newly found capacity. In point of fact, we could state that it makes an uncritical use of whatever it receives from the outside. The body interacts with objects that generate only the states of pleasure; it enjoys simple interactions with people, sexual contacts, physical exercise or acts of consumption. In this respect, it is submitted to the super-ego's commands present in its daily life. No distance towards these commands is yet present nor is the ego feeling any urge to reach it. It has not yet developed any knowledge of its own capacities. It frequently experiences frustration when its wishes are unfulfilled but it does not realise it is able to change the very structures of its environment for its own good.

A film that, it may be argued, depicts an experience originating from the pre-genital phase of the sexual-perverse position is 'The Truman Show'. This film is a satirical portrayal of life in contemporary capitalist consumption society. The key protagonist of this film, Truman Burbank, lives on the film set of a TV-show without realising it. His relatively carefree and happy life in a wealthy suburb is daily gazed at by millions of viewers. The invisible cameras continually record his daily successes and failures, daily states of pleasure and pain. Truman's life is portrayed as a life full of lies. All of his friends are actors. The audience does not seem to care and enjoys the fantasy of a happy life in a small and wealthy American town. Nevertheless, this idyllic life comes to an end. Truman eventually becomes suspicious and begins to realise that something is wrong with his environment. He wants to gain control of his own life and liberate himself from the world of lies. In an act of heroism, he escapes from his own imprisonment. He comes to realise that another, real world, exists. Truman's attempt at his liberation, not foreseen by the makers of the show and in fact wildly opposed by them, is received enthusiastically by the enormous audience of the show. They sympathise with Truman who is finally able to exercise control over his own life. They admire him for becoming a true master of the latter. The stage of pre-genital, uncritical sexuality is left

---

[84] This paragraph is based on the statement from the chapter 'Thirty-Second Series on the Different Kinds of Series': '*Or, dans les différents moments de la sexualité que nous avons considérés précédemment, nous devons distinguer des espèces de séries très différents. En premier lieu, les zones érogènes dans la sexualité prégénitale: chacune s'organise en une série, qui convérge autour d'une singularité représentée le plus souvent par l'orifice entouré de muqueuse.*' (LdS 261), (LoS 225).

[85] Deleuze remarks: '*En tous ces sens, une série liée à une zoné érogène paraît avoir une forme simple, être homogène, donner lieu à une synthèse de succession qui peut se contracter comme telle, et de toute manière constitue une simple connexion.*' (LdS 262), (LoS 225).

behind. As will be argued in the last two chapters, a victory such as Truman's, can be only partial. The remainder of the current chapter is devoted to an analysis of the conditions of possibility for a break-through similar to the one realised by Truman. This will show how an ego may start to believe in its own capacities to change its environment and demonstrate how genital sexuality contributes to that belief.

6. Genital sexuality

The analysis of the properties of the sexual-perverse position has until now been limited to its pre-genital phase. The surface of the body has been described as the Harlequin's cloak. It consists of various zones, concentrated around membranes or orifices. These zones and the corresponding singular points generate various series that organise experience. The ego of the pre-genital phase is therefore split up into many instances. This state of relative disintegration comes to an end during the genital phase. The experience becomes unified. Deleuze develops an alternative to Freud's and Lacan's theories about genital sexuality and the Oedipus complex here, basing it yet again on the work of Klein. The image of the phallus that plays a central role in the genital phase of the sexual position is not the mark of sexual difference. It is not a symbol of power; nor does it structure the symbolic order. The ego, strengthened by this image, starts to believe in its own restorative capacities. It begins to relate differently to its environment from the manner which structuralist psychoanalysis would expect. How then, in Deleuze's view, does a more unified experience emerge?

A preliminary coordination of the splintered psychic experience comes into existence long before the emergence of the image of the phallus. The initial coordination occurs already in the early stages of the pre-genital phase and is achieved in a threefold manner.[86] This coordination is first of all reached by contiguity.[87] The separate stimulations of various zones are coordinated

---

[86] I comment here upon the passage which follows: '*Là encore nous devons faire intervenir l'ensemble de la position sexuelle, avec ses éléments successifs, mais qui empiètent si bien les uns sur les autres que le précédent n'est déterminé que par son affrontement avec le suivant, ou se préfiguration du suivant. Les zones ou surfaces érogènes prégénitales ne sont pas séparables du problème de leur raccordement. Or il est certain que ce raccord s'opère de plusieurs façons: par contiguïté, dans la mesure où le série qui se développe sur l'une est prolongée dans une autre série; à distance, dans la mesure où une zone peut être repliée ou projetée sur une autre, et fournit l'image dont l'autre se satisfait; et surtout indirectement, dans le stade du miroir de Lacan.*' (LdS 233), (LoS 200).

[87] I refer here to: '*par contiguïté, dans la mesure où le série qui se développe sur l'une est prolongée dans une autre série*' (LdS 233), (LoS 200).

when occurring at the same moment. In the case of a little child a stimulation of the skin leads to the expectation of an approaching oral pleasure. The child connects the experience of being caressed with the subsequent experience of being fed. A series that emerges around one zone – in this case the skin – is extended into the vicinity of another series – here emerging around the oral zone. The oral pleasure, experienced during eating, is connected to the pleasure of being held and caressed. The second manner in which coordination of the various zones is achieved is by distance. In this case one zone is folded or projected into another.[88] One zone produces an image that accompanies the pleasure experienced in another zone. This coordination occurs for example when a child sucks a finger or when it masturbates. Two different erotogenic zones – the finger and the oral zone, or the hand and the genital zone – are coordinated during a common pleasurable activity. The image of the finger is projected onto the oral zone. The finger produces an image by which the oral zone is satisfied. Another recognised example is that of the lips, kissing themselves.[89] The lips themselves furnish an image by means of which they are satisfied.

The third method of coordinating the splintered experience of pleasure is the mirror stage described by Lacan.[90] A child notices its own image in the mirror between six and eighteen months of age.[91] This time it suddenly realises that it is seeing itself in the mirror and starts to identify with it. This act of observing oneself in the mirror generates a state of narcissistic pleasure that leads to fundamental consequences. The child suddenly realises that it possesses a hand, head, lips, legs and other body parts. Its own fragmented body suddenly appears as a unity. Its various parts appear to be related to one another. This image strengthens the splintered ego. It allows the latter to believe in its own powers. The ego develops an image of itself, an ego-ideal that guarantees its unity. This image becomes a source of self-confidence. The mirror stage announces the beginning of an imaginary relationship with the environment.[92] For Lacan, this orientation to an external image

---

[88] Here I refer to: 'à distance, dans la mesure où une zone peut être repliée ou projetée sur une autre, et fournit l'image dont l'autre se satisfait' (LdS 233), (LoS 200).

[89] Cf. Laplanche and Pontalis (1967: 43), (1973: 44).

[90] I am referring here to: 'et surtout indirectement, dans le stade du miroir de Lacan.' (LdS 233), (LoS 200).

[91] Refer: Lacan 1966: 93, Ecrits I; also: Laplanche and Pontalis (1967: 453), (1973: 249).

[92] The emergence of the imaginary order leads to projections of various images onto the environment. According to Lacan, difficulties in distinguishing between these images and reality emerges at the same moment. Only the awareness of the existence of the symbolic order's rules – the structure of the language and society – will bring about a more realistic relationship with the environment.

is of fundamental importance; it is a sign of each human subject's state of perpetual alienation. The ego cannot constitute itself as a unity, without an exterior image of itself, without exteriority. Deleuze, while not rejecting the existence of the mirror stage in *The Logic of Sense,* nevertheless does not regard the relationship with exterior images as fundamental for the emergence of a unified experience of the ego. The visual experience is less important than the non-visual one. A unified ego does not emerge out of the experience of alienation only.

The three processes mentioned, merely mark the beginning of the process of coordination.[93] Deleuze stresses that, normally, the full integration of the partial erotogenic zones is solely furnished by the image of the phallus, projected onto the genital zone.[94] It is the said image that eventually unifies the fragmented experience. Before embarking upon an in-depth discussion of the characteristics of this image, one should first answer the question of why so much attention is paid to the experiences of the genital zone. Why does Deleuze consider them to be strong enough to cause the integration of the ego? Why does he choose to pay little attention to the visual experience of the complete body perceived in the mirror? The pages of *The Logic of Sense* do not provide a clear answer to this question. We can speculate that the genital zone plays a privileged role only because its stimulation is more intense than that of other zones. As Deleuze states, usually, the genital experience overshadows others and must hence necessarily lead to domination by this zone. The strength of the genital zone may be supported by biological arguments. The zone allows for procreation and is, as a result, additionally heavily invested in by the self-preservation drive. Humans need to concentrate on their genital experiences in order to secure the survival of the species. The importance of the self-preservation drive clearly does not entirely disappear in the sexual-

---

[93] I am here referring to the following passage: '*Reste que la fonction d'intégration directe et globale, ou de raccordement général, est normalement dévolu à la zone génitale. C'est elle qui doit lier toutes les autres zones partielles, grâce au phallus. Or, à cet égard, le phallus ne joue pas le rôle d'un organe mais celui d'image particulière projetée sur cette zone privilégiée, aussi bien pour la fille que pour le garçon*' (LdS 233), (LoS 200).

[94] Deleuze distinguishes here between the phallus as an image projected onto the genital zone and the physical organ, the penis. It has been noted above that the images projected on the various zones are not visual in nature. Deleuze also stresses here that the dominance of the genital zone is fundamental only in general or in normal situations. He states: '*Reste que la fonction d'intégration directe et globale, ou de raccordement général, est normalement dévolu à la zone génitale.*' (LdS 233), (LoS 200). This statement implies that a similar role may be fulfilled by another organ. Genital sexuality does not have to produce the strongest drive. The images projected on other zones can become as equally significant as the image of the phallus. They may play a similar role in the process of genesis as this image and may coordinate the various experiences.

perverse position.[95] Social arguments might be advanced as well; without doubt, the child's environment frequently stresses the importance of the erotogenic zone. A boy and a girl become aware of belonging to a particular sex or gender very early in their lives. They are frequently made aware of it. A boy possesses a different reproductive organ to that of a girl. They also quickly derive their identity from the genital zone. It is consequently also the environment that allows for the projection of an image of the phallus on their genital zones.

Deleuze understands the role of the image of the phallus in a very particular way. It is not a mark either of sexual difference or of power. The image of the phallus is an image of a reparative organ that is projected onto the body's genital zone for both a boy and a girl. To be able to understand the nature of this image properly, one must more precisely analyse the role of the genital zone in the previous positions. In the schizoid position the genital organs belong to the depths.[96] They generate experiences of satisfaction when stimulated, and of tension and subsequent fear when no stimulation or overstimulation occurs. A schizoid person fears the penis or vagina of the depths. These organs can quickly become bad partial objects and lead to a state of fear that increases due to the projection of (their) own aggression. A schizoid person introjects the penis or vagina proper to the depths when it causes a pleasurable experience but wants to get rid of it when the negative tension reaches a certain threshold. In that instance, the bad penis or bad vagina are phantasmatically thrown out or projected onto the outside world.[97] This projection damages the environment or the mother's body. Such aggressive projection will inevitably occur when the sexual partner is perceived as a partial object. This person is seen as the source of tension when the pleasurable experiences fail to occur. The ego suddenly projects the simulacrum of a bad penis onto that person

---

[95] A similar argument is offered by Freud in the first version of his '*Three essays*'. For Freud, the genital sexuality represses the polymorph-perverse one so that the excitations of the various erotogenic zones lose importance. Genital sexuality becomes the most fundamental part of psychopathology (see i.a. Laplanche and Pontalis 1967: 243-244; 1973: 133). The conflict between the polymorph-perverse sexuality and the genital one was of lesser significance for Freud in his later work. From 1914 onwards, more emphasis was placed on the oedipal conflict, as became visible in the analysis of little Hans (See a.o. van Haute & Geyskens 2012: 26).

[96] Deleuze makes the following statement: '*C'est que l'organe du pénis a déjà toute une histoire liée aux postions schizoïde et dépressive. Comme tout organe, le pénis connaît l'aventure des profondeurs où il est morcelé, mis dans le corps de la mère et dans le corps de l'enfant, agressé et agresseur, assimilé à un morceau de nourriture vénéneux, à un excrément explosif;*' (LdS 233), (LoS 200).

[97] Deleuze remarks: '*où il est morcelé, mis dans le corps de la mère et dans le corps de l'enfant, agressé et agresseur,*' (LdS 233), (LoS 200).

who is then regarded as the true source of tension. The will to control and even damage the other follows naturally; the partner must be forced to have sexual intercourse. Another example of sexual behaviour generated by the genital zone in the schizoid position is hypersexuality.[98] A nymphomaniac aims at continuous discharges of the tensions generated by the genital zone. Such discharges are only able to be achieved by a continuous introjection of good partial objects; by frequent sexual intercourse. Hyposexuality, on the other, occurs due to the existence of a defence mechanism. The ego protects itself against the bad penis and bad vagina – the stressful genital experiences – by resisting all possible states of genital arousal.[99] The hyposexual person fears the damage that may be caused to their own body and to the body of the other. The penis or vagina of the schizoid position is hence experienced as an explosive organ or explosive excrement, according to Deleuze.[100]

The introduction of the dimension of the heights, characterising the depressive position, changes the relation towards the genital experiences.[101] The release of tension becomes less important or, rather, is endured in a new manner. The genital experiences refer to an idol and must express the love given to the ego by this object. However, while the genital activity must realise a state of perfection proper to this object, in this instance, the ego necessarily fails in these attempts. Building upon Klein's work, Deleuze moreover stresses that the penis and vagina (breast) of the heights are attributed to both parents. The parents form a perfect unity. The mother possesses the good penis and the father the good feeding breast.[102] Signs of an orientation towards a complete

---

[98] See Klein 1997: 199.

[99] For a similar analysis *cf.* Klein, who states: 'Her fear of the sexual act is thus based both on the injuries she will receive from the penis and on the injuries she will herself inflict on her partner. Her fear that she will castrate him is due partly to her identification with her sadistic mother and partly to her own sadistic trends.' Klein does not yet systematically distinguish between the paranoid-schizoid and manic-depressive positions in this text. She makes no distinction yet between the identification with the sadistic mother (complete object, the super-ego) and her own sadistic tendencies, which are central in the paranoid-schizoid position.' (Klein 1997: 204).

[100] Deleuze states: '*Comme tout organe, le pénis connaît l'aventure des profondeurs où il est morcelé (..) à un excrément explosif.*' (LdS 233), (LoS 200).

[101] I refer here to this passage: '(..) *et il ne connaît pas moins, l'aventure de la hauteur où, comme organe complet et bon, il donne amour et sanction, tout en se retirant pour former la personne entière ou l'organe correspondant à la voix, c'est-à-dire l'idole combinée des deux parents*'. (LdS 233), (LoS 200).

[102] See M. Klein (1952: 219), and Laplanche and Pontalis (1967: 303), (1973: 70). Deleuze remarks: '*pour former la personne entière ou l'organe correspondant à la voix, c'est-à-dire l'idole combinée des deux parents*'. (LdS 233), (LoS 200). (…) '*et surtout le bon objet de la hauteur était à la fois pénis et sein comme organe complet, mère pourvue d'un pénis et père pourvu d'un sein.*' (LdS 238), (LoS 204).

good organ, representing the united parents, are present in masochism. A masochist subjects himself to a woman with a penis, one who carries all characteristics of an idol. He desires a woman who possesses the complete good organ belonging to the heights. The clothes that are worn by the idealised woman must for example suggest the presence of both the penis and the good feeding breast.[103]

The shift to the depressive organisation of the genital experience is also visible in the case of a child hearing parental coitus, states Deleuze.[104] In the schizoid position, the sound of coitus is experienced as a threat. It is perceived as a furious attack. Coitus is full of aggression. In the depressive position on the other hand, this sound becomes an organised voice. It now refers to a higher order. The sound refers to an idol. The perfection and completeness of the coitus heard by the child should be realised. Genital sexual experience organised by the depressive position can be enormously frustrating exactly due to the unbridgeable distance towards the good object – the united penis and breast (vagina) of the heights. The continuous striving for perfection may in that case result in the loss of interest in sexuality. The union with the partner that is to be reached, for example during sexual intercourse, appears as impossible. The idol – the united parents – can never be made present. Inevitably, an endless search for a perfect partner naturally follows. In the case of a manic response to the loss of the good object of the heights, the consequences are different; any sign that might shatter belief in the existence of the idol is resisted. While the need exists for relationship to be perceived as perfect, nevertheless confrontation with reality is seldom avoided. The manic person is doomed to discover that the perfection at which he is aiming is impossible to attain.

The emergence of the sexual position leads to a further change in the organisation of experiences generated by the genital zone. Similarly to the other erotogenic zones in the sexual position, the experience of the genital zone is organised by a specific image projected onto the zone by the ego. In the case of the genital zone it is the image of the phallus. According to Deleuze, this image is initially projected by both a boy and a girl.[105] Deleuze's understanding of the role of this image differs from Lacan's view. The image of the phallus is not

---

[103] See Deleuze: *Presentation de Sacher Masoch.* (PSM 60), (CC 68).

[104] I here refer to the following sentence: '*(Parallèlement, le coït parental, d'abord interprété comme pur bruit, fureur et agression, devient une voix organisée, même et y compris dans sa puissance de se taire et de frustrer l'enfant).*' (LdS 233), (LoS 200).

[105] As Deleuze states: '*Or, à cet égard, le phallus ne joue pas le rôle d'un organe, mais celui d'image particulière projetée sur cette zone privilégiée, aussi bien pour la fille que pour le garçon.*' (LdS 233), (LoS 200).

a signifier that marks an irreducible sexual difference.[106] It is not a symbol of power inscribed on the body by the symbolic order. The image of the phallus is an image of an organ capable of healing and unifying. It is an image that allows the ego to undo the experience of shattering and fragmentation found in the environment. Deleuze's analysis of the characteristics of the image of the phallus is partially based upon the work of Melanie Klein. The phallus can take on the role of a reparative organ only in the instance of the step from the schizoid to the depressive position and from the depressive position towards the sexual one.[107] The existence of the good complete object, in particular, is of fundamental importance for the emergence of this image. The genital zone and especially the penis must cease to be experienced as a bad partial object.[108] Klein frequently discusses the transformations of genital sexuality. According to her, the sense of pride derived from the possession of a penis allows a boy to defend himself against paranoid-schizoid fears. The attacks by bad partial objects cannot harm him anymore. The psychic representation of the penis is able, according to her, to become a good internal object.[109]

[106] See a.o. Laplanche and Pontalis (1967: 312), (1973: 313).

[107] To a certain extent, Deleuze follows Melanie Klein. He remarks: '*C'est de tous ces points de vue que Mélanie Klein montre que les positions schizoïde et dépressive fournissent les éléments précoces du complexe d'Œdipe; c'est-à-dire que le passage du mauvais pénis à un bon est la condition indispensable pour l'accession au complexe d'Œdipe en son sens strict, à l'organisation génitale et aux nouveaux problèmes correspondants.*' (LdS 233), (LoS 200).

[108] Deleuze, citing Klein from the work *The Psychoanalysis of Children*, observes: '*Sur le mauvais et le bon penis, cf. Mélanie Klein, par exemple La Psychanalyse des enfants, p. 233, p. 265. M. Klein marque avec force que le complexe d'Oedipe implique la position préalable d'un « bon pénis », aussi bien que la libération des pulsions libidinales à l'égard des pulsions destructrices: « C'est seulement quand un petit garçon croit fortement à la bonté de l'organe génital masculin, celui de son père comme le sien propre, qu'il peut se permettre de ressentir ses désirs génitaux à l'égard de sa mère…, il peut faire face à la haine et à la rivalité que fait naître en lui le complexe d'Œdipe »(Essayas de psychanalyse, tr. M. Derrida, Payot, p. 415). Ce qui ne veut pas dire, nous le verrons, que la position sexuelle et la situation œdipienne ne comportent pas leurs angoisses et leurs dangers nouveaux; ainsi une peur spécifique de la castration. Et s'il est vrai que, dans les stades précoces d'Œdipe, le surmoi dirige avant tout sa sévérité contre les pulsions destructrices, « la défense contre les pulsions libidinales fait son apparition dans les dernières phases » (La Psychanalyse des enfants, pp. 148-149).*' (LdS 234), (LoS 353). The topic of castration will be returned to in Chapter five.

[109] Klein puts this in the following words: 'They (characteristics determining the development of a boy - PS) may be summed up as follows: (1) The anxiety arising from his earliest danger-situations – his fears of being attacked in all parts of his body and inside it – which include all his fears deriving from the feminine position, are displaced on to the penis as an external organ, where they can be more successfully mastered. The increased pride the boy takes in his penis, and all that this involves, may be said to be the method of mastering those fears and disappointments which his feminine position lays him open to more particularly. (2) The fact that the penis is a vehicle first of the boy's destructive and then of his creative omnipotence, enhances its significance as a means of mastering anxiety. Moreover in thus fulfilling all these functions – i.e. in promoting his sense of omnipotence, his reality-testing

The penis strengthens the feeling of omnipotence. It also contributes to the strengthening of the sense of reality.

Klein stresses moreover that a similar kind of imagination also emerges amongst girls. Moreover, in this case the genital sexuality and related states of pleasure are able to annul the paranoid-schizoid and manic-depressive fears and frustration.[110] In the same way as a boy, a girl could also believe in the existence of a good sexual organ that may become a part of her unconscious during the predominance of the manic-depressive position. Possession of this internal good genital organ allows her to believe in her own reparative capacities. Similarly to the boy, she is provided with a sense of pride and empowerment. Genital activity becomes a manner of undoing the harm attributed to the outside world. The emergence of sexuality that is separated from aggression is perceived as a precondition for the development of a satisfying love life. Sexual intercourse is in that case accompanied by the phantasm of a good penis and a good vagina (or feeding breast). The woman can identify with the good mother and believe that intercourse will not harm her or her partner. She is unconsciously convinced of her restorative capacities. The fragmentation characterising both her own inner life and that of her partner is cancelled out.[111]

In his analysis of the properties of the image of the phallus Deleuze further builds upon Klein's theory.[112] He distinguishes the sexual position as such and

---

and his relation to objects, and, by means of those functions, in serving the dominating function of mastering anxiety – the penis, or rather its psychic representative, is brought into specially close relation with the ego and is made into a representative of the ego and the conscious; while the interior of the body, the imagos and the faeces – what is invisible and unknown, that is – are compared to the unconscious.' (Klein 1997: 252).

[110] As Klein writes: 'It is now her father who, in her phantasies, makes restitution to her mother and gratifies her by means of his health-giving penis; whilst her mother's vagina, originally a dangerous thing in phantasy, restores and heals her father's penis which it has injured. In thus looking upon her mother's vagina as a health- and pleasure-giving organ, the girl is not only able to call up once more her earliest view of her mother as the "good" mother who gave her suck, but can think of herself, in identification with her, as a healing and giving person and can regard the penis of her partner in love as a "good" penis. Upon an attitude of this kind will rest the successful development of her sexual life and her ability to become attached to her object by ties of sex no less than of affection and love.' (Klein 1997: 220).

[111] For a slightly different discussion of Klein's account of female sexuality see Kristeva (2001: 123).

[112] I refer here to the following passage: '*Ces nouveaux problèmes, nous savons en quoi ils consistent: organiser des surfaces et opérer leur raccordement. Justement, comme les surfaces impliquent en dégagement des pulsions sexuelles à l'égard des pulsions alimentaires et des pulsions destructrices, l'enfant peut croire qu'il laisse aux parents la nourriture et la puissance, et en revanche espérer que le pénis, comme organe bon et complet, va venir se poser et se projeter sur sa propre zone génitale, devenir le phallus qui « double » son propre organe et lui permet d'avoir des rapports sexuelles avec le mère sans offenser le père.*' (LdS 234), (LoS 201).

119

puts more emphasis on the importance of the process of defusion of the drives in this position. Belief in the reparative capacities of the phallus is only able to emerge when the libido is fully defused or separated from both the destructive drives and the self-preservation drive. This defusion leads to an increased sense of security. The child is certain about being fed by its parents and believes that they will not misuse their power.[113] It equally believes in their good intentions and ceases to project aggression onto them. This feeling of security subsequently leads to a belief in its own good intentions. The penis of the heights – the good and complete object of the heights – is now projected onto the genital zone.[114] The genital zone receives all of its positive characteristics. The ego believes not only in the good nature of the idealised others, but in its own goodness too. It claims possession of an idealised good object. The image of the phallus allows it to believe in its own capacity to restore the damage found in the environment. A sharp distinction is made here between the image of the phallus and the penis of the heights. The phallus is not a lost object that resides in the heights. This image accompanies a full belief in the possession of reparative capacities. No lack must be masked. The ego becomes fully narcissistic. No threat is yet looming on the horizon. The new image is able to play an important role in sexual intercourse. For Deleuze, the image of the phallus fulfils a role similar to the one of the good penis and the feeding breast for Klein. The ego is convinced that it can restore the fragmented body of the partner. No aggression is expressed. The partner is not an object that must be controlled and possessed. The pleasure aimed at ceases to refer to an ideal state that is impossible to realise. The image of the phallus allows for reparation. The other clearly profits from the actions of the ego.

The same image of the phallus may also guide the behaviour of a therapist or a physician. She is not guided by aggression but, rather, unconsciously perceives herself as capable of restoring the damage found in others. The others, in her view, will only profit from these interactions. In the same vein, a father or a mother can act in terms of a similar image. He or she believes in this instance in their own capacity to raise the children. The mother or the father are not engaged in any struggle with the children, who are no longer considered to be dangerous partial objects. Nor are they confronted with an experience of failure with respect to their role. The care for the children ceases to refer to an

---

[113] I here comment on this passage: '*l'enfant peut croire qu'il laisse aux parents la nourriture et la puissance*' (LdS 234), (LoS 200).

[114] Here I refer to this passage: '*et en revanche espérer que le pénis, comme organe bon et complet, va venir se poser et se projeter sur sa propre zone génitale, devenir le phallus qui « double » son propre organe et lui permet d'avoir des rapports sexuelles avec le mère sans offenser le père.*' (LdS 234), (LoS 201).

unreachable idol of the heights. The narcissistic parent is convinced that the liberation from aggression and the development of good intentions allows her or him to become a good parent. The state of incompleteness, attributed to the children, is undone by own actions. Similarly, the unconscious idol might also guide an artist who sublimates the genital drive of the sexual position. Her art is experienced as solutions to the existing problems of the audience. The artist is convinced that her work can, for example, eradicate or express and release the suffering and pain of the spectators. She is convinced that her work can heal the wounds of others.

7. The Oedipus complex[115]

The increased self-confidence of the genital phase of the sexual-perverse position plays a fundamental role in the Oedipus complex, as it is understood by Deleuze.[116] The purpose of the image of the phallus is not to penetrate or to empty out. This role is assigned only to the simulacrum of the penis of the schizoid position. The image of the phallus is a reparative instrument of the surface,[117] eradicating the suffering characterising the previous positions. A child is now unconsciously convinced that it can restore the body of the mother without competing with the father.[118] The body of the mother is no longer wounded by the aggressive attacks of the bad internal objects, among which is the internal penis of the depths. In the genital phase of the sexual position, the child is aiming rather at undoing those wounds. It still remembers its own anger, expressed when it was not fed or taken care of adequately. It

---

[115] This is my first sketch of Deleuze's account of the Oedipus complex. Its full form, including its consequences, are provided in Chapter five. Here, I am following Deleuze's original text; he has already introduced this notion in the chapter on sexuality.

[116] I comment here upon the following passage: 'Car c'est cela qui est essentiel: la précaution et la modestie de la revendication œdipienne, au départ. Le phallus comme image projetée sur la zone génitale, n'est nullement un instrument agressif de pénétration et d'éventration. Au contraire, c'est un instrument de surface, destiné à réparer des blessures que les pulsions destructrices, les mauvais objets internes et le pénis des profondeurs ont fait subir au corps maternel, et à rassurer le bon objet, à le convaincre de ne pas se détourner (les processus de « réparation » sur lesquels insiste Mélanie Klein nous paraissent en ce sens appartenir à la constitution d'une surface elle-même réparatrice).' (LdS 234), (LoS 201).

[117] Deleuze adds a systematic distinction to the work of Klein. Reparation is possible mainly due to the emergence of a surface. Deleuze states: '(les processus de « réparation » sur lesquels insiste Mélanie Klein nous paraissent en ce sens appartenir à la constitution d'une surface elle-même réparatrice).' (LdS 234), (LoS 201).

[118] I refer here to this passage: 'Au contraire, c'est un instrument de surface, destiné à réparer des blessures que les pulsions destructrices, les mauvais objets internes et le pénis des profondeurs ont fait subir au corps maternel' (LdS 234), (LoS 201).

121

now blames itself for the state of disintegration of the environment and aims to restore it.[119]

The projection of the image of the phallus on the genital zone is equally important for the relationship of the ego to the good object of the heights.[120] The ego now believes in its capacity to reassure the good object. It is confident that its liberation from aggression is sufficient to convince it not to turn away any longer. It is convinced that the good object does not have to fear the id any more. A physician driven by reparative capacities not only believes in his capacity to heal the patient, he also does not doubt the goals of his actions. He recognises what for him is a good quality of life and cannot imagine that physical health might not be its main constituent part. Similar, narcissistic appropriation of the good object of the heights is present among the viewers of various television series about healthcare (*House, ER*), criminality (*NCIS*), problematic children (*Supernanny*) or property renovation. The viewers admire the capacities of the main protagonists and firmly believe that the good life, both unreachable and never truly defined, is attainable. A good life is able to be realised once we have access to fantastic health care, with an equivalent of *Dr House* in our vicinity: this is realisable once the state institutions, such as the police or NCIS, fully exercise their power. The good life is achieved once the right parental techniques, or the advice of the *Supernanny*, have been applied in order to eliminate the excessive and aggressive behaviour of the children.

The emphasis placed on the reparative capacities of the image of the phallus may be read as an implicit critique of Freud's understanding of the Oedipus complex. Aggression, fears and subsequent guilt, central to Freud's analysis, are entirely absent here.[121] For Freud, nothing but competition between the father and his son can exist. Both desire the mother, but only one of them can be the true object of her affections. The competition leads to a prohibition imposed upon the boy by his father. The son must learn to accept that the mother does not belong to him. This point is, for example, visible in the analysis of little Hans's case. According to Freud, the different phobias of the

---

[119] The question remains why only the body of the mother and not of the father is experienced as disintegrated. Deleuze does not provide us with a clear answer. This topic will be analysed further in Chapter five.

[120] I refer here to: '*et à rassurer le bon objet, à le convaincre de ne pas se détourner*' (LdS 234), (LoS 201).

[121] Deleuze states this as follows: '*L'angoisse et la culpabilité ne dérivent pas du désir œdipien d'inceste; elles se sont formées bien avant, l'une avec l'agressivité schizoïde, l'autre avec la frustration dépressive.*' (LdS 234), (LoS 201).

little boy are only attributable to the Oedipus complex.[122] Little Hans is in love with his mother and desires her exclusive attention. He initially fails to accept that such a relationship is impossible. He is driven by an aggression towards his father, but also starts to fear the latter's response. He develops a fear of castration. This aggression and fear are nevertheless never uttered or consciously experienced. Their expressions are directly repressed. The fear of castration is unconscious. The sense of reality prevents the expression of aggression towards a figure as important as the father. The boy develops agoraphobia and a fear of horses instead; he becomes extremely anxious about being bitten by a horse.[123]

Deleuze's analysis allows for a different understanding of this case. We can hardly speak of Oedipus here. Fear of the horse experienced by little Hans is schizoid in nature and contains no characteristics of the sexual position.[124] As pointed out by Klein in her reinterpretation of Hans's phobias, the fear emerges during a temporary regression to the schizoid position. Such a conflict can occur only if this is the case. The horse was merely an attacking bad partial object.[125] Klein's analysis also clarifies why this schizoid episode was of relatively short duration. Little Hans was capable of quickly overcoming these schizoid tendencies because he had already established strong ties with his parents. The boy had developed a good complete internal object and had already developed the manic-depressive position. Klein even stresses that the boy might have already evolved strong genital sexuality and narcissism, which Deleuze speaks about in his analysis of the sexual position. It was thus no coincidence that the fear of the horses was merely temporary. Equally, the feeling of guilt, so central to the Freudian analysis of the Oedipus complex, emerges prior to the sexual position Deleuze speaks about.[126] It is possible to trace it to the depressive position where the ego is confronted with unfulfillable demands. The boy does not experience the feeling of guilt because he represses the aggression towards his father but rather because he fails to fulfil the demands

---

[122] Freud, S., (1909), 'Analysis of a phobia in a five-year-old boy', in Freud (1955).

[123] See among others: 'Let me summarize the results that had so far been reached. Behind the fear to which Hans first gave expression, the fear of a horse biting him, we had discovered a more deeply seated fear, the fear of horses falling down; and both kinds of horses, the biting horse and the falling horse, had been shown to represent his father, he was going to punish him for the evil wishes he was nourishing against him.' (Freud 1909, in Freud 1955: 126).

[124] I am referring to: 'elles (fears – PS) se sont formées bien avant, l'une avec l'agressivité schizoïde,' (LdS 234), (LoS 201).

[125] See also Klein, M., (1997: 158-161).

[126] I here refer to: 'la culpabilité (…) se sont formées bien avant, (…) avec la frustration dépressive.' (LdS 234), (LoS 201).

of the environment. A similar process might have occurred in Hans's case. In their analysis of the case, Deleuze and Guattari emphasise similar points. The origin of the phobia has absolutely no connection with the mother and the father. The child does not desire the mother nor fear the father. Rather, the phobia may be traced to the prohibitions imposed upon little Hans. His self-confident explorative activity is limited by his environment. The parents do not allow the vigorous boy to play outside with other children, nor is he allowed to sleep in the apartment of a neighbour. According to Deleuze and Guattari his self-confidence is undermined. Exactly such prohibitions cause a temporary regression and the development of his phobia of the horses.[127] His capacity to explore the world is nevertheless equally quickly restored.

According to Deleuze, the Oedipal desire, proper to the sexual position, does not lead to the emergence of any fear or guilt.[128] Oedipus is a peacemaker. He does not differ much from the Greek and Roman hero, Hercules, the son of Zeus, born from a relation of the God with a human. Hercules is a powerful hero, who continually tempts fate. He remains victorious in the face of all the initially insurmountable obstacles, set up by his stepmother Hera, his father's jealous wife. After surmounting all the obstacles, Hercules achieves a place in the pantheon of the Greek gods. He becomes immortal because of his powers and bravery. Oedipus does not differ greatly; he is also capable of heroic actions. He chases away the infernal power of the depths and the celestial power of the heights, argues Deleuze.[129] Just like Hercules, he is tempting fate. He does not want to slay his father. Neither does he wish to make his mother suffer. Oedipus desires to avert this fate at all costs. After discovering his destiny, he decides to flee. What is regarded as his parental

---

[127] The following chapters will return to this case study and especially to the role played by the horse. It must nevertheless be emphasised that Deleuze and Guattari conceptualise the role of the genital zone and the phallus differently from what is elucidated here. For them, the male organ is part of a larger assemblage (*agencement*). Its role is more determined by its environment than Deleuze explicitly allows for in his analysis here. See *L'interprétation des énoncés*, in DRF: 81, (TRM 90).

[128] I comment here upon the passage which follows: '*Le désir œdipien serait plutôt de nature à les conjurer. Œdipe est un héros pacificateur du type herculéen. C'est le cycle thébain. Œdipe a conjuré la puissance infernale de profondeurs, il a conjuré la puissance céleste des hauteurs et revendique seulement un troisième empire, la surface, rien que la surface – d'où sa conviction de ne pas être fautif, et la certitude où il était d'avoir tout arrangé pour échapper à la prédiction.*' (LdS 234), (LoS 201).

[129] I refer here to the following passage: '*Œdipe a conjuré la puissance infernale de profondeurs, il a conjuré la puissance céleste des hauteurs et revendique seulement un troisième empire, la surface, rien que la surface.*' (LdS 234), (LoS 201).

home is left behind.[130] Oedipus cannot live in the world he is destined to live in. His mother must not be violated, while his father may not be assassinated. His intentions are good. Oedipus is innocent and, in his naiveté, he believes that his fate can be averted. He is convinced that sufficient precautionary measures have been taken.[131] He is certain that renouncing aggression, and the lack of will to subvert the father's authority, are enough.

One can therefore conclude that Oedipus does not live in the world of the depths. He discovers a new territory: that is, the surface.[132] The image of the phallus allows him to act without aggression. It is this image that traces a line on the surface without violating it.[133] The image of the phallus fertilises the thin surface as a ploughshare would, states Deleuze. The phallus does not destroy. It plays a twofold role. Most importantly it contributes to the emergence of a complete surface of one's own body. It ties together the separate erotogenic zones.[134] It ensures their connection and duplication (*doublure*). A unified surface of the body emerges. The original partiality of experience is overcome. Experience generated by each separate surface now contributes to a unified experience. The already existing partial entities become part of an overarching entity. The second function of the line drawn by the image of the phallus on the surface considers the world outside of the body. As is more extensively developed in the next chapter, the development of genital sexuality leads to an important change in the nature of the images of the parents.[135] Deleuze subscribes to a theory according to which the development of genital sexuality leads to the development of a clear distinction between the images of both

---

[130] Oedipus arrives in Thebes and kills a man who blocks his way. Subsequently, he solves the Sphinx's puzzle and marries with the countries Queen. The slain man proves to be his own father, the woman his mother. The consequences of his deeds are analysed in the next chapter.

[131] Here I refer to the following passage: '*d'où sa conviction de ne pas être fautif, et la certitude où il était d'avoir tout arrangé pour échapper à la prédiction.*' (LdS 234), (LoS 201).

[132] I am referring to the passage which follows: '*il a conjuré la puissance céleste des hauteurs et revendique seulement un troisième empire, la surface, rien que la surface*' (LdS 234), (LoS 201).

[133] As Deleuze states: '*Ce point, qui devrait être développé par l'interprétation de l'ensemble du mythe, trouve une confirmation dans la nature propre du phallus: celui-ci ne doit pas s'enfoncer mais, tel un soc qui s'adresse à la mince couche fertile de la terre, il trace une ligne à la surface.*' (LdS 235), (LoS 201).

[134] I refer here to this passage: '*Cette ligne, émanée de la zone génitale, est celle qui lie toutes les zones érogènes entre elles, donc en assure le raccord ou la doublure, et fait de toutes les surfaces partielles une seule en même surface sur le corps de l'enfant.*' (LdS 235), (LoS 201).

[135] I here have the following passage in mind: '*C'est dans cette phase phallique œdipienne qu'un net clivage des deux parents s'opère, la mère prenant sur soi l'aspect d'un corps blessé à réparer, et le père, d'un bon objet à faire revenir; mais surtout c'est là que l'enfant poursuit sur son propre corps la constitution d'une surface et l'intégration des zones, grâce au privilège bien fondé de la zone génitale*' (LdS 235), (LoS 201).

parents. The child starts first of all to perceive the mother as lacking something. It begins to phantasmatically experience her body as incomplete. It also starts to see itself as an entity that restores this incompleteness. In this sense, the image of the body of the mother differs from the schizoid simulacrum of the mother. The simulacrum does not refer to any experience of unity, given the fact that the child does not yet have a clear conception of a complete object. It can consequently never aim at restoring the latter. Such activity only becomes possible in the sexual position, given the awareness of the existence of the mother as a complete and perfect idol of the depressive position. The genital sexuality also generates a new image of the father, who is not experienced as a good object of the heights. The image gains the characteristics of an object that must be rediscovered. The image of the phallus now leads to a peculiar conviction on the part of the ego, which is now convinced that it is able to make the father return.[136] It believes that it can terminate his retreat. As will be discussed in the next chapter, both images may be projected onto various other objects.

8. The genital phase of the sexual-perverse position: relationship to structures

The development of the genital phase of the sexual position changes the ego's relationship to the structures of sense. It has already been noted that the schizoid position is characterised by an independent production of sense. The ego constructs its own meaningful world by means of simulacra, despite not being aware of the existence of the structures of sense existing in its environment. This limited awareness leads to an incapacity to truly influence and change the environment. In the depressive position, on the other hand, the ego starts to acknowledge the presence of the external structures of sense. It is slowly deprived of the world of self-constructed simulacra. It subjects itself to the external ordering of sense, despite its incapacity to comprehend the inner dynamics of this ordering. The pre-genital phase of the sexual position introduces a minor shift as regards the depressive relationship with the structures of sense. The ego ceases to perceive itself as an inferior instance. It increasingly sees itself as a fully developed member of its environment. It enjoys the separate experiences of pleasure. Nevertheless, the ego or rather the egos cannot yet influence their environment. The only experiences they can

---

[136] I refer here to the following passage: '*Bien plus, elle est censée refaire une surface au corps de la mère elle-même, et faire revenir le père retiré.*' (LdS 235), (LoS 201).

enjoy are the ones allowed for by the already existing structures of sense. The separate experiences do not yet form a unity. The only synthesis of experience, present in this position, is connective in nature.

The emergence of the sexual position's genital phase leads to a change. The image of the phallus truly strengthens the ego. The separate egos are now tied together; a unified experience is formed and a particular kind of narcissism emerges. The slavish subjection to the external order slowly disappears. The image of the phallus strengthens the belief of the ego in its capacity to influence the environment. The environment does not have to consist of separate and chaotically related separate entities as was the case up until now. The ego is convinced that it can construct a well-functioning whole; in other words, it considers itself capable of constructing the structures of sense. The image of the phallus allows the ego to believe that it is the centre of the universe. It believes that it can restore the unity of the world without any exercise of force or aggression, and truly believes in its own good intentions.

The sexual position's genital phase is, moreover, characterised by a new synthesis. The connective syntheses are now over-determined by a conjunctive synthesis.[137] The experiences of separate zones, organised in various series, are tied together. The image of the phallus links the divergent series of experience together.[138] These divergent series begin to converge around a centre. The partial egos become less important so that the ego establishes a new unity. The various activities of the body are now less coincidental and start to be oriented towards a particular goal envisaged by the ego. The activity receives a clearly defined direction.

This change may be clarified by the previously mentioned example of the *Truman Show*'s main protagonist. Truman suddenly discovers that his life is a farce. He senses that there exists a completely different world outside of his safe suburb. Departing from the TV-show appears to be a heroic mission. The directors do not want him to leave as his departure would inevitably mark the end of a popular and profitable show. Truman prevails through a

---

[137] I offer a simplified explanation of the following passage from the 'Thirty-Second Series on the Different Kinds of Series' here: '*Mais, en second lieu, il est clair que le problème de raccordement phallique des zones érogènes vient compliquer la forme sérielle: sans doute les séries se prolongent-elles les unes les autres, et convergent autour du phallus comme image sur la zone génitale. Cette zone génitale a elle-même se série. Mais elle n'est pas séparable d'une forme complexe qui subsume maintenant des séries* hétérogènes, *une condition de* continuité ou de convergence *ayant remplacé l'homogénéité; elle donne lieu à une synthèse de* coexistence et de coordination, *et constitue une* conjonction *des séries subsumées.*' (LdS 262), (LoS 225).

[138] For a brief analysis of the phallus' role of coordination in *The Logic of Sense* see Žižek, (2004: 90). It must be noted that Žižek pays little attention to the influence of Klein on Deleuze. He is equally silent about the critique of Lacan implied by this analysis.

massive storm on a lake and reaches the border of his own world. Reminiscent of Oedipus, he attempts to alter his own destiny. He does not resign but leaves the TV-show that has been his whole life. He takes his life into his own hands. The spectators of the TV-show are thrilled by this sudden and unexpected change of the plot. Show's ratings rise to unprecedented heights. Each member of the public wants to believe that he can also exercise control over his own life. Truman departs and begins his own life. However, as I will argue in the next chapter, imagining such a heroic escape generates its own problems.

9. Conclusion

The sexual-perverse position develops later than the schizoid and depressive positions. It is characterised by the emergence of the surface of the body as a separate and new topological dimension. It was also pointed out that the sexual position is characterised by an increase in the importance of narcissism. The ego liberates itself from submission to the demands of the depths and the heights. One of the main events causing the emergence of the sexual position was the defusion of the drives. In the sexual-perverse position, the libido or the sexual drives have been separated from the death drive and the self-preservation drive. The states of pleasure cease to be pure states of discharge. I also noted that the sexual position is divided into a pre-genital and genital phases. The initial fragmented experience is unified by means of the image of the phallus projected onto the genital zone. This image strengthens the ego's narcissistic belief in its own reparative capacities. The ego becomes less dependent on the good object of the heights and on the direct demands emerging in the depths.

The analysis of the nature of the image of the phallus also allowed Deleuze to rethink the nature of the oedipal desire. The image of the phallus does not presuppose a competition and struggle with the real or symbolic father. Neither does it express a will to possess the mother. On the contrary, this image expresses the will of the child to restore the body of the mother and his will to render the retreated father present. Moreover, the image of the phallus is not a signifier that is inscribed on the body by the symbolic order. Akin to the other images and objects, it emerges out of the direct physical interactions of the body with its environment. This particular image emerges due to a projection of the characteristics of the good object of the heights on the genital zone. In the next chapter, the reader will nevertheless observe that the sense of self-confidence, discussed here, will be lost. The narcissistic belief in one's own reparative capacities is put to the test within a short period of time. The ego is directly confronted with the threat of castration. As we will additionally notice, this analysis will differ greatly from the Freudian and structuralist accounts. The loss of the image of the phallus is not the end of the dynamic genesis.

The development of the sexual position has also implied a change with respect to the relationship to language and the structures of sense. The slavish submission to those structures has been terminated. The ego slowly gains control of language and of the structures of sense. It increasingly considers itself capable of amending them, perceiving itself as a producer of sense. We have understood that in the pre-genital phase the ego executes the connective synthesis while in the genital phase it executes a conjunctive one. In the next chapter I will observe how the destruction of narcissism also changes the ego's relationship to the structures of sense. Control over those structures will prove to be illusory. A new type of relationship with the environment and the structures of sense will nevertheless appear to be possible.

This chapter has also allowed one to briefly reflect upon the broader development of Deleuze's thought concerning desire. It has been indicated that in his work with Guattari, Deleuze was equally interested in the experiences characteristic of the sexual-perverse position. It was evident that both writers analyse desire that does not involve the death drive and is hence not primarily aiming at discharge. I have mentioned the example of the Chinese sexual practices, described in *A Thousand Plateaus*, that are not aiming at a direct release of tension but at the generation of a particular amount of pleasure instead. Another topic that is present in both *The Logic of Sense* and books such as *Anti-Oedipus* is the Oedipus complex. In their common work, Deleuze and Guattari emphasise the dominant role of narcissism in contemporary consumerist society and indeed criticise all the social and political practices – amongst which is psychoanalysis – that support an uncritical construction of such forms of subjectivity. A similar critique is implicitly found in *The Logic of Sense*. Narcissism is not unavoidable and can be challenged. As will become clear, the decline of narcissism does not have to lead to a regression to previous positions. It can be overcome in the development of a proper form of the phantasm. As will become evident, the non-narcissistic phantasms that will be analysed in the following chapters play a crucial role in the work of Deleuze and Guattari as well. They constitute a basis for the construction of social and political practices that may become an alternative to the formation of desire within contemporary consumerist society.

CHAPTER 5

Oedipus complex and beyond

1. Introduction

In the previous chapter I analysed the pre-genital and genital phases of the sexual position. This chapter is devoted to an analysis of the castration or Oedipus complex and the phase that follows the development of that complex. I will demonstrate that the analysis of this complex is inspired by Melanie Klein and aims attempts to be a genuine alternative to its structuralist version. The Oedipus complex can only be thought of given the existence of the preceding positions and particularly the distance from aggression and violence reached only in the sexual position. As we have already noticed, the image of the phallus reveals the good intentions of the ego. It unifies the fragmented surface of its own body, aims to repair the wounded body of the mother and makes the retreated father present. As will become evident, this state of narcissistic self-confidence is quickly challenged. The ego loses the image of the phallus during a confrontation with the unforeseen consequences of its own actions. Neither Oedipus nor Hercules are able to avert their fate. Oedipus kills his father and marries his own mother. Thebes's citizens banish him from the city when the truth is revealed. Hercules is poisoned by his jealous wife and burns himself to death on a pyre.

Deleuze's analysis does not stop here. It is possible to move beyond the Oedipus complex and endure the loss of the image of the phallus. A post-castration phase appears to be full of possibilities. I will show that this new phase is characterised by the emergence of a new topological instance: the metaphysical or spiritual surface that separates itself from the bodily surface.[1] It is a surface that allows for a construction of sense. As we will see the metaphysical surface cannot be equated with the notion of the symbolic order, known from Jacques Lacan's work. This surface is never primary with respect to the body. Rather, it emerges out of the body and continually allows for the bodies expression. The separation between them is attained only upon the demise of the Oedipus complex. At that moment, the surface of sense allows not only for the sublimation of bodily desire, but also for an independent production of symbols. The demise of narcissism furthermore leads to a new relation of the ego towards the already present structures of sense. The ego

---

[1]   The exact meaning of the term will be provided below.

appears to be unable to construct a unity, but does not resign. It becomes an instance that accompanies the continual movement and change of the structures of sense. It participates actively in the process of construction of sense.

The present chapter is an analysis of the 'Twenty-Ninth Series – Good Intentions Are Inevitably Punished'. The first part takes the form of a further analysis of a point that was introduced in Chapter four; in it, I examine the emergence of the good intentions and analyse the nature of the oedipal desire. The second section is devoted to the analysis of the castration complex and its consequences. It examines the development of the metaphysical surface and the changed nature of the relationship between body and thought. This part of the chapter introduces the concept of event and investigates processes of sublimation, symbolisation and negation (*dénégation*). A section of this chapter focuses on the analysis of the nature of the drives that invest the metaphysical surface. We will see how Deleuze understands the process of desexualisation of the libido. The final part of the chapter concentrates on the analysis of some of the problems confronted by thought on the metaphysical surface.

2. Oedipal desire and narcissism[2]

The unification of the surface of the body by means of the image of the phallus leads to an emergence of a coherent psychic experience.[3] The hitherto weak ego is strengthened. As has been observed, the physical surface is not only present in the sexual position but also already plays an important role in the

---

[2] I offer a brief analysis here of paragraphs three and four of the chapter 'Twenty-Ninth Series – Good Intentions Are Inevitably Punished'. I chose to change the original structure of the chapter for reasons of argument. The analysis developed here is a further elaboration of the topics already discussed in Chapter four. Paragraphs one and two of the text of Deleuze are discussed later in the text.

[3] I refer to: '*La surface a une importance décisive dans le développement du moi; Freud le montre bien, lorsqu'il dit que le système perception-conscience est localisé sur la membrane qui se forme à la surface de la boule protoplasmique. Le moi, comme terme du « narcissisme primaire », gît d'abord en profondeur, dans la boule elle-même ou le corps sans organes. Mais il ne peut conquérir une indépendance que dans « auto-érotisme » avec les surfaces partielles et tous les petits moi qui les hantent. Alors la véritable épreuve du moi est dans le problème du raccordement, donc de son propre raccordement, quand la libido comme énergie superficielle l'investit dans un « narcissisme secondaire ». Et, nous le pressentions tout à l'heure, ce raccordement phallique des surfaces, et du moi lui-même à la surface, s'accompagne d'opérations qualifiées d'œdipiennes: c'est cela qu'il faut analyser. L'enfant reçoit le phallus comme une image projetée par le bon pénis idéal sur la zone génitale de son corps.*' (LdS: 237), (LoS: 203).

depths. The physical surface is a membrane that separates the inside of the organism from the outside. Here Deleuze follows both Simondon and Freud. The membrane protects the inside of the body from a violent overstimulation,[4] allowing the body to act in an appropriate fashion and to select only the stimuli that are relevant for its survival. The interaction with the environment is possible only because of the limitations imposed by the membrane. Already, in the depths, the surface is the first location of the ego. It is a body without organs, protecting the inside of the organism against an inevitable destruction by overstimulation.[5]

The ego of the depths is nevertheless still very vulnerable, particularly due to its relationship with the id. This situation changes gradually due to the emergence of the object of the heights. A true strengthening of the ego occurs only with the development of the autoeroticism of the sexual position. Only the secondary narcissism, the investment (cathexis)[6] in the image of the phallus by the libido, allows the ego to act in its environment with a sense of self-confidence.[7] The good, ideal penis of the heights, is projected on the genital zone of the body.[8] This investment in the genital zone has far

---

[4] Deleuze writes: '*Freud le montre bien, lorsqu'il dit que le système perception-conscience est localisé sur la membrane qui se forme à la surface de la boule protoplasmique.* (LdS 237), (LoS 203). Here, Deleuze is referring to the following passage of '*Beyond the pleasure principle*': 'This little fragment of living substances is suspended in the middle of an external world charged with the most powerful energies; and it would be killed by the stimulation emanating from these if it were not provided with a protective shield against stimuli.' (Freud 1961: 21).

[5] Here, Deleuze follows the second topological model proposed by Freud. Freud considers narcissism to be the most fundamental for the relationship of the ego with its environment. It does not emerge secondarily at the moment when the libido turns itself away from the more primary investment in objects in order to invest in the ego. The existence of this kind of primary narcissism has been widely discussed in psychoanalytic literature. Laplanche and Pontalis, for example, criticise this definition because it leads to a disappearance of the distinction between autoeroticism and narcissism. For Laplanche and Pontalis, the notion of narcissism must imply an investment in the ego by the libido. Such investment can only be secondary. (Laplanche and Pontalis 1967: 44, 1973: 46, 70). Melanie Klein has also criticised the notion of primary narcissism. According to her, the child is always already oriented towards other objects. In the very beginning of life, the mother is, for example, a primary object of desire. As already indicated in the analysis of the simulacrum of the body without organs, Deleuze distances himself from Klein in this respect.

[6] I use the term investment in this text rather than the term cathexis, frequently used in the translations of the work of Freud.

[7] Deleuze remarks: '*Mais il ne peut conquérir une indépendance que dans « auto-érotisme » avec les surfaces partielles et tous les petits moi qui les hantent. Alors la véritable épreuve du moi est dans le problème du raccordement, donc de son propre raccordement, quand la libido comme énergie superficielle l'investit dans un « narcissisme secondaire ».* (LdS 237), (LoS 203).

[8] For the meaning of this term, refer to Chapter four. Here I am referring to the following passage: '*L'enfant reçoit le phallus comme une image projetée par le bon pénis idéal sur la zone génitale de son corps.*' (LdS 237), (LoS 203).

reaching consequences for the relationship towards the objects in the ego's environment.[9] The subject perceives himself as capable of changing its world. Secondly, he also becomes more and more aware of the existence of the sexual difference, which is a new development. In the previous positions the sexual difference did not play a significant role. In the schizoid position, the mother's inside contains both a breast and a multiplicity of good and bad penises. In addition, the father possesses not only a penis but also the feeding breast. Both parents fulfil similar roles. Both take care of the child and cause various states of tension. This lack of strict separation is also present in the depressive position where both parents incorporate the good object of the heights. Both possess the feeding breast and the good penis of the heights.[10] The parents are idealised. They are the source of security and love. This unity disappears in the genital phase of the sexual position. The object of the heights is now split into two halves. The initial unity of the idol of idealised parents is broken down. The child starts to distinguish between an image of the father and an image of the mother.[11] This change's first cause is the appropriation of the good object of the heights by the ego. The parents no longer have to be idealised and can now be perceived as lacking something. The ego considers itself to be strong enough to act as a good object itself. The narcissistic ego projects its own previous state of disintegration onto the new images of the parents and subsequently

---

[9] As Deleuze avers: '*Ce don (surinvestissement narcissique d'organe), il le reçoit comme la condition par laquelle il peut opérer l'intégration de toutes ses autres zones. Mais voilà qu'il n'accomplit pas ce travail de production de la surface sans introduire ailleurs des changements très importants. D'abord il clive l'idole donatrice ou le bon objet de la hauteur. Les deux parents se trouvaient combinés précédemment, suivant des formules bien dégagées par Mélanie Klein: le corps maternel des profondeurs comprenait une multiplicité de pénis comme objets partiels internes; et surtout le bon objet de la hauteur était à la fois pénis et sein comme organe complet, mère pourvue d'un pénis et père pourvu d'un sein.*' (LdS 238), (LoS 204).

[10] I refer to: '*Les deux parents se trouvaient combinés précédemment, suivant des formules bien dégagées par Mélanie Klein: le corps maternel des profondeurs comprenait une multiplicité de pénis comme objets partiels internes; et surtout le bon objet de la hauteur était à la fois pénis et sein comme organe complet, mère pourvue d'un pénis et père pourvu d'un sein.*' (LdS 238), (LoS 204).

[11] I am alluding to: '*Maintenant, croyons-nous, le clivage se fait ainsi: des deux disjonctions subsumées par le bon objet, indemne-blessé, présent-absent, l'enfant commence par extraire le négatif, et s'en sert pour qualifier une image de mère et une image de père. D'une part il identifie la mère au corps blessé comme première dimension du bon objet complet (corps blessé qu'il ne faut pas confondre avec le corps éclaté ou morcelé de la profondeur); et d'autre part il identifie le père avec la dernière dimension, le bon objet comme retiré dans sa hauteur. Et le corps blessé de la mère, l'enfant prétend le réparer avec son phallus réparateur, le rendre indemne, il prétend refaire à ce corps une surface en même temps qu'il fait une surface pour son propre corps. Et, l'objet retiré, il prétend le faire revenir et le rendre présent, avec son phallus évocateur.*' (LdS 238), (LoS 204).

claims the capacity to complete them.[12] The mother is now perceived as a broken object.[13] Her body misses a penis. It is wounded. This state allows the narcissistic ego to conceive of itself as capable of restoring this body again into the state of a complete good object. The ego is convinced that the wound can be healed.[14] Deleuze emphasises here that the image of the mother proper to the sexual position differs from the simulacrum of the fragmented body of the mother of the depths.[15] The image of the body of the mother is directly related to a state of unity that is not found in the depths. The narcissistic ego of the sexual position wishes to restore this unity, an activity impossible to conceive of in the schizoid position. It not only wants to protect itself and her from the attacks of the bad partial objects by diminishing their impact but rather to restore the unity of the surface of the body of the mother.[16] She must become a good and complete object again. This new image of the mother may play a fundamental role in love relationships. A narcissistic partner of either sex might be convinced about the existence of the capacity to restore the wounded body of the partner. He or she may now perceive her- or himself as a missing part of the other.

The image of the father is endowed with a different characteristic.[17] The father is not a figure of authority. On the contrary, he becomes a retreated

---

[12] I have in mind: '*des deux disjonctions subsumées par le bon objet, indemne-blessé, présent-absent, l'enfant commence par extraire le négatif, et s'en sert pour qualifier une image de mère et une image de père.*' (LdS 238), (LoS 204).

[13] I am commenting on: '*D'une part il identifie la mère au corps blessé comme première dimension du bon objet complet.*' (LdS 238), (LoS 204).

[14] Deleuze does not completely clarify why the images of the mother and the father take on these particular roles. He does not refer to the contribution of culture. One could, for example, stress that normally speaking, contemporary patriarchal society forces the children to develop these two images in order to support the present structure of power. In that case, the images of the parents would not directly refer to the real bodies of both parents, but would, rather, be two signifiers proper to the symbolic order that is entangled with a particular power structure. Nevertheless, Deleuze's main aim, in *The Logic of Sense*, is to show that these images emerge in the interaction with the real bodies of the parents of both sexes and may only secondarily be attributed to external structures. The patriarchal division of power is in this respect not the primary cause of the emergence of the sexual difference that characterises this position.

[15] Here I refer to: '*(corps blessé qu'il ne faut pas confondre avec le corps éclaté ou morcelé de la profondeur)*' (LdS 238), (LoS 204). Deleuze stresses this point because the schizoid position lacks a simulacrum of a good and complete object. The fear of regression to the schizoid position is only able to emerge given the existence of the depressive position.

[16] I have in mind: '*Et le corps blessé de la mère, l'enfant prétend le réparer avec son phallus réparateur, le rendre indemne, il prétend refaire à ce corps une surface en même temps qu'il fait une surface pour son propre corps.*' (LdS 238), (LoS 204).

[17] I refer to: '*et d'autre part il identifie le père avec la dernière dimension, le bon objet comme retiré dans sa hauteur…. Et, l'objet retiré, il prétend le faire revenir et le rendre présent, avec son phallus évocateur.*' (LdS 238), (LoS 204).

and absent object that can be made present only by the ego itself. It is the ego that feels entitled to execute the role of authority. It may, for example, claim to have possession of a special kind of knowledge. A narcissistic lover may be convinced that he knows what is good for the other, whereas a philosopher can claim an access to the world of ideas. In both cases, this leads to a narcissistic conviction of one's own capacity, to determine the life of others.

For Deleuze, the separate images of both parents form the core of the Oedipus complex.[18] According to him, the narcissistic child is driven by good intentions. It wants to restore the wounded body of the mother and to make the retreated father present. Initially its narcissistic self-confidence results only in good consequences. The ego is free from feelings of fear and guilt. It is not in a state of conflict with its environment nor with the parental figures.[19] The aggression and self-preservation drives have been left behind. The desire for the mother is experienced as safe and entirely unproblematic. The child completes the mother. It takes on the role of the father. Nevertheless it is not aware of any danger. It does not compete with the latter. No aggression is present. The ego merely assumes that it is capable of restoring her wounded body. The ego also assumes that it can make the father return. It is convinced that his absence and apparent lack of authority is only temporary. Its actions can reverse this state and will in the end also benefit the father.

The Oedipus complex is of great importance for Deleuze. It marks the true birth of morality, which is not imposed upon the ego from the outside.[20] It cannot be equated with a slavish obedience to the commandments of the object of the heights. The good intentions are a prolongation of the innocent

---

[18] Deleuze puts this as follows: '*Chacun dans l'inconscient est le fils de divorcés, qui rêve de réparer la mère et de faire venir le père, de le tirer de sa retraite: telle nous semble la base de ce que Freud appelait le « roman familial », qu'il rattachait au complexe d'Œdipe. Jamais l'enfant n'eut de meilleures intentions dans sa confiance narcissique, jamais il ne se sentira aussi bon, et, loin de se lancer dans une entreprise angoissante et coupable, jamais dans cette position il ne s'est cru aussi proche de conjurer l'angoisse ou la culpabilité des positions précédentes.*' (LdS 238), (LoS 204).

[19] I am referring to: '*C'est vrai qu'il prend la place du père, et la mère pour objet de son désir incestueux. Mais le rapport d'inceste comme de procuration n'implique pas ici la violence: nulle éventration ni usurpation, mais au contraire un rapport de surface, un processus de réparation et d'évocation où le phallus opère une doublure en surface. On ne noircit, on ne durcit le complexe d'Œdipe au à force de négliger l'horreur des stades précédents où le pire s'est passé, et à force d'oublier que la situation œdipienne n'est atteinte que dans la mesure où les pulsions libidinales ont pu se dégager des pulsions destructrices.*' (LdS 238), (LoS 204).

[20] I am referring to: '*L'inceste avec la mère par réparation, le remplacement du père par évocation, ne sont pas seulement de bonnes intentions (car c'est avec le complexe d'Œdipe que naît l'intention, notion morale par excellence). A titre d'intentions, ce sont les prolongements inséparables de l'activité la plus innocente apparemment, celle qui consiste pour l'enfant à se faire une surface d'ensemble de toutes ses surfaces partielles, en utilisant le phallus projeté par le bon pénis d'en haut, et en faisant bénéficier les images parentales de cette projection.*' (LdS 239), (LoS 204).

activity concerning the ego's own experience. To be truly moral, the ego must become independent of the object of the heights.[21] Here, Deleuze emphasises the significance of a forgotten part of a famous phrase by Freud describing morality. According to Freud, the normal human being is not only more immoral than he thinks, but also more moral than he suspects.[22] On the one hand, the 'morally' conscious individual always denies the degree to which he or she blindly pursues pure states of pleasure. The identification with the super-ego leads to a distancing from the id. At the same time, however, the ego that identifies with the super-ego mistrusts itself too much. It underestimates its own hidden capacity to oppose the destructive drives. Only this lack of appreciation of its own good intentions leads to a choice for strong external institutions, in order to combat the destructive urges of the id. The presence of the hidden morality is confirmed by the fascination of the audience with the figure of Hercules. The audience perceives itself to be as equally carefree and innocent as he is. It is fascinated by his attempts to create a better world. Hercules expresses a will to pursue a better world, one with no inner aggression or fear; proving that it is possible to distance oneself from aggression and also that it is feasible to live in proximity to the good object of the heights. Likewise, the tragedy of Oedipus has a similar impact on the unconscious.[23] His story proves that morality in general is not only to be found outside of the subject, but also deep down in its core.[24] Oedipus gathers his courage and leaves his parental house with his belongings in a sack on his back. He is prepared to leave everything behind in order to construct a better world. He is convinced that this painful decision will avert his fate. He wants to save both of his parents from a horrible destiny. Unconsciously, the spectators of this tragedy cherish a similar image of themselves.

---

[21] Here, Deleuze takes a position opposite to the one adopted by Freud in '*Civilisation and its Discontents*'. According to Freud, super-ego's strong intervention ego is necessary to restrain the id that is dominated by the destructive drives. For Deleuze, the development of the dimension of the height is an important, but at the same time insufficient, condition for morality.

[22] I refer here to the following passage: '*Quand Freud remarque que l'homme normal n'est pas seulement plus immoral qu'il ne le croit, mais plus moral qu'il ne s'en doute, c'est vrai avant tout par rapport au complexe d'Œdipe. Œdipe est une tragédie, mais c'est le cas de dire qu'il faut imaginer le héros tragique gai et innocent, et partant d'un bon pas.*' (LdS 239), (LoS 205).

[23] I have in mind: '*Oedipe est herculéen, parce que lui aussi, pacificateur, veut se constituer un royaume à sa taille, royaume des surfaces et de la terre. Il a cru conjurer les monstres de la profondeur et s'allier les puissances d'en haut. Et, inséparable de son entreprise, il y a réparer la mère et faire venir le père: le vrai complexe d'Œdipe.*' (LdS 239), (LoS 205).

[24] It remains outside of this book's scope to analyse the implications of this statement for Deleuze's ethics.

3. Castration complex

The belief in reparative capacities must inevitably be challenged. The secondary narcissism, guaranteed by the image of the phallus, might disappear. The tender and fragile surface runs the risk of being destroyed. Castration seems inevitable. In this case, Hercules is an exemplary hero.[25] His good intentions turn against him. His stepmother, the goddess Hera (Juno), is jealous and full of resentment and his attempts at restoration have no chance of success when confronted by her anger and strength. Hera drives him to madness, resulting in his taking the lives of his own children. She also feeds the jealousy of his second wife. Deianeira does not believe in the sincerity of Hercules' love. She attempts to save their relationship by sending him a tunic as a gift, believing that only this tunic will revitalise his love. It appears to be drenched in the blood of the centaur Nessos[26] and is lethal. The tunic shrinks and burns her husband's skin, causing his flesh and bones to become visible. Deianeira is accused of treason and commits suicide while Hercules burns himself on a pyre in order to end his torment as soon as possible. He is rescued by the Gods who make him immortal as a reward for his heroic deeds. He therefore gains access to Olympus and marries Hebe, the goddess of youth.

Why are the ancient heroes such as Hercules doomed to perish?[27] Why are their good intentions turning against them? How can we explain the necessity of the loss of narcissism? Why are they castrated? Deleuze mentions a number of reasons. The first one is found in Melanie Klein's work. The

---

[25] Deleuze notes: '*Il faut donc imaginer Œdipe non seulement innocent, mais plein de zèle et de bonnes intentions: deuxième Hercule qui va connaître une expérience douloureuse semblable*'. (LdS 236), (LoS 205).

[26] The centaur who wants to kidnap Deianeira is killed by Hercules.

[27] I am referring to: '*Mais pourquoi ses bonnes intentions semblent-elles se retourner contre lui? D'abord en raison de la délicatesse de l'entreprise, la fragilité propre des surfaces. On n'est jamais sûr que les pulsions destructrices, continuant à agir sous les pulsions sexuelles, ne dirigent pas leur travail. Le phallus comme image à la surface risque à chaque instant d'être récupéré par le pénis de la profondeur ou celui de la hauteur; et ainsi d'être châtré comme phallus, puisque le pénis des profondeurs est lui-même dévorant, castrant, et celui de la hauteur frustrant. Il y a donc une double menace de castration par régression pré-œdipienne (castration-dévoration, castration-privation). Et la ligne tracée par le phallus risque de s'engouffrer dans la profonde* Spaltung; *et l'inceste de revenir à l'état d'une éventration qui serait aussi bien celle de la mère que de l'enfant, à une mélange cannibalique où le mangeur est aussi bien mangé. Bref, la position schizoïde et même la position dépressive, l'angoisse de l'une et la culpabilité de l'autre, ne cessent pas de menacer le complexe d'Œdipe; comme dit Mélanie Klein, l'angoisse et la culpabilité ne naissent pas de l'entreprise incestueuse, elles l'empêcheraient plutôt de se former, et la compromettent constamment.*' (LdS 236), (LoS 202).

surface is fragile.[28] It is a delicate veil that covers the self-preservation drive and the destructive drives of the depths. A person who has developed the surface knows the dangers of the depths. He knows that the destructive drives can gain strength and fears their capacity to destroy the surface. The liberated sexual drives are quickly able to reconnect with the destructive drives. Following Klein, we can cite the example of a happy marriage that could turn into complete chaos and struggle after a trivial incident. The partner may cease to be perceived through the prism of the image of the mother that is to be restored and become a bad partial object. Behaviour that has been perceived as an expression of love and gratitude towards the narcissistic ego, may suddenly become an expression of aggression. The image of the phallus might suddenly lose its reparative characteristic and change into an aggressive penis of the depths.[29] The behaviour that initially expressed love may suddenly turn into an aggressive will to possess and control the partner. The loss of the initial good intentions is also able to lead to a regression towards the depressive position.[30] In that case the image of the phallus becomes an idol or a frustrating penis of the heights. The relationship becomes an obligation. A person regressing to this position is only able to aim at the realisation of an unreachable ideal. The subject loses self-confidence and ceases to believe in his capacity to restore the damage attributed to the partner. The good intentions disappear, and depression or mania attempts to mask its own failure to become its destiny. A scientist led by good intentions may equally be castrated and regress to the previous positions. She might suddenly come to realise that the nature of her motivation has changed. She is no longer passionate about her work but, rather, full of aggression towards others. The success of others could suddenly provoke a sense of being directly attacked. In a case of regression to the depressive position a manic or depressive relation towards one's own work is a consequence. The success of others becomes a sign of his or her own failure.

The two forms of castration, identified by Deleuze on basis of Klein's work, are castration-devouring (*castration-dévoration*) and castration-deprivation

---

[28] I allude to: '*D'abord en raison de la délicatesse de l'entreprise, la fragilité propre des surfaces.*' (LdS 236), (LoS 202).

[29] Here I refer to: '*Le phallus comme image à la surface risque à chaque instant d'être récupéré par le pénis de la profondeur ou celui de la hauteur; et ainsi d'être châtré comme phallus, puisque le pénis des profondeurs est lui-même dévorant, castrant, et celui de la hauteur frustrant.*' (LdS 236), (LoS 202).

[30] I have in mind: '*puisque le pénis des profondeurs est... frustrant*' (LdS 236), (LoS 202).

(*castration-privation*).[31] They reappear at the moment when the line drawn by the image of the phallus on the surface becomes threatening, causing the surface to disintegrate. The separate erotogenic zones cease to be united. A deep split (*Spaltung*) is revealed. Incest, that is, the attempt to heal the wounded body of the mother, transforms itself into a schizoid act of aggression. The will to make the retreated father present turns into a schizoid act of violence. The father returns. Narcissism becomes a violent rebellion against his authority.

This analysis of castration, based upon the Kleinian concepts, has its limits. According to Deleuze, the danger of regression to the previous positions is of fundamental importance, but at the same time is not the only challenge faced by the ego.[32] The dangers proper to the sexual position must first be understood thoroughly before one can speak of regression to the previous positions. The sexual position is characterised by a third form of castration that cannot be reduced to the previous two.[33] This third form of castration alone must be understood as the proper form of the castration complex.[34] The defusion of the drives, reached in the sexual position, is not directly reversed. Deleuze emphasises that the object of the heights or the super-ego initially supports the ego in its struggle against the destructive drives. The defusion should not be reversed. The ego is initially protected; however, this support is not unconditional. The strengthening of the narcissistic oedipal desire must

---

[31] I refer to: '*Il y a donc une double menace de castration par régression pré-œdipienne (castra-tion-dévoration, castration-privation). Et la ligne tracée par le phallus risque de s'engouffrer dans la profonde* Spaltung; *et l'inceste de revenir à l'état d'une éventration qui serait aussi bien celle de la mère que de l'enfant, à une mélange cannibalique où le mangeur est aussi bien mangé.*' (LdS 236), (LoS 202).

[32] I comment on: '*Pourtant cette première réponse n'est pas suffisante. Car la constitution des surfaces n'en a pas moins pour principe et intention de séparer les pulsions sexuelles des pulsions destructrices en profondeur, et rencontre à cet égard une complaisance certaine de la part du surmoi ou du bon objet des hauteurs. Les dangers de l'entreprise œdipienne doivent donc aussi venir d'une évolution interne; bien plus, les risques de confusion, de mélange corporel, invoqués par la première réponse ne prennent tout leur sens qu'en fonction de ces nouveaux dangers sécrétés par l'entreprise œdipienne elle-même. Bref, celle-ci engendre nécessairement une nouvelle angoisse qui lui est propre, une nouvelle culpabilité, une nouvelle castration qui ne se réduit pas aux deux précédentes — et à laquelle seule convient le nom de « complexe de castration » en rapport avec Œdipe. La constitution des surfaces est le plus innocent, mais innocent ne signifie pas sans perversité. Il faut croire que le surmoi abandonne sa bienveillance première, par exemple au moment d'Œdipe, quand on passe de l'organisation des surfaces partielles prégénitales à leur intégration ou raccordement génital sous le signe du phallus. Pourquoi?*' (LdS 237), (LoS 203).

[33] I refer to: '*Les dangers de l'entreprise œdipienne doivent donc aussi venir d'une évolution interne; bien plus, les risques de confusion, de mélange corporel, invoqués par la première réponse ne prennent tout leur sens qu'en fonction de ces nouveaux dangers sécrétés par l'entreprise œdipienne elle-même.*' (LdS 237), (LoS 203).

[34] I have in mind: '*— et à laquelle seule convient le nom de « complexe de castration » en rapport avec Œdipe*' (LdS 237), (LoS 203).

inevitably lead to a reversal in the relation between the ego and the super-ego. The latter becomes increasingly less benevolent.[35] Deleuze claims that the super-ego eventually ceases to support the perverse desire. The activity made possible by the image of the phallus appears to be increasingly outside of the super-ego's control. The ego appears to be increasingly disobedient.[36] Is Deleuze making use of a Lacanian argument here and claiming that the ego must come to realise that it can never claim the possession of the phallus? Does it have to come to realise that it is only his property? As we will see below, this is not the case.

According to Deleuze, the story of Hercules is again exemplary of what happens to the ego in this phase.[37] Hercules faces two enemies.[38] The first emerges from the depths: it is Hera or fate, who symbolise the aggression of both the id and of the environment.[39] Hercules is already prepared to face this enemy. He already knows the destructive urges. His good intentions are developed exactly out of the confrontation with these drives. Hercules is constantly aware of the fact that the self-preservation drive and the death drive may gain victory over, and destroy, his good intentions. The image of the phallus is a weapon against his fate. The world must be liberated from the bad

---

[35] I am referring to: '*La constitution des surfaces est le plus innocent, mais innocent ne signifie pas sans perversité. Il faut croire que le surmoi abandonne sa bienveillance première, par exemple au moment d'Œdipe, quand on passe de l'organisation des surfaces partielles prégénitales à leur intégration ou raccordement génital sous le signe du phallus. Pourquoi?*' (LdS 237), (LoS 203).

[36] Deleuze does not discuss this topic further in *The Logic of Sense*. In his later collaboration with Guattari, he emphasises the importance of the social environment for the formation of individual desire. Society makes us behave in a certain way and robs us of self-confidence. This super-ego's interference is dependent on the type of society. In Chapter three of *Anti-Oedipus*, Deleuze and Guattari analyse the interventions proper to societies organised by the primitive, barbaric and capitalist modes of production. The first two modes limit desire and produce relatively rigid structures. Capitalism, on the other hand, leads to a break with those forms of organisation. The super-ego allows for certain ways of experimentation and transgression of the law, which the super-ego initially tries to impose upon it. Only this mode of production truly strengthens the narcissistic tendencies. Nevertheless, in this case also, a true independence, with respect to the commandments of the super-ego, is impossible. See also: Eugene Holland (1999), and Laermans (2009), in van Tuinen *et al.*, (2009).

[37] I am alluding to: '*Mais pourquoi tout tourne-t-il si mal? Pourquoi la nouvelle angoisse et la nouvelle culpabilité comme produites? Pourquoi déjà Hercule trouvait-il en Junon une marâtre pleine de haine, résistant à toute offre de réparation, et en Zeus un père de plus en plus retiré, se détournant de plus en plus après avoir favorisé?*' (LdS 239), (LoS 205).

[38] Here I refer to: '*On dirait que l'entreprise des surfaces (la bonne intention, le royaume de la terre) ne rencontre pas seulement un ennemi attendu, venu des profondeurs infernales qu'il s'agissait de vaincre, mais aussi un ennemi inattendu, celui de la hauteur, qui rendait pourtant l'entreprise possible et ne peut plus la cautionner. Le surmoi comme bon objet se met à condamner les pulsions libidinales en elles-mêmes.*' (LdS 239), (LoS 205).

[39] In individual psychology we could speak of a person's own aggression that is subsequently projected outside.

partial objects, as they appear in the myth. Hercules undertakes to perform the twelve labours in restitution for the crimes he has committed against his own family. He is constantly on the edge of failure, but keeps on trying.

The true new enemy, underestimated by Klein, comes from the heights. As Deleuze argues, the good object ceases to authorise (*la cautioner*) the existence of the sexual surface. It takes on the role of the super-ego and starts to condemn the libidinal drives.[40] This is striking, as it was initially responsible for the emergence of the sexual surface itself.[41] The good object starts to behave towards the ego in a manner similar to the way in which Zeus treats Hercules. Initially he supports him and is proud of each of Hercules' victories, but eventually withdraws his support. He does not pay enough attention and does nothing to stop the revenge of Hera. In a similar manner, the good object no longer supports the activity of the ego and keeps it at a distance. It ceases to acknowledge the good nature of its actions and particularly their consequences. How does the ego come to discover the painful truth?[42] What are the now mistrusted consequences of its actions? Deleuze emphasises the visual aspects of the development of the child. As stated above, the ego has phantasmatically separated the images of both parents. Both belong to separate sexes. This separation leads to a discovery. The child sees something it should not have seen, according to Deleuze. It comes to the realisation that the wounded body of the mother cannot be repaired. Her body appears to be marked by an unbridgeable lack.[43] The mother is not only threatened by the bad partial objects, but also the bad internal penises projected into her body during the schizoid position. The lack, that was supposed to be reversed, is permanent. Her body is castrated; its surface lacks a penis. This leads to a loss

---

[40] I comment on: '*mais aussi un ennemi inattendu, celui de la hauteur, qui rendait pourtant l'entreprise possible et ne peut plus la cautionner. Le surmoi comme bon objet se met à condamner les pulsions libidinales en elles-mêmes.*' (LdS 239), (LoS 205).

[41] In the terminology of Klein, we could state that the super-ego becomes stronger. Klein describes the relation between ego and the super-ego as follows: 'The kind super-ego (the benign internal object) acts as a spur for ego-development and enables the ego to expand and venture forth no less than the threatening super-ego (the strict internal father) prohibits activities. In many instances the young child dares to undertake something new because his parents encourage him to do so, and when he trusts them his self-confidence is greater.' (Heimann, in Klein *et al.* 1952: 138).

[42] I am referring to: '*En effet, dans son désir d'inceste-réparation, Œdipe a vu. Ce qu'il a vu (le clivage étant fait), et qu'il ne devait pas voir, c'est que le corps blessé de la mère ne l'est pas seulement par les pénis internes qu'il contient, mais en tant que manquant de pénis à la surface, comme corps châtré. Le phallus en tant qu'image projetée, qui donnait une force nouvelle au pénis de l'enfant, désigne au contraire un manque chez la mère.*' (LdS 239), (LoS 205).

[43] I comment on: '*c'est que le corps blessé de la mère ne l'est pas seulement par les pénis internes qu'il contient, mais en tant que manquant de pénis à la surface, comme corps châtré.*' (LdS 239), (LoS 205).

of the narcissistic feeling of omnipotence. The child is most disenchanted by the discovery of the existence of unalterable laws and comes to realise that very little can be done to reverse them. The body of the mother structurally lacks an organ that is considered to be the precondition for the emergence of a unified experience. After this discovery, the image of the phallus can only refer to a lack found in the body of the mother, argues Deleuze.[44] All attempts to heal this wound will fail. A person perceived by means of the image of the mother cannot be healed.[45]

According to Deleuze, the discovery of the lack characterising the body of the mother leads to an even more threatening observation.[46] It is now equally threatened by the discovery that the penis can only be the property of the father.[47] Deleuze's interpretation of this discovery differs from the one developed by Lacan in his early seminars. Lacan emphasises that a child can never claim possession of the phallus.[48] Castration is equal to a discovery that the phallus is not the property of the child but of the symbolic father. In

---

[44] I have in mind: '*Le phallus en tant qu'image projetée, qui donnait une force nouvelle au pénis de l'enfant, désigne au contraire un manque chez la mère.*' (LdS 239), (LoS 205).

[45] Deleuze does not discuss the distinction between the experiences of a boy and a girl here. We can nevertheless assume that a girl also discovers a similar lack that characterises her own body. Just as in case of the boy, this discovery leads to a loss of belief in one's own reparative capacities and a capacity to control one's own environment. The lack of a penis is a sign of her incapacity to protect it. In that sense, it makes a girl more fragile than a boy. In phantasy, a penis still remains an organ that is able to exercise control over bad partial objects. An analysis of a trauma in the case of a girl may be found in Klein's work, where she states: 'The possession of an external penis would help to convince the girl in the first place that in reality she has that sadistic power over both her parents without which she cannot master her anxiety, and in the second place that the penis, as a means of sadistic power over her objects, is evidence that the internalized dangerous penis and the introjected objects can be overcome; so that having a penis ultimately serves to protect her own body'. (Klein 1997: 215). The lack of a penis must lead to the development of a fear that is stronger than the fear of the boy. Below I will cite examples that could help the reader to visualise the impact of this realisation for the psyche.

[46] I discuss: '*Or cette découverte menace essentiellement l'enfant; car elle signifie (de l'autre côté du clivage) que le pénis est la propriété du père, et qu'en prétendant faire revenir celui-ci, le rendre présent, l'enfant trahit l'essence paternelle qui était dans le retirement, et qui ne pouvait être trouvée que comme retrouvée, retrouvée dans l'absence et dans l'oubli, mais jamais donnée dans une simple présence de « chose » qui dissiperait l'oubli.*' (LdS 240), (LoS 206).

[47] In their later analysis of castration, Deleuze and Guattari emphasise a different point (DRF 91), (TRM 82). The conflict with the father is enforced upon the child from outside. The child does not ascribe the phallus to the father by itself. Rather, it is infected with the Oedipal virus. In the little Hans's case, the parents understand his behaviour solely in oedipal terminology. His sexuality is reduced to two options, female or male. For the time being, it seems that Deleuze discusses a different problem in this case. I return to this topic below.

[48] Evident is a clear similarity with Lacanian understanding of the Oedipus complex. According to Lacan, the child starts to realise that the phallus is the property of the father. Only the father can restore the broken body of the mother. See i.a. Seminar 1956-1957, *La Relation d'objet*.

consequence, to assure the proper psychic functioning of a child, either a real father or a real mother must take on the role of the symbolic father upon him- or herself. One of them should facilitate the entrance of the child into the symbolic order. He or she must break the imaginary unity established between the child and the imaginary mother. Only a subject castrated by the symbolic father can enter the symbolic order.

In his analysis of the castration complex, Deleuze claims that castration does not lead to the necessary acceptance of the authority of the symbolic father. It is not equal to a realisation that the phallus is his property. To the contrary, it emerges once the child realises that it has gone too far by fully appropriating this image. This act of appropriation is a betrayal of the essence of the father, understood as the good object of the heights. The narcissist attempts to make the father present, while it should have respected its retreat. The father should have been found, as if recovered, states Deleuze.[49] The subject should have realised that the father has retreated and can be recovered only in absence and in forgetfulness (*dans l'absence et dans l'oubli*).' A father can never simply be made present as a thing. Forgetting belongs to his essence. It is exactly one's inability to treat the father as such, and not the incapacity to recognise the symbolic father's authority, that results in the traumatic consequences. The ego was too arrogant. Its attempt to eliminate forgetting, by making the object of the heights present, is a mistake. This is visible in Oedipus's case, who was too naive in his belief in his own good intentions. He was careless, wrongly assuming that leaving the house of his parents would be enough to avert fate. It was incorrect to assume that he truly possessed the right kind of knowledge. Narcissism had catastrophic consequences.

The castration complex is hence proper to the sexual position only.[50] The observation of the body of the mother leads to a loss of the image of the phallus and subsequent disintegration of the physical surface. The child discovers that the body of the mother misses an organ that is supposed to guarantee its unity and comes to the conclusion that it faces a similar fate. A total destruction of the barely acquainted unified experience emerges. The child loses its self-confidence and feels increasingly powerless. The castration is also accompanied by a growing feeling of guilt seemingly imposed upon the

---

[49] I refer to: '... *et qui ne pouvait être trouvée que comme retrouvée...*,' (LdS 240), (LoS 205).

[50] I am referring to: '*Il devient donc vrai, à ce moment, qu'en voulant réparer la mère l'enfant l'a châtrée et éventrée, et faire venir le père, l'enfant l'a trahi et tué, transformé en cadavre. La castration, la mort par castration, devient alors le destin de l'enfant, réfléchie par la mère dans cette angoisse qu'il éprouve maintenant, infligée par le père dans cette culpabilité qu'il subit maintenant come signe de vengeance.*' (LdS 240), (LoS 206).

child by the father.[51] The child sees itself not only as the source of the wound on the body of the mother, but also feels guilt about the reckless appropriation of the object of the heights. This abolishment of the distance towards the object of the heights has changed the father into a corpse.[52] The ego develops an image of a punishing father, of the father who takes revenge for the violence committed towards the mother and for the betrayal of his essence.[53] The father takes away its most precious possession, the narcissistically invested genital organ.[54] The line traced by the phallus on the surface of the body ceases to unite the experience and alters into a marker of castration. The surface falls apart.

It is important once again to stress that the castration complex in its proper form differs from the two castrations experienced by the ego in the previous two positions.[55] The castration of the depths is characterised by the experience of devouring and absorption (*dévoration-absorption*). During the process of the introjection of partial objects, the child phantasises that it is castrated from within by an introjected bad partial object. It is attacked from within. This experience is in fact close to what Freud himself understood by the castration complex. We may claim that in his analysis, the father fulfils the role of a threatening bad partial object. The father is idealised only at the level of consciousness. At the unconscious level, he is a competitor who wants to punish his son for the pursuit of the son's desire. Castration, as discussed by Freud, is equal to a fear of being punished by the father for the genital desire

---

[51] I comment on: '*infligée par le père dans cette culpabilité qu'il subit maintenant come signe de vengeance*' (LdS 240), (LoS 206).

[52] I discuss: '*et faire venir le père, l'enfant l'a trahi et tué, transformé en cadavre.*' (LdS 240), (LoS 206).

[53] Deleuze does not here consider the influence of the society on the development of the child. The image of the father is connected at this point with the function of the super-ego, disciplining the child. The father threatens the child with castration, given the internal dynamic of its genesis. In my opinion, Deleuze does not wish to refer here to the child's increased understanding of the environment.

[54] I consider: '*Toute l'histoire commençait par le phallus comme image projetée sur la zone génitale, et qui donnait au pénis de l'enfant la force d'entreprendre. Mais tout semble se terminer avec l'image qui se dissipe et qui entraîne la disparition du pénis de l'enfant. La « perversité », c'est le parcours des surfaces, et voilà que se révèle quelque chose de faussé dans ce parcours. La ligne que le phallus traçait à la surface, à travers toutes les surfaces partielles, n'est plus que le tracé de la castration où le phallus se dissipe lui-même, et le pénis avec lui.*' (LdS 240), (LoS 206).

[55] I have in mind: '*Cette castration, qui mérite seule le nom spécifique de « complexe », se distingue en principe des deux autres castrations, celle de la profondeur par dévoration-absorption, celle de la hauteur par privation/frustration. C'est une castration par a*dsorption, phénomène de surface: ainsi les poisons superficiels, les poisons de la tunique et de la peau dont brûle Hercule, ainsi les poisons sur des images ne fût-ce que contemplées, comme ces enduits vénéneux sur un miroir ou sur un tableau qui inspirent le théâtre élisabéthain.*' (LdS 240), (LoS 206).

towards the mother. The castration complex also differs from castration by the object of the heights. This latter castration presupposes the existence of an unreachable idol. It is equal to the feeling of lack and frustration (*privation-frustration*). The ego of this position is in fact castrated from the very beginning. It is structurally unable to obtain the retreated and unreachable object and develops all kinds of strategies to mask the persistent feeling of lack.

The castration proper to the sexual-perverse position takes the form of *ad*sorption, a phenomenon of the surface.[56] In chemistry, adsorption occurs when molecules of a gas or a fluid stick to the surface of another solid matter or fluid. They cover it with a thin layer that can be subsequently removed, together with the surface of the object. This process is fundamental for the purification of water. Cleaning molecules attach themselves to polluted particles and allow for their removal. The physical surface is subjected to a similar fate. As in the case of Hercules, the tender and fragile layer, consisting of unified partial zones, is covered by a poison and is subsequently destroyed.[57] The poisoned tunic, soaked in the blood of Nessos, burns away Hercules's skin, who becomes defenceless and unprotected from the outside world. The surface disappears prematurely, before it was even allowed to develop fully.[58] It is destroyed before a child was able to exercise its own heroic deeds, before it was able to express its own reparative tendencies. The paralysis brought about by the castration complex causes a subsequent regression to the previous positions. The dangerous depths and their 'cannibalistic mixtures' are revealed again. The ego is confronted with a deep *Spaltung*. Its world is again reduced to bad partial objects. Aggression and death dominate over the libidinal drives. The attempts at reparation disappear. The body of the mother is torn into pieces, while the father once again appears to be a competitor. The vain attempts to overcome the depths are destroyed.

According to Deleuze, in the end castration not only concerns genital sexuality but also all events in private and public life.[59] Castration is an event

---

[56] I comment on: '*C'est une castration par ad*sorption, phénomène de surface' (LdS 241), (LoS 206).

[57] I refer to: '*C'est une castration par ad*sorption, phénomène de surface: ainsi les poisons superficiels, les poisons de la tunique et de la peau dont brûle Hercule …*' (LdS 241), (LoS 206).

[58] I discuss: '*Mais, justement, c'est en vertu de sa spécificité que cette castration retrouve les deux autres et que, phénomène de la surface, elle semble en marquer l'échec ou la maladie, la moisissure prématurée, la manière dont la surface pourrit prématurément, dont la ligne à la surface rejoint la profonde* Spaltung, *et l'inceste des surfaces le mélange cannibalique en profondeur – conformément à la première raison que nous invoquions tout à l'heure.*' (LdS 241), (LoS 206).

[59] Deleuze states the following in his chapter on the phantasm: '*Ce ne sont pas davantage les meurtres de pères, les incestes, les empoisonnements et éventrations qui manquent dans l'histoire publique et privée*' (LdS 245), (LoS 210). I will analyse this passage further in chapter six.

that is faced by everybody acting out of good intentions.[60] What kinds of actions are accompanied by the image of the castrated mother? Naturally, the functioning of this image is probably most intensely expressed in a person's love life. The attempts to restore one's own partner are frequently doomed to fail. The problems remain unresolved or are even aggravated by a narcissistic partner. One of the most drastic cinematic examples of such a situation can be found in Żuławski's film *Possession,* with Isabelle Adjani in the leading role. A husband, who overestimates his reparative capacities, in fact contributes to his wife's increasing madness. All his attempts to help her fail and, in reality, aggravate her situation. The woman appears to be possessed. She is in love with a terrifying monster and is capable of committing several murders in order to protect this repulsive object of her love. The most interesting part of the film is that the beast appears to be the male protagonist's mirror image. Adjani is possessed by something that lies deep in the male character itself. The narcissistic male protagonist is the actualisation of evil. The film ends tragically. Both the wife and her husband die at the end. The only character to survive is the mirror image of the man. The spectator, who has initially identified with the male protagonist, is left confused. The narcissist male is not only failing in his attempts to help his wife, but is in fact the true and hidden source of her suffering.[61] A similar situation is found in the *Antichrist* by Lars von Trier, where an equally narcissistic male protagonist, William Dafoe, attempts to offer psychological help to his own wife, who suffers greatly after the loss of a child. His self-confidence is quickly challenged. Her mental condition deteriorates. She does not want to lose her husband and begins to be suspicious about his intentions. Eventually she loses control over herself and becomes violent. The male character survives her attacks and is in the end forced to kill her in order to survive. Corresponding to the case of the Adjani in *Possession,* the husbands are the source of these women's problems.

The emergence of the castration complex also has an impact on the ego's relationship to the object of the heights. As I have indicated, the image of the father alters since the ego has betrayed his essence and changed him into a cadaver.[62] The good object has not been kept at a distance. The first

---

[60] I refer to: '*Il devient donc vrai, à ce moment, qu'en voulant réparer la mère l'enfant l'a châtrée et éventrée.*' (LdS 240), (LoS 206).

[61] At first sight *Repulsion* by Polański seems to display a similar structure and also describes the process of a woman becoming possessed. Nevertheless both stories have little in common. *Repulsion* is built upon the image of a hysterical woman's suffering from androphobia. The man's and the environment's contribution towards her madness plays hardly any role, and does not shatter but instead strengthens the narcissistic beliefs of the main male protagonist.

[62] I refer to: '*et faire venir le père, l'enfant l'a trahi et tué, transformé en cadavre.*' (LdS 240), (LoS 206).

point Deleuze attempts to make is the importance of prudence. The object of the heights cannot be made fully present. Anyone blindly convinced of the capacity to overcome this distance runs a risk of failure. This might be the case for any intellectual convinced about fully possessing knowledge that can be used for the benefit of humanity. He or she runs the risk of turning the theory into a dead letter. Many bureaucrats, intellectuals and artists who completely endorsed and supported the communist regimes in the Stalinist period were overcome by a similar fate. They lost their belief in their good intentions. In their eyes, Marxism has turned into a dead letter. They had been too easily convinced about the truth they possessed. Their belief in Stalin's application of Marxism was blind. A conviction that a new and perfect society was being realised led to an all too easy justification of the committed atrocities.[63] Marxism died for many at the moment when the crimes committed were revealed.

Similar phantasms did not characterise the supporters of all totalitarian regimes. In the case of National-Socialism one can hardly speak of a behaviour guided by the image of the phallus. Their state of disenchantment must have been entirely different. The image of the phallus, as noted, is of a reparative organ that allows for a distance towards aggression. The motives of National-Socialists were different. Their relationship to the object of the heights was only a way of protecting the ego against the attacks of the bad partial objects. Most Nazi soldiers and bureaucrats committed crimes in order to get rid of bad partial objects. Germany was to be liberated from the enemies of the Aryan race: the Jews, Communists, homosexuals and others.[64] Their possible identification with the object of the heights, expressed in the adoration of the *Führer*, Germany or the Aryan race, was, first of all, part of their struggle against such objects. In communist regimes, similar motivations were far more marginal and visible in the first years of the struggle against aristocracy and the wealthy bourgeoisie. The best example of the castration complex and activity led by the image of the dead father is visible in the case of the French 'new philosophers'. In the nineteen seventies, intellectuals such as Henry-Lévi and Glucksmann lost their passionate belief in Maoism. Long after the revelations of the extreme degree of Stalinist terror, they also came to realise that the

---

[63] For an analysis of such dilemmas, see for example Czesław Miłosz (1953), '*Captive Mind*', London: Vintage Books.

[64] An example of an official who is wrongly convinced about the good intentions of his work would be Commander Neigel in *See: Under Love* by David Grossman. Neigel is a devoted follower of the Nazi ideology. His interaction with the writer Ansjel Wasserman changes the situation. Neigel slowly starts to identify with the victims of his camp. He loses his belief in the good object of the heights, is unmasked by one of his assistants and is in the end forced to commit suicide.

communist revolution had frequently led to violence and heavy repression. The Cultural Revolution in China was typical in this respect. The confrontation with those results was unbearable for these initially devoted Maoists. The Marxist theory could no longer be subjected to a productive critique but had turned into a dead letter. Their disenchantment became the leading force of their subsequent philosophical project. The main image supporting their work was that of a dead father. Their critique of totalitarian systems could not point in the direction of any alternative. The new philosophers were unable to reconnect with their own original good intentions. Starting with the moment of castration, their project became entirely negative.[65]

The topic of castration also appears in the later collaboration of Deleuze with Guattari. No profound contradiction exists in the manner by means of which this topic is approached during both periods of Deleuze's work.[66] The topic of castration, is for example, discussed in Deleuze and Guattari's analysis of Little Hans's case study.[67] Both authors stress that the little patient of Freud is initially very excited by the possibilities of exploring the world around him. Little Hans is strongly interested in his environment and wants to play with other children. He is also very interested in girls as his sexuality awakens. Hans wants, for example, to sleep over at his neighbour's, Mariedl. According to Deleuze and Guattari, agoraphobia and fear of horses cannot be attributed to the fear of castration, as Freud claims. They are caused by the confrontation with the limits and demands posed by the parents instead. Their style of upbringing is the root of the problems.[68] Little Hans is not allowed to sleep at the house of Mariedl or to play with children of working class origins. His parents do not realise that these prohibitions have a tremendous impact on the very essence of his life and produce a state of fear. The subsequent interpretation of his behaviour by his parents only aggravates the situation. Little Hans is infected with the Oedipal virus. He must surrender himself to a certain kind of sexuality.[69] Freud is, to a high degree, held responsible. He convinces Hans's parents that the fear of the horses is an expression of a hidden and more primary fear of the father. The boy's interest in the girl from

---

[65] According to Deleuze, the new philosophers do not produce new and relevant philosophy. They are entirely reactive against their former ideals. They feed themselves with the corpses of the gulag's victims, he states. They pay no attention to the true causes of resistance of the victims, their true vitality. See: *À propos des nouveaux philosophes et d'un problème plus général,* (DRF 127), (TRM 145). For a more extensive discussion of this confrontaion, see also Dosse (2007: 441).

[66] See i.a. Žižek (2004: v).

[67] See Freud (1909) and DRF 90-101, TRM 145.

[68] DRF 81, TRM 92.

[69] Deleuze and Guattari note: '*On lui inocule le virus Oedipe.*' (DRF 82), (TRM 91).

the neighbourhood is interpreted as an expression of a more primary love of the mother. The phobias are interpreted merely as conscious expressions of those repressed fears. The boy must be afraid of being castrated. The child who cannot enter into an open conflict with his father transforms this unconscious fear into a conscious fear of the horses. Deleuze and Guattari entirely disagree with this analysis. For them, Freud wrongly understands the motives of the boy. Little Hans is not afraid of losing his penis but of losing his freedom to act. He loses the different methods of exploring the world around him and, subsequently, the multiplicity of sexes. The sexuality of the boy is reduced to a single sex.[70] Both authors stress that the horse plays a completely different role from that imagined by Freud. The animal is not a symbol representing the father. Little Hans is affected by this animal, which, just like him, is mistreated by his masters. The animal expresses pride. It does not only suffer, but is capable of biting back. It is angry and active.[71] Little Hans engages in the process of becoming-animal.

The Logic of Sense does not explicitly express a similar critique, but this does not imply that it is absent. One can claim that the analysis of the castration complex in *The Logic of Sense* speaks, in fact, of a similar kind of loss. Little Hans might lose his self-confidence, supported by his strongly developed genital sexuality. After his loss of the image of the phallus he is no longer able to engage his environment in various ways. His carefree explorations are stopped. Hans is effectively castrated; he is therefore afraid and feels guilty. His parents have deprived him of his narcissism. He is unable to understand the prohibitions imposed upon him. The becoming-horse is the only fragile response that allows him to recover the early independence and optimism.

The emergence of the castration complex has important consequences for the relationship of the subject with the structures of sense. After claiming the capacity to generate and change those structures, he is now confronted with the consequences of its actions. The structures cannot be transformed as easily as he has thought. The unity cannot be imposed upon the reality.

---

[70] As Deleuze and Guattari state: '*Et comme chacun de nous entre dans beaucoup d'agencements, chacun de nous entre dans beaucoup d'agencements, chacun de nous a* n *sexes. Quand l'enfant découvre qu'il est réduit à un sexe, mâle ou femelle, c'est là qu'il découvre son impuissance: il a perdu le sens machinique et n'a plus qu'une signification d'outil. Alors en effet, l'enfant entre dans la dépression. On l'a abime, on lui a volé les sexes innombrables !*' (DRF 83), (TRM 93).

[71] Deleuze and Guattari observe: '*Devenir animal, se lancer dans un tel agencement, c'est un quelque chose de grave. Mais bien plus, le désir affronte ici directement sa propre répression. Dans l'agencement cheval, le pouvoir d'être affecté se trouve rempli par des affects de domestication, d'impuissantation, de brutalité subie, non moins que de puissance et de fierté, de force active.*' (DRF 90), (TRM 99). The theme of becoming-animal is discussed more extensively also in Chapter six.

His own activity appears to have led only to negative consequences. The conjunctive synthesis has not been completed. The ego cannot but lose trust in its own capacities. It ceases to conceive of itself as capable of influencing the structures of language and society. It seems that it can only resign itself and accept its own limitations. This emergence of the sense of loss can nevertheless be prevented. The first solution Deleuze alludes to is prudence. Narcissism must be exercised in a proper manner. A person believing in their reparative capacities must understand their own limitations. They must understand the possible negative consequences of their actions. This is nevertheless not the only proposed solution. The castration complex is not the end of the dynamic genesis. The physical surface does not have to disappear, nor does it have to be continually reconstructed. The adsorption of the sexual surface may be accompanied by the emergence of a new topological dimension: the metaphysical surface. Thought can liberate itself from the body, which allows for the development of a new relationship of the ego with the structures. I analyse this process in the following part of this chapter.

4. Emergence of the metaphysical surface[72]

The first part of this chapter was devoted to the analysis of the castration complex. The narcissistic ego that has lost the image of the phallus is confronted with the images of the castrated mother and of the dead father. It runs a great risk of returning to the depths. The emerging *Spaltung* (split) on the surface of the body nevertheless does also hold a possibility. Castration is not the end of the dynamic genesis, but instead allows for an opening towards a new topological dimension, the metaphysical surface or the surface of pure thought. This surface emerges after or beyond (*meta*) the physical surface. It not only allows for the expression of the bodily desire but also for the liberation of thought from the body. New symbols, which cease to be merely sublimations of problems concerning the body, are constructed. As will become evident, the symbols and phantasms begin to express the engagement of the body with a broader social and political environment. This implies a separation from a structuralist psychoanalysis. The metaphysical surface is not given a-priori and is able to become an independent dimension only as a result of the castration complex. In the rest of this chapter I first analyse

---

[72] It must be noted here that Deleuze does not make it clear whether the developments discussed here have the status of a separate position. For this reason I speak here of the post-castration phase.

the contribution of the castration complex and of the good intentions to the emergence of the metaphysical surface. I furthermore analyse the conceptual framework used by Deleuze to analyse the relationship between thought and body after castration, a framework that aims to replace the philosophy of representation. Additionally, I analyse the role of the concept of the event, the nature of the energy investing the metaphysical surface and the problems encountered by the liberated thought. It will be observed that in this case the analysis differs from possible similar accounts developed in structuralist psychoanalysis.

5. The decline of the good intentions

The ego, deprived of the image of the phallus, is unable to act; the images of the castrated mother and dead father paralyse it. Every act increases the sense of guilt. The ego expects to do only harm. The mother will be castrated once again, while the father will be assassinated. The world will not change and will remain broken and incomplete. Resignation and regression that appear to be inevitable are not the only outcome of the castration complex. The dynamic genesis does not end with the discovery of a narcissistic wound.[73] The discovery of a new bodily image and the liberation of thought on the metaphysical surface allow the ego to move beyond narcissism.[74] But how does Deleuze conceptualise the emergence of these new dimensions? To understand this, he first points to the necessity to think of the nature of the good intentions in a new manner. Normally, the intentions are thought of by means of a distinction between an accomplished action (*action réellement fait*) and a wanted action (*l'action voulue*).[75] The intentions are equated with a wanted action. A person has good intentions when he or she, for example, consciously wants to help another human. This consciously wanted action is subsequently contrasted with an accomplished action. The results of an action that are achieved, in reality fulfil a fundamental role. They in fact form

---

[73] I refer to: '*Pourtant l'histoire ne s'arrête pas là. Le dégagement avec Œdipe de la catégorie éthique d'intention est d'une importance positive considérable.*' (LdS 241), (LoS 206).

[74] I have in mind the following passage from the chapter 'Thirty Fourth Series of Primary Order': '*Que la surface métaphysique à son tour ne soit nullement identique à une conscience n'a rien d'étonnant si l'on songe que les séries d'amplitude qui la caractérisent débordent essentiellement ce qui peut être conscient et forment un champ transcendental impersonnel et pré-individuel.*' (LdS 285), (LoS 244).

[75] I am referring to: '*Mais ce serait une erreur de penser la bonne intention, et sa perversité essentielle, dans le cadre d'une simple opposition de deux actions déterminées, celle qui est voulue et celle qui est faite.*' (LdS 241), (LoS 207).

the base upon which to judge the intentions. The good intentions may be contested in a case where the results of an action are negative.

This conceptual framework is commonly used to understand the intentions of the ego in the oedipal situation. It allows the ego itself to understand and relate to its own actions.[76] In this case the good intentions appear to have negative consequences only. The wounded body of the mother is not welded into a unity. The father is not rendered present, but is assassinated instead. The ego perceives itself as the cause of those actions because it is not yet able to understand its lack of omnipotence. The reduction of its good intention to a determined wanted action (*l'action voulue*) leads to it being discredited by an accomplished real action (*action réelment fait*). The ego begins to question its own motives, its good intentions being forgotten.[77] The ego cannot accept the consequences of its own actions because the sight of the destroyed bodies is extremely unsettling and it cannot handle the truth.[78] It does not want to assume this responsibility since the weight of guilt is too heavy. The death of the father and castration of the mother must therefore be the consequence of others' actions. The ego wants to liberate itself from guilt; it must forget everything and deceive itself. The only manner of coping with the consequences of one's actions is repression; in other words the accomplished action (*l'action réellement fait*) and the determined wanted action are negated by the ego.

Denial of responsibility is most clearly visible in the famous statement frequently uttered by Europeans throughout their violent history: '*Wir haben es nichts gewusst*'.[79] 'It was not me', 'I did not want it', 'I have killed without knowing' are uttered by both perpetrators and witnesses. Both deny their original intentions. The wanted action, for example, the will to achieve a pure new society that has been liberated from elements considered dangerous, is repressed from consciousness. Their awareness about their own contribution to the various murders reaches consciousness only in a negative fashion, by means of the statements mentioned above. This denial has been expressed in various ways within different European nations after the Second World War. It is visible in Polish cinema after the war in the figure of a '*Volksdeutsch*'.

---

[76] I comment on: '*A première vue il n'y a que du négatif dans la bonne intention qui tourne mal: l'action voulue est comme niée, supprimée par ce qui est réellement fait; et aussi bien l'action réellement faite est déniée par celui qui l'a faite et qui en récuse la responsabilité (ce n'est pas moi, je n'ai pas voulu cela, « j'ai tué sans savoir »).*' (LdS 241), (LoS 207).

[77] I refer to: '*l'action voulue est comme niée, supprimée par ce qui est réellement fait*' (LdS 241), (LoS 206).

[78] I am referring to: '*et aussi bien l'action réellement faite est déniée par celui qui l'a faite et qui en récuse la responsabilité.*' (LdS 241), (LoS 206).

[79] Deleuze refers to this problematic in these words: '*(ce n'est pas moi, je n'ai pas voulu cela, « j'ai tué sans savoir »).*' (LdS 241), (LoS 206).

This figure allows the Poles to negate the feelings of guilt. The memory of collaboration or of the hidden and sometimes explicit participation in the destruction of European Jews by part of the population is repressed. An example of this mechanism is visible in the 1947 movie by Aleksander Ford, called *Ulica Graniczna*. The movie depicts the story of a number of Jewish inhabitants of wartime Warsaw, who are delivered to the Nazis. The director does not present the collaborating neighbours as ethnic Poles, but rather as Poles of German origin. Making use of this distinction masks the feeling of guilt. This figure allows the Poles to repress the fresh memory of betrayal, theft of the possessions and the occupation of the social and economic roles of their former Jewish neighbours.[80] The figure of the '*Volksdeutsch*' plays a double role. Guilt is not entirely repressed as the ego does not entirely eliminate the memory of its actions and hidden wishes. The figure of the *Volksdeutsch* allows for the resurfacing of this memory in an inverted manner.[81]

According to Deleuze, the opposition between the two kinds of determined action, the wanted and accomplished action (*action determinable voulue, action effectivement faite*) is nevertheless inadequate for a proper understanding of human action. The relation between the sexual and metaphysical (spiritual) surfaces is inadequately represented.[82] The nature of both the determined wanted and accomplished actions must be thoroughly reconceptualised. Neither action has to be thought of as determined. In Nietzschean terms one can argue that a conceptual framework which understands both actions as determined does not allow for an expression of active forces and strengthens the reactive ones.[83] Uncritical application of such concepts in order to understand human action must lead to a state of resignation. Deleuze develops an alternative framework. Firstly, I analyse the concepts by means of which

---

[80] A recent study of this topic is that by: J. Gross (2006), '*Fear: Anti-Semitism in Poland after Auschwitz: An Essay in Historical Interpretation*', New Jersey: Princeton University Press; and Gross, J. (2011): *Złote żniwa. Rzecz o tym, co się działo na obrzeżach zagłady Żydów*, Znak, Kraków. See also A. Leder, (2014), *Prześniona Rewolucja*, Warszawa: Krytyka Polityczna.

[81] It must be noted here that this example does not fully cover the nature of the problematic discussed. In the examples of Nazism and anti-semitism, one can hardly speak of good intentions as initially guiding action.

[82] I comment on: '*Mais ce serait une erreur de penser la bonne intention, et sa perversité essentielle, dans le cadre d'une simple opposition de deux actions déterminées, celle qui est voulue et celle qui est faite. D'une part, en effet, l'action voulue est une image d'action, une action projetée; et nous ne parlons pas d'un projet psychologique de la volonté, mais de ce qui le rend possible, c'est-à-dire d'un mécanisme de projection lié aux surfaces physiques. C'est en ce sens qu'on peut comprendre Œdipe comme la tragédie de l'Apparence. Loin d'être une instance des profondeurs, l'intention est le phénomène d'ensemble de la surface, le phénomène qui correspond adéquatement au raccordement des surfaces physiques.*' (LdS 241), (LoS 207).

[83] See i.a. LdS 305, LoS 264.

he attempts to understand the wanted action; the re-conceptualisation of the accomplished action follows subsequently.

According to Deleuze, good intentions are not equal to a wanted action. Intentions have little to do with the psychological framework that places the conscious subjective will as its cornerstone.[84] Good intentions are not a property of consciousness. They cannot be comprehended by referring to a consciously pursued goal. A determined wanted action is always dependent upon a more fundamental unconscious phantasmatic life. The good intentions are dependent upon the existence of a fully unconscious image that is made possible by the projection of the good object of the heights onto the genital zone of the physical surface.[85] According to Deleuze, this mechanism alone allows for a proper understanding of the tragedy of Oedipus, which does not reveal an unconscious relationship to familial figures. We do not unconsciously love our mothers. Neither do we want to kill our fathers for the prohibitions imposed on our desire. The tragedy testifies to the existence of an unconscious image. It reveals its existence and subsequent demise, showing that we can be guided by a particular will. The spectators recognise first of all an urge to act, one that can never be captured by the analysis of the personages present in the tragedy.[86] According to Deleuze, Oedipus is a tragedy of semblance (*apparence*) due solely to the existence of the mechanism of projection and the existence of a certain image that guides action.[87]

The image expressing the good intentions does not disappear entirely after the event of castration. It alters in nature. With the decline of the Oedipus complex, intention becomes a phenomenon of the entire (*ensemble*) surface.[88]

---

[84] I refer to: '*et nous ne parlons pas d'un projet psychologique de la volonté*' (LdS 241), (LoS 207).

[85] I am referring to: '*D'une part, en effet, l'action voulue est une image d'action, une action projetée;(…) c'est-a-dire d'un mécanisme de projection lié aux surfaces physiques.*' (LdS 241), (LoS 207).

[86] It must be noted that there is no inconsistency between the remarks by Deleuze in *The Logic of Sense* and his critique of psychoanalysis and its use of tragedy both in *Difference and Repetition* and *Anti-Oedipus*. Deleuze criticises the theatrical understanding of the unconscious found in psychoanalysis for its inability to understand the productive processes characterising desire. Psychoanalysis makes use of structural oppositions between characters in order to understand human desire. For Deleuze and Guattari the unconscious must be understood as a factory which is connected to the outside world. The conflicts found in the unconscious are consequences of problems also found in the outside world. The image of the phallus should be understood as part of a similar machine.

[87] I have in mind: '*…mais de ce qui le rend possible, c'est-à-dire d'un mécanisme de projection lié aux surfaces physiques. C'est en ce sens qu'on peut comprendre Œdipe comme la tragédie de l'Apparence.*' (LdS 241), (LoS 207).

[88] I refer to: '*Loin d'être une instance des profondeurs, l'intention est le phénomène d'ensemble de la surface, le phénomène qui correspond adéquatement au raccordement des surfaces physiques.*' (LdS 241), (LoS 207).

I have already shown how the notion of the image has changed its nature during the previous phases of the sexual position.[89] It emerged after the defusion of the libido from the death and the self-preservation drives. In the pre-genital phase the images designate the superficial objects of various partial zones. They accompany local experiences of pleasure. During the subsequent genital phase, the image of the phallus becomes fundamental and furnishes the coordination of the various partial zones. The emergence of the Oedipus complex leads to the emergence of two separate images of the parents. The ego is paralysed by the image of the wounded mother and of the dead father.

The decline of the Oedipus complex does not lead to a complete disappearance of the images. A regression to the previous positions is not the only option. A new image designating an action in general (*l'action en général*) emerges.[90] How can one understand the nature of this image that appears after the loss of narcissism? After castration, the ego ceases to believe in its own omnipotence. The image also ceases to designate a particular action. This was still the case with the image of the phallus that had a relationship with the images of the parents. The new image, on the other hand, designates an action in general, an action that concerns the surface.[91] It concerns all action (*toute l'action*) that spreads itself out at the surface and is able to haunt it (*hanter*), argues Deleuze. The demise of the image of the phallus does not eliminate the attempts to undo the fragmentation found in the outside world. The action must restore the surface.[92] What alters is the way in which this goal is reached. The image is entirely separated from references to human figures. It is not referring to the attempts to form the surface of one's own body or that of another human. In the post-castration phase the ego becomes part of the world. The other becomes part of a larger whole. He or she becomes its expression or actualisation. The image which guides action now refers to this whole.[93]

---

[89] I comment on: '*La notion même d'Image, après avoir désigné l'objet superficiel d'une zone partielle, puis le phallus projeté sur la zone génitale, puis les images parentales pelliculaires issues d'un clivage, désigne enfin l'action en général,…*' (LdS 241), (LoS 207).

[90] I am referring to: '*La notion même d'Image, … désigne enfin l'action en général, qui concerne la surface, non pas du tout telle action particulière, mais toute l'action qui s'étale en surface et qui peut la hanter (réparer et évoquer, réparer la surface et faire venir a là surface).*' (LdS 241), (LoS 207).

[91] '*mais toute l'action qui s'étale en surface et qui peut la hanter*' (LdS 241), (LoS 207).

[92] I refer to: '*non pas du tout telle action particulière*' (LdS 241), (LoS 207).

[93] The analysis of this topic is found in Appendix 4, 'Michel Tournier and the world without others', See for example the following passage: '*Et quand nous désirons autrui lui-même, sur quoi portait notre désir sinon sur ce petit monde possible exprimé, qu'autrui avait le tort d'envelopper en lui, au lieu de le laisser flotter et voler au-dessus du monde, développé comme un double glorieux?*' (LdS 364), (LoS 313).

The good intentions triumph exactly when they cease to concern the figures of the parents and become directed at a broader environment.

An example that will allow one systematically to differentiate between actions guided by the image of the phallus or the subsequent oedipal images on the one hand and the non-narcissistic, non-oedipal action in general on the other, is discussed in Appendix IV of *The Logic of Sense*, called 'Michel Tournier and the world without others'. There, Deleuze analyses Tournier's book '*Friday, or, The Other Island*.' The central figure of this book, Robinson Crusoe, shipwrecked on a deserted island, undergoes a crucial shift in his mental life. Tournier analyses the progressive abandonment of an orientation towards other humans. Crusoe abandons his initial and highly successful attempts to control the uncivilised island. The cultivation and stockpiling of crops ceases to be his major activity. He stops acting as the master of the island. Crusoe discovers a less narcissistic attitude towards it. Tournier shows how he becomes part of the island, how he dissolves within it. This is particularly visible in the moments when Crusoe discovers that his presence leads to the emergence of a new species of flowers. He beings to perceive them as the offspring of their mutual and unplanned interactions. The image of the phallus disappears. This initial discovery is strengthened by the appearance of the Native American, Friday, who is abandoned on the island by his tribe. He shows Crusoe how to relate to the island in a non-narcissistic manner. The confrontation with the arrogant and aggressive crew of a vessel that is eventually able to rescue both Crusoe and Friday after a decade spent together is devastating for Crusoe. He can no longer live among people unable to develop a similar relationship with their environment. His relation to the it is too precious to be lost through contact with them; consequently, he does not leave the island and stays behind with one of the members of the crew.[94]

Similar examples of actions guided by the image of the action in general can also be found, for example, in *A Thousand Plateaus*.[95] Deleuze and Guattari

---

[94] As Deleuze states: '*La nature et la terre ne nous disaient-elles pas déjà que l'object du désir n'est pas le corps ni la chose, mais seulement l'Image? Et quand nous désirons autrui lui-même, sur quoi portait notre désir sinon sur ce petit monde possible exprimé, qu'autrui avait le tort d'envelopper en lui, au lieu de le laisser flotter et voler au-dessus du monde, développé comme un double glorieux? Et quand nous contemplons ce papillon qui butine une fleur reproduisant exactement l'abdomen de sa femelle et qui en sort portant sur sa tête deux cornes de pollen, il apparaît que les corps ne sont que des détours pour atteindre aux Images, et que la sexualité réalise d'autant mieux et plus promptement son but qu'elle économise ce détour, qu'elle s'adresse directement aux Images, et finalement aux Eléments libérés des corps. La conjugaison de la libido avec les éléments, telle est la déviation de Robinson; mais toute l'histoire de cette déviation quant aux buts, c'est aussi bien le « redressement » des choses, de la terre et du désir.*' (LdS 364), (LoS 313).

[95] See: (MP 292-308), (ATP 239 – 252).

devote their analysis to various processes of becoming, such as becoming-animal, becoming-woman, becoming-Jewish or becoming-imperceptible. I have already indicated how, in the case of Little Hans, the confrontation with the superior power of the rigid laws governing his environment does not destroy him. The boy develops a new, non-phallic relationship with his environment. He engages in the process of becoming-animal. He is affected by the persistent power and pride of the horses, unchanged despite the continuous abuse they suffer.[96] Becoming-animal allows the little boy to remain strong notwithstanding the confrontations he has to endure. He still believes in himself and acts independently. A similar image might also be found in David Grossman's book about the Shoah: 'See under: Love.' Initially the reassurance Grossman tries to convey faces the direct risk of failure. The incredible and fascinating stories told in the book hardly bring about any comfort. The disintegration and trauma described in the book are too deep to be reversed. Narcissism is not restored and the consolation remains highly artificial. The writer seems unable to impose order upon the chaos he encounters. Grossman's aim is nevertheless not to restore a belief in humanity. The image of a wounded mother does not prevail; neither is it again replaced with the image of the phallus. The various characters of the novel, or rather the reader herself, cease to experience guilt regarding their incapacity to restore the world to a state of relative calm and unity. The life of the various characters expresses the existence of a different image. At various moments the characters engage in *becomings* that are no longer human. They frequently engage in becoming-animal, as is the case with Kazik who lives his whole life within a day. Likewise the becoming-salmon of the writer Bruno Schulz no longer feeds any narcissistic tendencies.[97]

---

[96] See: (DRF 82), (TRM 92) and (MP 315), (ATP 257).

[97] Grossman's attempt to overcome the traumatic experiences of the Holocaust differs greatly from the statements of directors such as Lanzmann or philosophers such as Adorno. Grossman makes the following point about his book: 'I wrote 'See Under: Love,' among other reasons, to restore my will to live and my love of life. Perhaps also to heal from the insult I felt on behalf of Bruno Schulz – the insult at the way his murder was described and "explained". (...) I also recall that, with the arrogance of a young writer, I told myself that I wanted to write a book that would tremble on the shelf. That the vitality it contained would be tantamount to the blink of an eye in one person's life. Not "life" in inverted commas, life that is nothing more than a languishing moment in time, but the sort of life Schulz gives us in his writing. A life of the living. A life in which we are not merely refraining from killing the other, but rather giving him or her new life, revitalising a moment that has passed, an image seen a thousand times, a word uttered a thousand times.' (The Guardian, 15 September, 2007). As will be discussed below, Deleuze's philosophy can be regarded as an attempt to overcome a deadlock similar to the one encountered by Grossman. In this respect, his philosophical project differs from that of Adorno, Lyotard and to a certain degree Derrida as well. See also Patton & Protevi (eds.), (2003).

The common conceptual framework that allows for the understanding of the human must nevertheless be rethought on another level too. It is not enough to rethink the nature of the determined willed action and to point to the importance of the body and the image it develops. The nature of the accomplished action must be reconceptualised as well. In the common conceptual framework, the accomplished action is equated with a determined action that can be opposed to the willed action.[98] The acting person is perceived as confronted with the consequences of his actions. He must gradually develop a sense of reality. The acting ego must discover that reality is organised by means of a limited number of rules. It must realise that its impact on the world can only be minimal. Emergence of such increased awareness of the laws governing reality is frequently depicted in tragedies. Oedipus comes to the realisation that one cannot escape these rules. He must learn to accept his fate. He was not destined to be only the saviour of Thebes and the lover of the queen. Instead, he was meant to become the cause of the misery of his city and to become the lover of his mother and murderer of his father. The determined action is an expression of the rules governing the world.[99]

Deleuze criticises this understanding of the accomplished action that is proper to what he elsewhere calls the philosophy of representation. The confrontation with the accomplished action does not, by definition, lead to an increased sense of the determined structures of reality. The ego is not confronted with unchanging structures, but rather with something that is highly indeterminate.[100] Accomplished action is first of all a mystery, an event.[101] It is something that arrives, something that happens to the ego. It refers to something that may come. The ego is taken by surprise. The accomplished action seems to be a result of its own actions but it is at the same time entirely separated from them. It is in fact not yet an action or a

---

[98] I refer to: '*Mais, d'autre part, l'action effectivement faite n'est pas davantage une action détermine qui s'opposerait à l'autre, ni une passion qui serai le contrecoup de l'action projetée.*' (LdS 241), (LoS 207).

[99] Pasolini's film about the tragedy of Oedipus depicts the moment of the confrontation with the laws of reality very well. Oedipus acts as if possessed when he kills his father and when he defeats the Sphinx. He seems to be willing to resist his own actions, but eventually acts according to the orders of the gods. The memory of these moments is entirely repressed making his discovery of own guilt highly painful.

[100] This claim is also made in *Difference and Repetition*, (DR 141), (DRE 107).

[101] I refer to: (the accomplished action – PS) *C'est quelque chose qui arrive, qui représente à son tour tout ce qui peut arriver, ou mieux encore quelque chose qui résulte nécessairement des actions et des passions, mais qui est d'une tout autre nature, ni action ni passion soi-même: événement, pur événement,* Eventum tantum *(tuer le père et châtrer la mère, être châtré soi-même et mourir).*' (LdS 241), (LoS 207).

passion.[102] It arrives in the ego as a pure Event, as an *Eventum tantum*. The ego is first of all confronted with uncertainty and chance. The sudden appearance of the event does not mean that order and structure are absent and lost. The ego attempts to restore order directly after the occurrence of an event. This takes place by means of thought and its concepts. When he is investigating the causes of Thebes' suffering, Oedipus is first convinced that he has done no harm. Somebody else must be the cause of his city's misfortunes. The shock caused by the discovery of his guilt is enormous, but is in fact also quickly absorbed. He directly attributes causes to what has happened. Thought seems to be incapable of truly establishing a relation with chance. The accomplished action ceases to be an even and quickly becomes a determined accomplished action. In this case the concept of fate or the will of the gods are held responsible for the difficulties of Thebes and the demise of Oedipus. Thought quickly restores order that has been temporarily undermined. The projection of an action onto a cerebral surface provides the body with words and meaning that stabilises its experience.[103] Thought allows for an understanding of Events. The accomplished action gains a name and a structure: it becomes part of a larger whole. A structure is hastily established, before any relationship with chance and chaos is able to develop.

Hence Deleuze's aim is to show that in the analysis of human action, a different conceptual scheme must be developed. The nature of intentions cannot be understood properly by departing from an opposition between two determined actions, the determined willed and accomplished action.[104] As he puts this: 'the intention takes the totality of every possible action and divides it into two.' It projects an action onto two screens, those of the physical and metaphysical surfaces. On each surface an action is organised according to the rules that are proper to it. On the physical surface an action appears as

---

[102] I am referring to: '*ou mieux encore quelque chose qui résulte nécessairement des actions et des passions, mais qui est d'une tout autre nature, ni action ni passion soi-même*' (LdS 241), (LoS 207).

[103] I comment on: '*Autant dire que l'action faite n'est pas moins que l'autre projetée sur une surface. Seulement, c'est une tout autre surface, métaphysique ou transcendantale.*' (LdS 242), (LoS 207). See also Marc de Kesel (2009: 139).

[104] I am discussing the following passage: '*Bref, l'intention comme catégorie œdipienne n'oppose pas du tout une action faite. Au contraire, elle prend l'ensemble de toute action possible et le divise en deux, le projette sur deux écrans, et détermine chaque côté conformément aux exigences nécessaires de chaque écran: d'une part toute l'image de l'action sur une surface physique, où l'action même apparaît come voulue et se trouve déterminée sous les espèces de la réparation et de l'évocation; d'autre part tout le résultat de l'action sur une surface métaphysique, où l'action même apparaît comme produite et non voulue, déterminée sous les espèces du meurtre et de la castration.*' (LdS 242), (LoS 208).

willed. It is an action that is guided by a physical image. The acting ego wants to restore and evoke. This projection is visible in the case of Oedipus, who initially intends to restore the damaged body of the mother and evokes the retreated father. Little Hans, on the other hand, does not lose the physical image guiding his actions and preserves a will to act, exactly at the moment of his greatest fears.[105] The boy does not give up. The second screen onto which the results of an action are projected is the metaphysical or cerebral surface. Here an action cannot appear as willed.[106] An action is directly experienced as having a reason, as having been produced. The ego searches for an explanation of its own actions. It refers to external circumstances and uses symbols. Oedipus alludes directly to fate and the gods because he cannot find any other explanations. This projection of an action on the metaphysical surface has severe consequences for the ego because the exclusive attention paid to an explanation leads to a repression of the good intentions. The subject becomes merely capable of stating that he did not wish to act as he did. An action appears on the metaphysical surface in the form of murder and castration, as Deleuze asserts.[107] It overcomes the ego and could not have been consciously willed. The metaphysical surface allows for all kinds of excuses, similar to those mentioned at the beginning of this chapter: 'I could not do otherwise', 'The circumstances forced me', 'It was the will of God/fate/physical processes and could not have been escaped.' Resignation is the usual result of this second projection.

6. Metaphysical surface and the drives

The metaphysical or cerebral surface thus becomes a fundamental topological dimension in the post-castration phase. The projection of an action onto this surface allows the ego to limit its own responsibility. Oedipus blames fate. The first thought arising in his consciousness is the same excuse, 'It was not me. I did not want it. I did not know.' Oedipus develops a symbol of negation. The images projected on the physical surface are forgotten. Action appears as determined; the ego consequently resigns itself to accepting the existing structures and their manner of describing failure. Nevertheless, Deleuze

---

[105] See: DRF 90, TRM 100.
[106] I am referring to: '*d'autre part tout le résultat de l'action sur une surface métaphysique, où l'action même apparaît comme produite et non voulue, déterminée sous les espèces du meurtre et de la castration.*' (LdS 242), (LoS 208).
[107] I refer to: '*déterminée sous les espèces du meurtre et de la castration.*' (LdS 242), (LoS 208).

attempts to distance himself from such an understanding of thought's nature. Thought is able to endure and relate to castration. He develops this point first in his analysis of the status of the drives that are proper to the metaphysical surface. According to him, this surface is invested by a new liberated energy that allows for a free production of symbols. In order to understand the nature of this energy, an analysis of the genesis of this surface together with the notion of the desexualised libido is presented here.

The metaphysical and physical surfaces are initially intertwined.[108] The former surface is initially responsible for attributing names to bodily experiences. The symbols it produces directly express the activity of the body, allowing for sublimation. The disintegration of the physical (sexual) surface is per se a bodily event. The loss of the image of the phallus does not concern the metaphysical surface as such.[109] How does the separation come about? Death and castration occurring on the physical surface represent only the first step, and are not the only condition of possibility for the emergence of the new surface. The castration complex is fundamental because it initiates the process of the transformation of the libido. This transformation alone clarifies the emergence of the new surface as an independent topological instance. The loss of the image of the phallus leads to a demise of secondary narcissism. The libido ceases to invest the surface of the body. Deleuze terms this process desexualisation.[110] It suddenly finds itself in a free state and starts to invest (cathex) in thought. The metaphysical surface liberates itself from the body and receives its own independent quantity of energy: an energy that is different in nature from the libido of the surface and also from the intertwined drives of the depths.

Deleuze's conception of the desexualised libido differs from that of Freud, who develops this notion among others in *The Ego and the Id*. Freud recognises the possibility of existence of a free energy that is independent of the ego and the id. This energy is capable of increasing the intensity of investment

---

[108] I am referring to: '*Encore allons-nous trop vite. Il est évident que le meurtre et la castration qui résultent de l'action concernent les corps, qu'ils ne constituent pas par eux-mêmes une surface métaphysique, et ne lui appartiennent même pas. Pourtant ils sont sur le chemin, une fois dit que c'est un long chemin jalonné d'étapes.*' (LdS 242), (208).

[109] I refer to: '*qu'ils ne constituent pas par eux-mêmes une surface métaphysique, et ne lui appartiennent même pas*' (LdS 242), (LoS 208).

[110] I comment here on: '*En effet, avec la « blessure narcissique », c'est-à-dire quand la ligne phallique se transforme en tracé de la castration, la libido qui investissait à la surface le moi du narcissisme secondaire connaît pour son compte une transmutation particulièrement importante: celle que Freud nomme désexualisation, l'énergie désexualisée lui paraissant à la fois alimenter l'instinct de mort et conditionner le mécanisme de la pensée.*' (LdS 242), (LoS 208).

(cathexis) of various objects by the libido and the destructive drives.[111] According to Freud, this displaceable energy is highly plastic. It facilitates easy discharge of tension and, as such, functions in the service of the pleasure principle.[112] Freud nevertheless also stresses that a true desexualisation solely occurs upon the emergence of narcissism. Desexualisation occurs when the ego is invested (cathexis) by the libido and the external sexual objects are abandoned. Deleuze chooses to distance himself from Freud's analysis on several points.[113] According to Deleuze, the source of the desexualised energy cannot be traced to the emergence of narcissism.[114] The narcissistic libido is fully sexual. It implies a relationship with objects. The ego of the secondary narcissism directly relates to the images of the parents. It wants to restore the disintegrated body of the mother and allow for the return of the retreated father. In Deleuze's account, desexualisation of the libido can only occur after the loss of the image of the phallus.[115] In this case alone, the world is no longer experienced by means of the images of the parents. To Deleuze, this does not mean that the interest in the external world as such is lost. It simply leads to

---

[111] Freud observes the following about the desexualised energy: 'We have reckoned as though there existed in the mind- whether in the ego or in the id – a displaceable energy, which, neutral in itself, can be added to a qualitatively differentiated erotic or destructive impulse, and augment its total cathexis (I use the term investment in this text – PS). Without assuming the existence of a displaceable energy of this kind we can make no headway. The only question is where it comes from, what it belongs to, and what it signifies.' (Freud 1923, in 1989: 648).

[112] Freud makes the following statement: 'It seems a plausible view that this displaceable and neutral energy, which is no doubt active both in the ego and the id, proceeds from the narcissistic store of libido – that it is desexualised Eros. (The erotic instincts appear to be altogether more plastic, more readily diverted and displaced than the destructive instincts). From this we can easily go on to assume that this displaceable libido is employed in the service of the pleasure principle to obviate blockages and to facilitate discharge.' (Freud 1923 in 1989: 649).

[113] It is doubtful whether Deleuze's discussion of the death-drive in Freud is entirely correct. Monique David-Ménard criticises Deleuze in her book 'Deleuze et la psychanalyse' (2005: 61-63) exactly on this point. I will nevertheless not engage with her critique in the discussion. My primary aim is not to clarify whether Deleuze provides us with a correct reading of Freud but to understand Deleuze's statements about the nature of the drives on the new surface. To make Deleuze's statements about Freud more comprehensible I will nevertheless still refer to work of the latter.

[114] I discuss: '*Nous nous séparons de l'expose freudien sur deux point. D'une part, Freud s'exprime souvent comme si la libido narcissique impliquait comme telle une désexualisation de l'énergie. Ce qui ne peut pas être maintenu dans la mesure où la moi phallique du narcissisme secondaire dispose encore de relations objectales avec les images de parents (réparer, faire venir); alors la désexualisation ne peut se produire qu'avec le complexe de castration défini dans sa spécificité.*' (LdS 243), (LoS 354).

[115] I examine: '*alors la désexualisation ne peut se produire qu'avec le complexe de castration défini dans sa spécificité.*' (LdS 243), (LoS 354).

an alteration of the image characterising the physical surface. The image of general action, considered above in the example of Tournier's discussion of Robinson Crusoe, emerges.[116] In his desire for the island, Crusoe does not sublimate the sexual desire towards others. The same happens to little Hans who engages in the process of becoming-animal.

The second difference between Freud and Deleuze's analysis of the desexualised energy concerns its so-called 'neutral' status.[117] I will discuss this topic briefly here and more extensively in Chapter six. For Freud, the desexualised energy is actually only free and displaceable initially. It strengthens either the libido, Eros or the death drive, Thanatos. At the same time the neutral energy receives characteristics that do not differ from those of the death drive.[118] The new energy is characterised as a mechanical inclination to return to a state of rest or death. It is a tendency to return to an inorganic state. Deleuze proceeds towards a different understanding of this notion. The desexualised energy has little in common with Thanatos. It is not a brute physical force, a tendency to return to a state of rest. The desexualised energy is not characterised by a negativity and immobility.[119] It is pre-individual (*pré-individuel*) and impersonal (*impersonnel*), contends Deleuze.[120] It refers to singularities unbounded by the form imposed on this energy by the ego. The new energy accompanies a state in which an organism relates to problems characterising its environment.[121] If one can speak of a

---

[116] See Michel Tournier, 'Friday, or the other Island' and Appendix 4 of *The Logic of Sense*.

[117] I refer to: '*D'autre part, Freud appelle <neutre> cette énergie désexualisée; il entend par là qu'elle est déplaçable et susceptible de passer d'Eros à Thanatos. Mais, s'il est vrai qu'elle ne se contente pas de rejoindre Thanatos ou l'instinct de mort, s'il est vrai qu'elle le constitue au moins sous la figure spéculative qu'il prend à la surface, <neutre> doit avoir un tout autre sens, que nous verrons dans les paragraphes suivants.*' (LdS 243), (LoS 354).

[118] Freud states this as follows: 'By thus getting hold of the libido from the object-cathexis, setting itself up as sole love-object, and desexualising or sublimating the libido of the id, the ego is working in opposition to the purposes of Eros and placing itself at the service of the opposing instinctual impulses.' (Freud 1923 in 1989: 649).

[119] I refer to the following statement: '*s'il est vrai qu'elle ne se contente pas de rejoindre Thanatos ou l'instinct de mort,*' (LdS 243), (LoS 354).

[120] In the chapter 'Thirtieth Series of the Phantasm' Deleuze observes: '*Il faut interpréter l'expression « énergie neutre » en ce sens: neutre signifie alors pré-individuel et impersonnel, mais ne qualifie pas l'état d'une énergie qui viendrait rejoindre un sans-fond, il renvoie au contraire aux singularités libérées du moi par la blessure narcissique*' (LdS 249), (LoS 213).

[121] In *Difference and Repetition* Deleuze critically discusses the role of the death drive in Freud's theory. He remarks, for example: '*Mais pourquoi Freud ainsi pose-t-il l'instinct de mort comme préexistant à cette énergie désexualisée, indépendant d'elle en principe? Pour deux raison sans doute, l'une renvoyant à la persistance du modèle dualiste et conflictuel qui inspire toute la théorie des pulsions, l'autre, au modèle matériel qui préside à la théorie de la répétition.(...) Mais de toute façon la mort, déterminée comme retour qualitatif et quantitatif du vivant à cette matière inanimée, n'a qu'une définition extrinsèque, scientifique et objective; (...) Mais en vérité*

death drive in this case, the death one speaks of is a matter of speculation. Death is a conceptual principle, constituted on the metaphysical surface. In *Difference and Repetition* Deleuze conceives of death in similar terms. Death emerges out of the relation of the organism to its environment. It is a problem that challenges the organism. Death primarily poses questions and requires solutions.[122]

One can illustrate these statements by citing the example of Deleuze and Guattari's analysis of the experience of Captain Ahab, the hero of Melville's *Moby Dick*. Ahab loses his leg during a hunt. After this accident he becomes obsessed with hunting a white whale. He wants to catch and destroy it at all costs. He succeeds, but also loses his ship and the crew. We could claim that Ahab is driven by the death drive. He wishes to destroy a certain object and ignores all the potential risks. His actions are not guided by the pleasure principle. Nevertheless, from the perspective of Deleuze and Guattari, this chase must be understood differently. Ahab's libido goes through a process of desexualisation. Ahab loses his leg and with it his belief that he is the absolute sovereign over the sea. He loses his narcissism. He realises that he is not a hero, but a labourer in an industrial whale hunt. This point is made apparent, for example, by the chapters of the book devoted to a rational analysis of the different techniques of whale hunting. This castration does not lead to a submission to a death drive, to a pure aggression. Ahab does not intend to eliminate all negative stimuli. He opens up to a free energy of the metaphysical surface instead, making a choice that is a response to particular circumstances and constructing a solution. The white whale is a symbol that allows him to relate to a world in which it is impossible to maintain one's narcissism. His destructive chase is his answer to the events that have changed his life.

From the analysis developed above one may conclude that castration and death play a double role.[123] They, firstly, threaten the body but also allow

---

la structure de l'inconscient n'est pas conflictuelle, oppositionnelle ou de contradiction, elle est questionnante et problématisante. La répétition n'est pas davantage puissance brute et nue, par-delà des déguisements qui viendraient l'affecter secondairement comme autant de variantes; elle se tisse au contraire dans le déguisement, dans le déplacement comme éléments constitutifs auxquels elle ne préexiste pas.' (DR 148), (DRE 112).

[122] I comment on: '*La mort est plutôt la forme dernière du problématique, la source des problèmes et des questions, la marque de leur permanence par-dessus toute réponse, le Où et Quand?qui désigne ce (non)-être où toute affirmation s'alimente.*' (DR 148), (DRE 112). This topic is discussed more extensively in Chapter six.

[123] I am referring to: '*Nous devons donc accorder aux thèmes de la mort et de la castration une double valeur: celle qu'ils ont dans la persévération ou la liquidation du complexe d'Œdipe et dans l'organisation de la sexualité génitale définitive, aussi bien sur sa surface propre que dans ses rapports avec les dimensions précédentes (positions schizoïde et dépressive);*' (LdS 242), (LoS 208).

for the development of the image of action in general. Secondly, castration and death contribute to the emergence of desexualised energy.[124] The libido ceases to invest only the body and is not characterising the new metaphysical surface, the surface of pure thought (*pensée pure*). The new phase announces a changed relationship between the body and thought. The emergence of the new surface now allows not only for sublimation but also for independent construction of symbols.[125] Sublimation occurs when the body projects itself on the metaphysical surface.[126] Thought is used only to express the underlying libidinal tendencies. As has already been observed, doctors, artists or scientists can sublimate the reparative tendencies in their work. Symbolisation differs in nature from sublimation.[127] The desexualised energy is capable of reinvesting everything that is projected onto the metaphysical surface by the body. Captain Ahab's destructive chase of the white whale clarifies this activity. The white whale is a symbol, a response to the problematic of castration that is bodily in nature. Ahab loses his narcissism and is confronted with the sheer banality of his own existence. Thought in this case not only expresses the bodily problematic but produces a symbol that allows it to relate towards the problematic field. The white whale offers a solution to the problems encountered by Ahab. It is a purely spiritual solution. The free desexualised energy is investing this symbol. This activity of thought is re-sexualised in a subsequent stage. Ahab enjoys his hunt physically. The free floating libido reinvests the physical surface and the desexualised libido is re-sexualised.[128]

A similar relationship between the physical problematic and the desexualised energy is also analysed by Deleuze in *Coldness and Cruelty* in his

---

[124] I refer to: '*mais, également, la valeur qu'ils prennent comme origine de l'énergie désexualisée et la façon originale dont cette énergie les réinvestit sur sa nouvelle surface métaphysique ou de pensée pure. Ce second processus — indépendant de l'autre dans une certaine mesure, puisqu'il n'est pas directement proportionnel à la réussite ou à l'échec de la liquidation d'Œdipe — correspond dans son premier aspect à ce qu'on appelle sublimation,*' (LdS 243), (LoS 208).

[125] I allude to: '*Ce second processus – …- correspond dans son premier aspect à ce qu'on appelle* sublimation*, et dans son deuxième aspect à ce qu'on appelle* symbolisation.' (LdS 243), (LoS 208).

[126] Deleuze gives a definition of what he understands by sublimation and symbolisation in the chapter 'Thirty-first series of thought': '*Nous appelions sublimation l'opération par laquelle le tracé de la castration devient ligne de la pensée, donc aussi l'opération par laquelle la surface sexuelle et le reste se projettent à la surface de la pensée. Nous appelions symbolisation l'opération par laquelle la pensée réinvestit de sa propre énergie tout ce qui arrive et se projette sur sa surface.*' (LdS 255), (LoS 219).

[127] I am referring to: '*et dans son deuxième aspect à ce qu'on appelle symbolisation.*' (LdS 243), (LoS 208).

[128] The analysis of the symbol's spiritual nature provided here is still partial. It will be developed further in Chapter six, on the phantasm.

discussion of masochism.[129] A masochist is not only sublimating the physical tendencies that characterise his desire, nor is he only submitting himself to an object of the heights. His submission to a mistress is also a solution to the problems in the social and political environment. The mistress is a symbol, invested by the desexualised libido. She is a spiritual answer to these problems. Masochism emerges in circumstances where the paternal law is exercised with particular authoritarian force. The masochist's practice is an act of resistance. He cannot tolerate the law and the feelings of guilt it imposes upon him.[130] A masochist disavows it by means of a contract with his mistress. Neither the father nor the institutions exercising the paternal law can torture him. The punishment, inevitable in contemporary society, is in his hands. The problems gain a spiritual solution. The organised sexual energy is first of all desexualised. It invests in a problematic field and is united around a symbol. But the masochist also experiences pleasure in pain. He particularly enjoys the state of suspension and waiting for the future physical torture. As in Ahab's case, the desexualised energy is re-sexualised in the actual activity of the masochist. He eventually experiences pleasure in enduring the physical and spiritual suffering.[131]

---

[129] Deleuze describes this process in *Coldness and Cruelty*, stating the following: '*au cœur du sadisme il y a l'entreprise de sexualiser la pensée, de sexualiser le processus spéculatif en tant que tel, en tant qu'il dépend du surmoi. (…) Sade montre que nulle passion, l'ambition politique, l'avarice économique, etc., n'est étrangère à la « lubricité »: non pas que celle-ci soit à leur principe, mais au contraire parce qu'elle surgit à la fin comme ce qui procède sur place à leur resexualisation. (…) Quoique la froideur masochiste soit d'une tout autre sorte, on y retrouve le processus de désexualisation comme condition d'une resexualisation sur place, par laquelle toutes les passions de l'homme, celles que concernant l'argent, la propriété, l'État, pourront tourner au bénéfice du masochiste. Et c'est bien là l'essentiel: que la resexualisation se fasse sur place, dans une espèce de saut. Là non plus, le principe de plaisir n'est pas détrôné. Il garde son pouvoir empirique. Le sadique trouve son plaisir dans la douleur d'autrui, la masochiste trouve son plaisir dans sa propre douleur, celle-ci jouant le rôle de condition sans laquelle il n'obtiendrait pas le plaisir.*' (PSM 102), (CC 118).

[130] I here consider the following passage from *Coldness and Cruelty*: '*Partant de l'autre découverte moderne, que la loi nourrit la culpabilité de celui qui y obéit, le héros masochiste invente une nouvelle manière de descendre de la loi aux conséquences: il « tourne » la culpabilité, en faisant du châtiment une condition qui rend possible le plaisir défendu. … Dans le cas du masochisme, toute la loi est reportée sur la mère, qui expulse le père de la sphère symbolique*'. (PSM 79), (CC 90). There is insufficient space here to discuss the topic of the law more extensively.

[131] I refer to the following extract from *Coldness and Cruelty*: '*Quoique la froideur masochiste soit d'une tout autre sorte, on y retrouve le processus de désexualisation comme condition d'une resexualisation sur place, par laquelle toutes les passions de l'homme, celles que concernant l'argent, la propriété, l'État, pourront tourner au bénéfice du masochiste. Et c'est bien là l'essentiel: que la resexualisation se fasse sur place, dans une espèce de saut. Là non plus, le principe de plaisir n'est pas détrôné. Il garde son pouvoir empirique.*' (PSM 102), (CC 118).

7. The crack in the metaphysical surface – the dangers of the post-castration phase

The two surfaces are brought into proximity when the bodily tendencies are projected onto the metaphysical surface and when the desexualised energy reinvests the bodily problematic.[132] Both surfaces encounter each other with particular force at a very specific point. This occurs when the trace of castration on the physical surface starts to correspond with the crack (*fêlure*) proper to the metaphysical surface.[133] The said surface itself can also encounter its own kind of impossibility, its own castration and death. Thought encounters its own un-resolvable problems. Deleuze addresses this topic throughout *The Logic of Sense*. According to him, sense is continually confronted with non-sense and the source of non-sense is not only found on the level of the body. Thought itself is characterised by its own paradoxes and pitfalls. By referring to the Lewis Carroll's work, for instance, Deleuze identifies the ambiguities present in our understanding of words. They frequently make hardly any sense. They not only lack sense but also express sense's overabundance. He demonstrates how communication and understanding may turn into a state of complete confusion.[134]

The idea of the crack on the metaphysical surface cannot be comprehended by referring to the Lacanian notion of the Real, as it is developed in his earlier work. The crack is not just continually resisting the activity of symbolisation; it does not only reveal the existence of the limits of thought. The crack discloses the true nature of the metaphysical surface. This surface does not consist of rigid structures. Instead, its nature can best be understood by means of the concept of the virtual.[135] The crack is an opening towards the pure line of Aiôn, a form of time that proceeds the chronological, organised time of

---

[132] I have this passage of *The Logic of Sense* in mind: '*Nous devons donc admettre que les métamorphoses ne s'arrêtent pas avec la transformation de la ligne phallique en tracé de castration sur la surface physique ou corporelle, et que le tracé de castration correspond lui-même avec une fêlure, sur une tout autre surface métaphysique incorporelle qui en opère la transmutation.*' (LdS 243), (LoS 208).

[133] I refer here to: '*et que le tracé de castration correspond lui-même avec une fêlure, sur une tout autre surface métaphysique incorporelle qui en opère la transmutation.*' (LdS 243), (LoS 208).

[134] A thorough analysis of the paradoxes of sense lies outside of the topic of this book. A discussion of this topic may be found in James Williams (2008).

[135] In Deleuze's analysis of the *Difference and Repetition* the virtual carries transcendental characteristics. It is the condition of possibility of the actual, constituting the ground allowing for its emergence that is continually questioned out of the actual.

Chronos.[136] Aiôn is an all-encompassing time structure, while Chronos on the other hand is merely its chronological and organised expression. Chronos actualises Aiôn and provides it with a liveable form. Aiôn is also never given as such. Its existence can be traced only through an analysis of its own actualisation. Just as with the virtual, Aiôn is not the realm of a true meaning. It cannot be compared to the Platonic ideas. It is instead a broader field of problems subsequently expressed by and narrowed down to the Chronos.[137]

The confrontation with the crack (*fêlure*) on the metaphysical surface, the pure line of Aiôn, leads to important consequences. It is one of the factors that contribute to a change (*transmutation*) of the image on the physical surface.[138] The ego is now capable of orienting itself to an instance outside of the realm of the actual: thought and body engage the metaphysical surface and the virtual. They start to actualise something new. According to Deleuze, this opening towards the virtual is also an opening towards the death drive in its speculative form.[139] A new and different production of desire becomes possible, one that allows for a production of symbols engaging the problematic field.[140]

Deleuze first of all mentions the dangers of the new discovery. As with the previous stages of the dynamic genesis, the last metamorphosis may also be very unsettling.[141] The crack might first of all lead to a complete breakdown of the metaphysical surface. The opening towards the pure line of Aiôn could fail

---

[136] I here refer to: '*Cette fêlure de la pensée, à la surface incorporelle, nous y reconnaissons la ligne pure de l'Aiôn ou l'instinct de mort sous sa forme spéculative.*' (LdS 243), (LoS 209). A comprehensive analysis of the metaphysical and ontological aspects of the concept of Aiôn also lies outside of the scope of this book. A consideration of this concept may be found in Bowden (2011: 22) as well as in James Williams (2008) and van Tuinen et. al. (eds.), (2009).

[137] For further analysis of this concept see i.a. LdS: 74-82, 95, 211, (LoS 58-65, 77, 180).

[138] I refer here to the following passage: '*Ce changement pose toute sorte de problèmes relatifs à l'énergie désexualisée qui forme la nouvelle surface, aux mécanismes mêmes de la sublimation et de la symbolisation, à la destinée du moi sur ce nouveau plan, enfin à la double appartenance du meurtre ou de la castration à l'ancien et aux nouveau systèmes.*' (LdS 243), (LoS 208).

[139] I am referring to: '*Cette fêlure de la pensée, à la surface incorporelle, nous y reconnaissons la ligne pure de l'Aiôn ou l'instinct de mort sous sa forme spéculative.*' (LdS 243), (LoS 209).

[140] The symbol can be regarded as a proper form of the phantasm and will be discussed more extensively in chapter six.

[141] I here comment on: '*En même temps on rappellera que cette dernière métamorphose encourt les mêmes dangers que les autres, et peut-être d'une manière encore plus aiguë: la fêlure risque singulièrement de briser la surface dont elle est pourtant inséparable, de rejoindre le simple tracé de la castration sur l'autre surface ou, pire, de s'engouffrer dans la* Spaltung *des profondeurs ou des hauteurs, emportant tous les débris de surface dans cette débâcle généralisée où la fin retrouve le point de départ, et l'instinct de mort les pulsions destructrices sans fond — suivant la confusion que nous avons vue précédemment entre les deux figures de la mort: point central d'obscurité qui ne cesse de poser le problème des rapports de la pensée avec la schizophrénie et la dépression, avec la* Spaltung *psychotique en général et aussi la castration névrotique, « car toute vie bien entendu est un processus de démolition », y compris la vie spéculative.*' (LdS 244). (LoS 209).

and become a source of various dangers. The ego runs the risk of regression. The crack may become the trace of castration on the physical surface. One could think here of a scientist who is convinced that scientific knowledge can provide solutions to most of the world's problems. Part one of the series *Dekalog* by Kieślowski offers an example of a scientist who loses faith in this way. The main protagonist, Krzysztof, is a scientist who completely believes in his own technical and theoretical knowledge. In this case, both narcissism on a personal level and belief in the capacities of science come together. Krzysztof is convinced that he is capable of fully understanding the weather patterns. His calculations allow him, for example, to measure the strengths of the ice. On a winter's day he predicts its thickness and allows his only son to go skating. His knowledge is tested because he is unable to include all possible variables that might determine the thickness of the ice. The story ends dramatically: his only son, the brilliant and touching Pawel, drowns. Somebody has set a campfire in the vicinity of the little lake. What is important for us is the end of the movie. Krzysztof is unable to endure the destruction of both his narcissism and the crack that tears the metaphysical surface to pieces. The film concludes with an open ending. The screen of the computer that has carried out all the calculations displays the message '*I am ready.*' Nevertheless, Krzysztof does not make additional calculations. He cannot trust and enjoy science any longer, nor does he find consolation in a religious belief. No system of thought can provide him with any sense of security. Krzysztof goes to the church and destroys an altar. He is alone and completely broken, holding a block of melting ice in his hand.[142] Both the metaphysical and physical surfaces disappear. Krzysztof is swallowed up by the depths. He disappears into a state of almost unbearable chaos. In this case both figures of death, differentiated by Deleuze become, once again, entangled.

The protagonist of Sacher-Masoch's *Venus in furs* meets a similar fate. At the end of the book, Severin loses control over his mistress, Wanda. Her relationship with a Greek man, who has initially perfectly fitted the masochist

---

[142] A similar Lacanian reading of this movie can be found in Žižek (2001, *The fright of real tears*, BFI Publishing). Of this movie Žižek observes: 'It is thus crucial not to read Decalogue 1 as simply asserting the unreliable and cheating nature of the "false God" of reason and science: its lesson is not that, when our reliance on the false idol of science (embodied in the father's personal computer) fails, we are confronted with a "deeper" religious dimension; on the contrary, when science fails us, our religious foundation is also shattered – this is what happens to the desperate father at the end of Decalogue 1.' (Žižek 2001: 121). The difference from our reading concerns a possible critique of the work of Kieślowski himself. He provides us only with an image of negative consequences: the father was not prudent enough. Kieślowski is unable to go beyond this point and allow for construction of symbols and phantasms in the sense that Deleuze employs.

universe, becomes a source of various dangers. The new partner does not accept the subjection of Wanda to the contract with Severin. He destroys the masochist universe by assuming the role of the sadistic father; his actions make it impossible for Severin to deny the existence of this figure of cruel authority. The Greek physically tortures him with a truly sadistic pleasure, a pleasure his mistress would never imagine experiencing.[143] Subsequently, Severin can only destroy the contract with Wanda. He stays behind, shattered. His depressive tendencies can no longer be expressed. The symbol produced on the metaphysical surface disappears as well, together with the surface, as an independent topological dimension. Severin has only one option left. He becomes a sadist himself. The woman he meets at the end of the book is not idealised any longer. She becomes his slave, nothing more than a source of direct pleasure. The problematic Severin sought to confront on this surface – not only personal but social and political in nature – ceases to be accessible. He no longer confronts the limits of thought or challenges the problematic of authority. The speculative death drive alters into pure aggression. The phantasm becomes a simulacrum of the depths. Severin disappears into a *Spaltung*.[144]

The relation between the crack on the metaphysical surface and the depths is nevertheless explored most profoundly in the work of French poet and actor Antoine Artaud.[145] According to Deleuze, Artaud was able to explore the dangers of this confrontation and has explored the process during which the speculative death drive, characterising the metaphysical surface, once again mingles with the destructive death drive of the depths (*les pulsions destructrices sans fond*). In *The Logic of Sense*, Deleuze compares his work with Lewis Carroll's. Both writers appear to be fascinated by the crack splitting the cerebral or metaphysical surface. Carroll's story of *Alice in Wonderland* is, for example, full of paradoxes and contradictions. Carroll displays the incompleteness and incoherence of sense, playfully exploring both the limitations and madness of thought. In his world, there exists an excess of

---

[143] In his book Deleuze denies the necessity of cooperation between a sadist and a masochist. Both live in different worlds and never encounter each other.

[144] Deleuze expresses this as follows in *Coldness and Cruelty*: '*la face virile* (of the Greek - PS), *marque au contraire le fin du phantasme et de l'exercice masochistes: quand le Grec prend le fouet et bat Séverin, le charme suprasensuel s'évanouit vite « rêve voluptueux, femme et amour » se dissipent.*' (PSM 57), (CC 64).

[145] I refer here to the following passage: *point central d'obscurité qui ne cesse de poser le problème des rapports de la pensée avec la schizophrénie et la dépression, avec la* Spaltung *psychotique en général et aussi la castration névrotique, « car toute vie bien entendu est un processus de démolition », y compris la vie spéculative.* (LdS 244), (LoS 209). For a more extensive analysis of the work of Artaud, see Chapter two.

sense. Sense continually unsettles the only superficially stable organisation of reality. Carroll's world is dominated by non-sense that allows for the overabundant production of sense. Despite the fascination with his world, Deleuze nevertheless points to a fundamental limitation of the extraordinary world of Carroll. The paradoxes concern only the surface of sense. They lack a profound connection with physical suffering. Carroll does not truly arrive in the vicinity of the *Spaltung* that tears thought apart and confronts it with its own physical madness.[146] His world is deprived of the depths. It does not reveal the dangers facing thought. Artaud, on the other hand, is capable of exactly such a revelation. His work reveals the painful interaction between the madness of the body and the madness of thought. His work makes plain that the speculative and productive death drive of the metaphysical surface remains connected to the aggressive death drive of the depths. Artaud suffered from schizophrenia and was simultaneously a celebrated artist and writer. Despite being hospitalised in mental institutions, he was able to escape the destruction of the depths, gaining control over his destructive drives. He was able to relate to his madness: for instance, in his performances and poetry, he was able to express the suffering of his schizophrenic body. But Artaud was capable of more. His breakthrough towards the metaphysical surface has also revealed the madness proper to thought. He has demonstrated that thought can disintegrate into madness and that it is possible to endure this process of disintegration. His screams do not belong to the world of schizophrenia only. They reveal its hidden core and its future possibilities.[147] Artaud has discovered the body without organs, as the possibility of transforming the continuous process of destruction characterising life,[148] showing that the ego of the surfaces continually faces the risk of regression to the depths and endures a world without any kind of order. He has proven that each thought expresses the most horrible madness. Demolition is the true face of life, including the speculative

---

[146] I here have in mind: '*Les séries de surface du type « manger-parler » n'ont réellement rien de commun avec les* pôles en profondeur *apparemment semblables.* (Deleuze speaks here about the opposition between the disintegrated body and the body without organs - PS) (...) *La coupure de surface n'a rien de commun avec la Spaltung profonde. La contradiction saisie dans une subdivision infinie du passé-futur sur la ligne incorporelle de l'Aiôn n'a rien à voir avec l'opposition des pôles dans le présent physique du corps.(...) A la surface même, on peut toujours trouver des morceaux schizoïdes, puisqu'elle a précisément pur sens d'organiser et d'étaler des éléments venus des profondeurs.*' (LdS 112), (LoS 92).

[147] I am referring to: '*Artaud est le seul à avoir été profondeur absolue dans la littérature, et découvert un corps vital et le langage prodigieux de ce corps, à force de souffrance, comme il dit.*' (LdS 114), (LoS 93).

[148] I refer to: '« *car toute vie bien entendu est un processus de démolition* »' (LdS 244), (LoS 209).

172

life, Deleuze argues. Schizophrenia, depression, and neurotic castration are present in each thought and are strengthened by madness proper to thought only. When properly handled, this speculative death drive may nevertheless become a source of hope. The process of demolition is able to allow for the emergence of new and adequate concepts, symbols and phantasms.

The analysis developed in this chapter has allowed us to reflect upon the relationship between the ego and the structures of sense. We have seen that the narcissistic ego, attempting to change those structures, is threatened with castration and eventually loses belief in its own reparative capacities. As we have noticed, the metaphysical surface provides it with clarifications for this failure. We have also observed that these explanations are never sufficient. The thought itself is confronted with a crack: the structures of sense are partial and lack coherence. They cannot be brought into a unity. The conjunctive synthesis that should have unified both individual experience and our conceptual understanding of reality is doomed to fail. Both the physical and metaphysical surfaces are in a state of continuous disintegration. For Deleuze, this failure still conveys a possibility. Thought does not have to provide a coherent system of sense because sense is virtual in nature. It is a broader problematic field that is expressed by thought. Thought actualises virtual sense. The confrontation between castration on the physical surface and the crack of thought allows for the emergence of a disjunctive synthesis. The ego renounces its attempts to master the structures of sense and becomes a participant in the construction of partial structures. It starts to participate in a more encompassing virtual environment, a topic that is explored more extensively in the next chapter.

8. Conclusion

This chapter was devoted to the analysis of two developments characterising the dynamic genesis. In the first part I analysed the castration complex. I demonstrated how Deleuze builds upon the Melanie Klein's work and distances himself from Freud and Lacan. The core of this complex does not consist of the confrontation with the symbolic father. The castration complex is equal to the loss of the image of the phallus. It designates the loss of belief in the reparative capacities of the ego. We have also seen that the castration complex does not imply the end of the dynamic genesis. Resignation and cognitive acceptance of one's own limitations, central to structuralist psychoanalysis, cannot be the purpose of the analysis of desire. In the phase after the castration, the architecture of the psyche is extended with a new topological dimension, the metaphysical or cerebral surface. Thought is liberated from the body. It ceases to sublimate the bodily desires and develops its own capacity to symbolise. The construction of sense becomes possible. In this chapter, I have also briefly analysed the nature of the drive characterising the new surface. This drive is not situated under the mastery of the pleasure principle, neither is it equal to a death drive that is understood as a mechanical tendency to return to the state of rest. The energy characterising the new surface is a desexualised and free moving libido. It is this drive that allows for continuous movement on a developing problematic field and is also able to explain the free production of symbols.

As preparation for analysis of the phantasm in Chapter six, several developments characterising the new surface have been discussed. Thought appears to be confronted with a crack (*fêlure*). It does not form a coherent whole but is continually disrupted by non-sense and is full of paradoxes and inconsistencies. Deleuze, moreover, points to the dangers appearing at the moment when the crack disrupting the metaphysical surface starts to correspond with castration that destroys the surface of the body. The ego disappears once again to the depths or heights, while thought loses its independence from the body. Nevertheless, this confrontation also carries possibilities. It could strengthen the new relationship with the environment; it may contribute to the formation of a proper form of the phantasm.

The dynamic genesis of sense is also a theory about the emergence of the structures of sense. In this chapter we have seen how, given the development of the castration complex, the ego loses its alleged grip on its world, being unable to unify its world by means of a conjunctive synthesis. Thought, developed on the metaphysical surface, initially allows it to develop explanations for this failure. This surface provides it with a system of representation that elucidates the actions of the body. As we have seen, such a complete explanation of actions appears to be impossible. Thought cannot construct a unified explanation. The crack on the metaphysical surface prevents it. Sense lacks coherence. It is excessive, overabundant and virtual. The ego is only capable of constructing partial structures of sense by means of the disjunctive synthesis.

Lastly, several points of similarity with other works by Deleuze and his later collaboration with Guattari have been revealed. Both the event of castration and the investment of the problems it generates by energy characterising the metaphysical surface are topics analysed in books such as *Coldness and Cruelty*. Similar points are nevertheless also made in the later analysis of, for example, the case study of little Hans or in the analysis of Ahab in *A Thousand Plateaus*. For instance, we have noticed how Little Hans is able to endure the confrontation with the limits imposed upon his desire by means of becoming-horse. This becoming must be understood as a non-narcissist investment of a symbol by a desexualised libido.

The second part of this chapter, that closely followed the arguments of only one chapter 'Twenty-Ninth Series – Good Intentions Are Inevitably Punished' of *The Logic of Sense,* still remained highly schematic. The developments characterising the metaphysical surface were discussed only partially. The next chapter is therefore devoted to a further analysis of the characteristics of the new surface and of the objects, the phantasm and the symbols, characterising it.

Chapter 6

The phantasm

1. Introduction

As I have argued, the dynamic genesis of sense is a theory focusing on the nature of desire, a theory describing the emergence of structures of sense and an important step in Deleuze's thinking about desire. The previous chapters have been devoted to the analysis of the various positions of desire and we have noticed that they are each characterised by different topological dimensions and by an orientation towards different objects. It has been observed that in the schizoid position, the ego orients itself towards simulacra; in the depressive position, to an idol and in the sexual positions to various images, amongst which is the image of the phallus. The sexual position itself does not only lead to the development of the metaphysical surface but also to the emergence of a new object – the phantasm. Its characteristics are the central topic of this chapter. Up until now, we have discussed the different ways in which phenomena, such as nationalism or love, may be experienced, arising out of the three analysed positions. In the schizoid position, a partner is treated as a partial object. He or she must be continually introjected in order to provide a direct release of tension. This experience is very different from the depressive one, where the partner is idealised. In this case, he or she fulfils the role of the object of the heights that protects and punishes the ego. The subsequent genital phase of the sexual position is characterised by other tendencies. A narcissistic lover believes in her capacity to restore the supposedly damaged inside of the partner. The analysis of the phantasm, alluded to in the previous chapter, will allow us to develop another perspective on this experience. Love can go beyond narcissism. It may lead to an opening towards the world. Partners might become mutual sources of events and open each other towards yet unforeseen ways of being.

The analysis of the phantasm will moreover allow us to shed more light on the concepts developed by Deleuze during his collaboration with Guattari. I will argue that concepts such as becoming-minoritarian, becoming-animal or becoming-imperceptible may be understood as phantasms or symbols, already analysed in *The Logic of Sense*. Little Hans's biting horse, Captain Ahab's white whale, the masochist's mistress in furs, Wolf-Man's wolves in the tree may all be considered as phantasms in the proper sense of the word. As will be argued, in his analysis Deleuze builds upon the Freudian theory of original fantasy. However, for Freud, those fantasies are generated by the confrontation of the ego with the universal questions and problems characterising human existence. Little Hans's or Wolf-Man's fantasies[1] are an expression of a confrontation with unresolvable problems of human sexuality. I will note that Deleuze follows Freud and psychoanalysts such as Laplanche and Pontalis just to a certain degree, in considering the problems facing the ego to be not only sexual in nature. Phantasms always emerge in a broader problematic field. The sexual experience of the body forms only a limited part of it. This point proves once again that Deleuze distances himself from structuralist psychoanalysis. As we shall see, a phantasm does not reveal a truth about the hidden sources of desire. It is, rather, a construction that guides desire and opens it up towards events.

To fully comprehend the nature of a phantasm, we need to understand additional concepts developed by Deleuze. In this chapter I discuss the concepts of event, counter-actualisation and pre-individual singularities. Furthermore, I also elaborate on the characteristics of the desexualised energy, already introduced in the previous chapter. This analysis will moreover allow me to respond to some of the critiques of Deleuze's notion of counter-actualisation. I will argue that Deleuze's philosophy is not vitalist in nature.[2] The phantasm does not allow for an expression of a deeper, underlying life force. It does not allow the subject to somehow reach transcendence, supposedly hidden deeper inside the immanence. A phantasm is not a spiritual instance that leads to a total disregard for tangible material circumstances. It is a construction that guides concrete actions. A phantasm is always a singular answer to a multiplicity of problems. Deleuze is also a philosopher of contingency. The problems which generate a phantasm may be continually changing. Nevertheless, this does not mean that their actualisation is submitted to an equal process of change. In fact, phantasms do not have to be continually reconstructed. In this respect, Deleuze agrees with Alain Badiou: we are surrounded by rigid structures of the actual. Change is a difficult process. The conditions under which the production of sense is possible must always be properly delineated. Finally I will show that a phantasm introduces an important change in the individual relationship with the structures of sense. It allows the ego to let go of its attempts to organise the environment according to its own wishes. The conjunctive synthesis is replaced by a disjunctive one. This chapter is devoted

---

[1] I write fantasy with an 'f' when referring to Freudian conception of original fantasy. The Deleuzian concept of the phantasm will continue to be written with a 'ph'.

[2] This interpretation can be found in the influential book by Peter Hallward, (2006).

to the analysis of the chapter 'Thirtieth Series of the Phantasm.' In the first part I discuss the relation between phantasm and event, considering why and how this notion may change psychoanalysis and suggesting that psychoanalysis can allow for a free construction of phantasms. The second part of the chapter is devoted to the analysis of the role of the ego in the original fantasy and in phantasm and to a further analysis of the specific nature of the energy that invests the metaphysical surface.

2. *The phantasm and the body*

In Chapter five I indicated that Ahab's actions cannot be understood simply by referring to the schizoid, depressive or sexual positions. The white whale is not only a bad partial object that must instantly be destroyed. Fear and a will to retaliate cannot explain the entire activity of the Captain. Neither is his hunt motivated by an orientation to an object of the heights. The white whale does not threaten an unreachable and perfect higher entity, for example, the elevated social status that protects Ahab's weak ego. The chase after the white whale is not a merely manic attempt to conceal the lost sense of pride. Furthermore, Ahab is not a narcissist: the hunt is not an expression of his reparative capacities. Wealth and fame are irrelevant. Nobody gains anything from his hunt. Something else is at stake here. Ahab responds to the problems he encounters in his environment. He comes to realise that the industrial whale hunt is denigrating for both animals and humans. His answer is the process of becoming-animal or becoming-whale. Ahab becomes part of the forces of the ocean, as Deleuze and Guattari state in *A Thousand Plateaus* as well as in *Essays Critical and Clinical*.[3]

Engaging in this process must be seen as a construction on the metaphysical surface. To fully understand the nature of this engagement we nevertheless have to fully understand the nature of a phantasm that may be constructed on this surface. According to Deleuze, the main characteristic of a phantasm is that it represents an event.[4] This indicates, first of all, that a phantasm is separate from the body. A phantasm is not a direct representation of the activity of a subject. It is not directly expressing its actual passions. A phantasm is not a

---

[3] Deleuze states, in *Essays Critical and Clinical* (ECC 88), (CeC 113) that Melville's heroes are driven by a particular kind of imagination that gives no space to oedipal desire. His heroes are not narcissistic nor are they directed at an image of the father. See also (CeC 99), (ECC 77) and (MP 298), (ATP 243).

[4] I refer to: '1°) *Il ne représente pas une action ni une passion, mais un résultat d'action et de passion c'est-a-dire un pur événement.*' (LdS 245), (LoS 210). The other characteristics will be discussed further on in the chapter.

visual expression of a subjective will.[5] Ahab's phantasm, for example, is not an expression of a projection of physical aggression onto the white whale. His phantasm is not an expression of a subjective will to destroy this partial object. On the contrary, the phantasm generates a particular relationship towards the actual passions of the subject. Rather, by representing an event, a phantasm represents the result of the passions and actions of a subject (*mais un résultat d'action et de passion*). The phantasm is related to Ahab's life in its totality. It emerges out of the diverse passions and experiences. I will try to clarify this point below.

To comprehend the specific ontological status of the phantasm, Deleuze initially refers to the nature of the images found in fantasies analysed in psychoanalysis.[6] These images are not only an expression of a distinct bodily state, but also of certain problems. This position is visible in the case study of the Wolf-Man. This highly neurotic patient was continually overwhelmed by unbearable anxiety attacks. According to Freud, the origin of those fears could be traced to his early childhood. At the age of four, his patient had developed a severe animal phobia that transformed into a neurosis with religious content in his adult life. According to Freud, the nature of the animal phobia is visible in the boy's well-known dream. Its content is described as follows: 'I dreamt that it was night and that I was lying in my bed. (My bed stood with its foot towards the window; in front of the window there was a row of old walnut trees. I know it was winter when I had the dream, and night-time.) Suddenly the window opened of its own accord, and I was terrified to see that some white wolves were sitting on the big walnut tree in front of the window. There were six or seven of them. The wolves were quite white, and looked more like foxes or sheep-dogs, for they had big tails like foxes and they had their ears pricked like dogs when they pay attention to something. In great terror, evidently of being eaten up by the wolves, I screamed and woke up.'[7]

Freud does not analyse the scene in the manner Klein would do. The wolves are not only considered to be bad partial objects that attack the weak ego. There is something more at stake here than physical state of fear. According to Freud the traumatic dream is an expression of an original fantasy that lies deeper in the unconscious. It is generated as a response to the problems encountered by the boy in the early stages of his sexual development. The Wolf-Man must have been confronted with the existence of an irreconcilable sexual difference

---

[5] Deleuze partially distances himself here from the Kleinian conception of the phantasm that does not allow for such a separation between individual will and phantasm.

[6] I refer to: '*La question: de tels événements sont-ils réels ou imaginaires? N'est pas bien posée.*' (LdS 245), (LoS 210).

[7] See Freud 1918 in 1955: 29.

after seeing the parental coitus.[8] He became anxious after having unravelled its meaning. Seeing the scene must have led to the identification with his mother and a realisation that he wanted to become the love object of his father. According to Freud, becoming such an object would only be possible if the castration that the boy fears occurred, as is supposedly visible in the dream.[9] The original fantasy, in this case the scene of parental coitus, is of the greatest importance, because it expresses the significance of the confrontation with the universal problem of developing sexuality. A vital point in Freud's analysis is that the scene visible in the original fantasy is not a constructive work of imagination. The events represented there cannot be fabricated: a topic of great significance in the debates between Freud and Jung.[10] According to Freud, the events must have been really observed during childhood. The creative work of imagination and the interactions with the environment only strengthen the impact of the original scene. The Wolf-Man was seduced by his sister, adored his father and had a particular relationship with his nanny. Increased interest in sexuality at the age of four, the reading of fairy tales such as Red Hat, seeing copulating dogs and later interactions with Freud indeed strengthened the impact of the original scene, but are not the main cause.[11]

---

[8] Freud expresses this as follows: 'The steps in the transformation of the material, 'primal scene - wolf story – fairy tale of "The Seven Little Goats"', are a reflection of the progress of the dreamer's thoughts during the construction of the dream: 'longing for sexual satisfaction from his father – realization that castration is a necessary condition of it – fear of his father'. It is only at this point, I think, that we can regard the anxiety-dream of this four-year-old boy as being exhaustively explained.' (Freud 1918 in 1955: 36).

[9] For the analysis of the explanation of the nature of the primary scene in Wolf-Man's case for both Freud and Lacan see also Van Haute (2001: 185). Lacan points to the conflict between the imaginary identification with the mother – identification that also generates the imaginary homosexual orientation to the father – and the symbolic father. The latter eventually strengthens the heterosexual object choice and allows for the diminishment of fears.

[10] Freud criticises Jung, among others, in the Wolf-Man's case study, Freud (1918 in 1955: 102). According to Freud, various fantasies discussed by Jung such as a fantasy of re-birth, must be traced back to original scenes, related to the development of sexuality. For a brief description of the conflict between Freud and Jung, see for example Jonathan Lear (2005: 109), *Freud*, New York: Routledge.

[11] Freud explains it in the following way: 'The view, then, that we are putting up for discussion is as follows. It maintains that scenes from early infancy, such as are brought up by an exhaustive analysis of neuroses (as, for instance, in the present case), are not reproductions of real occurrences, to which it is possible to ascribe an influence over the course of the patient's later life and over the formation of his symptoms. It considers them rather as products of the imagination, which find their instigation in mature life, which are intended to serve as some kind of symbolic representation of real wishes and interests, and which owe their origin to a regressive tendency, to a turning-away from the tasks of the present.' (Freud 1918 in 1955: 49).

According to Deleuze, the dispute between Jung and Freud about the status of the memories constituting the original fantasy is not the appropriate point of departure for the analysis of phantasms.[12] Their nature cannot be understood in terms of the opposition between the real and the imaginary. It is insufficient to claim that the phantasm is either an event observed in reality or a work of the imagination. The phantasm must be understood on the basis of the distinction between an event (*événement*) and the corporeal state of affairs (*l'état de choses corporel*). According to Deleuze, a phantasm that represents an event indeed originates in the physical or corporeal state of affairs (*état de choses corporel qui le provoque*).[13] Both the passions of the body and the personal history have indeed a fundamental impact on its emergence, as visible in the analysis of the Wolf-Man. Nevertheless, the phantasm has a different ontological status from the body. It is submitted to different laws and logic. The Wolf-Man's phantasm, his becoming-wolf, or, if the reading of Freud is correct, the original fantasy of the coitus of the parents represents an event. The phantasm expresses the whole personal (physical) history of the boy. It is a construction that is a response to and a transformation of this history. The phantasm is itself an event. It emerges out of the material circumstances and directly affects the body. After its emergence, the Wolf-Man's life is directly distorted. The boy becomes anxious and develops various new symptoms. We have in fact encountered similar kinds of events before. Castration by adsorption or the death of the father, both discussed in chapter five, are also events that differ in nature from their corporeal causes.[14] Castration is a sudden discovery of one's own powerlessness. It is caused by material circumstances but it differs in nature from these causes. The ego is suddenly powerless.

Deleuze differentiates between different causes that contribute to the emergence of an event and a phantasm. A phantasm has, first of all, endogenous and exogenous physical causes.[15] The former may be a hereditary constitution,

---

[12] I am referring to: '*La question: de tels événements sont-ils réels ou imaginaires? N'est pas bien posée. La distinction n'est pas entre l'imaginaire et le réel, mais entre l'événement comme tel et l'état de choses corporel qui le provoque ou dans lequel il s'effectue. Les événements sont des effets (ainsi « l'effet » castration, « l'effet » meurtre du père...).*' (LdS: 245), (LoS 210).

[13] Deleuze comments: '*La distinction n'est pas entre l'imaginaire et le réel, mais entre l'événement comme tel et l'état de choses corporel qui le provoque ou dans lequel il s'effectue.*' (LdS 245), (LoS 210).

[14] I have in mind: '*Les événements sont des effets (ainsi « l'effet » castration, « l'effet » meurtre du père...).*' (LdS: 245), (LoS 210).

[15] I am alluding to: '*Mais précisément en tant qu'effets ils doivent être rattachés a des causes non seulement endogènes, mais exogènes, états de choses effectifs, actions réellement entreprises, passions et contemplations réellement effectuées (...) Nous parlons des causes endogènes (constitution héréditaire, héritage phylogénétique, évolution interne de la sexualité, actions et passions introjetées) non moins que des causes exogènes.*' (LdS 245), (LoS 210).

phylogenetic heritage, internal evolution of sexuality and introjected actions and passions. A hereditary constitution may, for example, determine the testosterone levels in the body. Boys with low levels of testosterone may develop phantasms that could allow for a compensation for a relative lack of aggression, important in a patriarchal society. Such a boy might develop a phantasm that could, for example, facilitate the development of a scientific career in order to compensate for the relative weakness of the body. The actual experiences of a body – the exogenous causes – can equally serve as causes of phantasms. The actions undertaken in reality or passions and contemplations effectively actualized, are an example.[16] A child, actually expressing aggression and anger towards its parents, might be shocked by a sudden outburst and may subsequently develop a phantasm to resolve this issue. An actually experienced, persistent state of fear could generate a phantasm of a threatening figure. This happened in the case of Judge Schreber, writer of the famous memoirs that were analysed by Freud. Schreber endured continuous states of fear during his childhood. He was submitted to particularly harsh methods of upbringing by his father, a famous German educationalist. Deleuze and Guattari stress that at various moments of his life Schreber was capable of liberating himself from those fears by the construction of another phantasm. He engaged in the process of becoming-woman.[17]

Both the actually occurring observations and the various physical states are thus of fundamental importance for the emergence of an internal phantasmatic life.[18] This point proves that Deleuze disagrees with the Jungian understanding of the working of fantasy. He clearly chooses the side of Freud in this debate. Phantasms are not only a work of imagination. They are not an actualisation of a deeper and unchanging layer of sense characterising human existence, but emerge in the confrontation with real events instead. We should never forget that children are observing both the body of the mother and the father in real life, Deleuze states.[19] Every child discovers the existence of, for example,

---

[16] Deleuze states: '*mais exogènes, états de choses effectifs, actions réellement entreprises, passions et contemplations réellement effectuées.*' (LdS 245), (LoS 210).

[17] See AO: 17, LAO: 24.

[18] Deleuze stresses that Freud also realises the importance of reality for the formation of fantasy. This is visible in his analysis of Wolf-Man's case. As Deleuze puts it: '*C'est pourquoi Freud a raison de maintenir les droits de la réalité dans la production des phantasmes, au moment même ou il reconnait ceux-ci comme produits qui dépassent la réalité*' (LdS 245), (LoS 210).

[19] I refer to: '*Il serait tout à fait fâcheux d'oublier ou de feindre d'oublier que les enfants observent réellement le corps de la mère, du père, et le coït parental, qu'ils sont réellement l'objet d'entreprises de séduction de l'adulte, qu'ils subissent des menaces de castration précises et détaillées, etc. Ce ne sont pas davantage les meurtres de pères, les incestes, les empoisonnements et éventrations qui manquent dans l'histoire publique et privée.*' (LdS 245), (LoS 210).

sexual differences by observing the sexual nature of relations between people and particularly its parents. Children are also seduced by adults (*enterprises de seduction de l'adulte*) in actual life, not in an imaginary one. Similarly, they are threatened by castration in a precise and detailed way. Deleuze nevertheless extends the Freudian analysis by developing an important point, already mentioned in analysis of little Hans: he material causes characterise not only private, but also public life.[20] The castration endured by little Hans does not concern his private life alone. The boy loses his narcissism but also has to submit to the rules of society. He is forced to understand his behaviour in terms of a dominant system of representation. He is disciplined, just like any other contemporary subject. The boy is trained in accepting the authority of, for example, a political leader or a boss. He is additionally trained to construct his own subjectivity by means of confessional techniques, brilliantly analysed not only by Deleuze and Guattari but also Foucault.[21] He loses his independent world of imagination.

3. The quasi-cause and the ideational surface[22]

We have already stated that the phantasm distinguishes itself from its physical causes. It is the expression of their effects.[23] The phantasm liberates itself from its physical causes. According to Deleuze, the phantasm can be defined as a noematic attribute.[24] A subject is intentionally oriented to such an object despite the fact that it is at the same time not a real physical object that may be directly perceived. The phantasm does not represent a quality proper to an actual object. Instead it represents an event separated from these actual

---

[20] I am referring to: '*Ce ne sont pas davantage les meurtres de pères, les incestes, les empoisonnements et éventrations qui manquent dans l'histoire publique et privée.*' (LDS 245), (LoS 210). See also DRF 82, TRM 92 and MP 314, ATP 258.

[21] See Foucault, M. (1978), *History of Sexuality, vol. 1, The will to knowledge*, New York: Pantheon Books.

[22] In this part of the chapter I refer more explicitly to Deleuze's ontology. Those theoretical insights must first of all contribute to our understanding of psychopathology. This might lead to a slight distortion of the discussed points. An interesting reading of the topic of quasi-causality can be found in chapter six of Jay Lampert (2006), *Deleuze and Guattari's Philosophy of History*, (2006), London: Continuum.

[23] I allude to: '*Reste que les phantasmes, au moment même ou ils sont des effets et parce qu'ils sont des effets, diffèrent en nature de leurs causes réelles.*'(LdS 245), (LoS 211).

[24] I refer to: '*C'est que le phantasme, à la manière de l'événement qu'il représente, est un « attribut noématique » qui se distingue non seulement des états de choses et de leurs qualités, mais du vécu psychologique et des concepts logiques.*' (LdS 246), (LoS 211).

qualities.[25] According to Deleuze, every object is in this respect both actual and virtual. It is both an event and an actualised entity possessing qualities. This distinction can be explained by referring to the example of death, analysed elsewhere in *The Logic of Sense*. Deleuze distinguishes between the physical death of the body on the one hand and death as an event. At first, death concerns just the physical body. It has a predictable impact on both the body and its environment. It leads to a disintegration of that body and usually causes grief among those left behind. Death is nevertheless also an event. This death can be expressed by the verb [to] 'die'. The effects of this kind of death are unpredictable. The event of death realises itself in the environment of the body in diverse ways that cannot be determined in advance. Death persists as a problem. It poses a challenge. In particular those who stay behind are forced to confront it in a variety of ways.[26] The death of a person does not have to lead to a destructive sense of mourning. It might, for example, also lead to the strengthening of the ties with other loved ones, equally affected by the event of the death. In this sense each one of us 'dies' in entirely different ways.

According to Deleuze, as a noematic attribute, the phantasm is primary with respect to both the psychological experience (*vécu psychologique*) and the concepts of logic.[27] A given phantasm may for example never be fully conscious. The Wolf-Man is slowly constructing an image of an event that has been disrupting his life during his analysis with Freud, without fully comprehending its meaning. It exceeds the possibilities of interpretation and is continually actualised in various unpredictable manners. The phantasm should hence be understood by means of the distinction between the virtual and the actual. It is virtual in nature. It escapes a precise determination and is

---

[25] Deleuze emphasises the differences of his own understanding of a noematic object from Husserl's analysis elsewhere in *The Logic of Sense*. According to him, Husserl understands the transcendental field, the field of the noema, only from the perspective of a subject. Deleuze on the other hand uses Sartre to state that the transcendental surface must be thought without any reference to a subject. The transcendental surface produces the subject and can as such never be equal to it. (see LdS 123-124, LoS 102). I lack the space here to fully analyse these points. The nature of the transcendental pre-individual surface will be analysed below.

[26] See for example Keith Ansel Pearson: 'The phantasm presents the event as a noematic attribute that renders it distinct from the actions, passions, and qualities of an actual state of affairs (a noematic attribute is a pure predicate that is different from the physical quality of a thing, for example 'to die' as opposed to the mere physical fact of one's empirical death). This is phenomenology's way of opening up an intentional consciousness by right, the positing and giving of sense.' *Notre Dame philosophical reviews*, 2007.03.06.

[27] See: '*C'est que le phantasme, à la manière de l'événement qu'il représente, est un « attribut noématique » qui se distingue (…) du vécu psychologique et des concepts logiques.*' (LdS 246), (LoS 211).

always only partially actualised. It represents something that can never be made entirely present. The white whale represents an event that is itself referring to a multiplicity of psychological, social, economic and political factors that concern Ahab's life. It brings them together but it does not allow for their full explication. The phantasm merely allows for a continual interaction between those factors, for a continually changing response. Another example of a phantasm is the figure of Joan of Arc.[28] A person affected by her actions is attracted to a multiplicity of possibilities. Joan of Arc might be a symbol of perseverance, courage, femininity but also patriotism. Her person is a symbol which lacks clearly defined characteristics. It refers to an instance that can never be rendered entirely present. Joan of Arc is a container for a multiplicity of scenarios that can be actualised in a variety of manners; for instance, a French nationalist will be drawn towards a scenario other than that of a feminist struggling for women's rights.

The difference between the phantasm representing an event and a state of affairs is also analysed by Deleuze in the 'Ninth series of problematic'. In an analysis of Protestantism, Deleuze makes a distinction between real (imperfect) events and ideal events. Basing his argument on the work of the German philosopher and poet Novalis, he analyses the difference between Protestantism as an ideal event on the one hand and Lutheranism as a real event on the other.[29] According to Deleuze, Protestantism is ideal or virtual in nature because it represents an ideal event. Protestantism does not possess clearly defined characteristics. It is, rather, an ideal instance aimed at by the various churches that act in real circumstances. Protestantism is an idea, emerging in a problematic field. It is to be actualised in a daily organised practice. Lutheranism, on the other hand, is such an actualisation. It is a real event that develops itself in particular circumstances, and is a spatio-temporal

---

[28] See: Lampert 2006: 99.

[29] I refer to the analysis of this topic in the 'Ninth series of the Problematic. Deleuze writes: '*Les événements sont idéaux. Il arrive à Novalis de dire qu'il y a deux trains d'événements, les uns idéaux, les autres réels et imparfaits, par exemple le protestantisme idéal et le luthérianisme réel. Mais la distinction n'est pas entre deux sortes d'événements, elle est entre l'événement, par nature idéal, et son effectuation spatio-temporelle dans un état de choses. Entre l'événement et l'accident. Les événements sont des singularités idéelles qui communiquent en un seul et même Événement; aussi ont-ils une vérité éternelle, et leur temps n'est jamais le présent qui les effectue et les fait exister, mais l'Aiôn illimité, l'Infinitif où ils subsistent et insistent. Les événements sont les seules idéalités; et, renverser le platonisme, c'est d'abord destituer les essences pour y substituer les événements comme jets de singularités. Une double lutte a pour objet d'empêcher toute confusion dogmatique de l'événement avec l'essence, mais aussi toute confusion empiriste de l'événement avec l'accident.*' (LdS 69), (LoS 53).

imperfect effectuation of the ideal or virtual Protestantism, states Deleuze.[30] In the case of Lutheranism we can speak of a doctrine that is a solution to the problems opened up by Protestantism. It actualises the choices for action opened up by the emergence of the latter. It is this actual doctrine and not its virtual counterpart that determines the behaviour of actual humans. The Lutheran church actualises virtual Protestantism. Protestantism is a phantasm, a quasi-cause of Lutheranism. Protestantism may in fact be described only by means of its actualisation in the actual Lutheran doctrine and practice.

We have seen that the phantasm belongs to an ideational or conceptual surface. The ideational surface separates itself from the physical one and is in fact used here as a synonym for the metaphysical surface. It is entirely spiritual. Deleuze notes moreover that this surface transcends the distinction between the inside and the outside.[31] As such, it precedes the distinction between a subject and an object. The ideational surface is the condition of possibility for the emergence of a distinction between the inside and outside of a subject. It is primary with respect to the intentional subject. The ideational surface brings 'its' internal and external sides into contact in order to unfold them onto a single side. The virtual emerges together with its actualisation. The inside and the outside of the subject emerge together with the unfolding of the ideational surface. The inside and the outside contribute to the emergence of the problematic field and are at the same time its solution. They actualise a solution to the emerging problems. The surface clarifies why and how an ego can engage in new relations with its environment. However, it can also always escape the limitations imposed upon it in the actualisation. In this sense the ideational surface fundamentally differs from the physical one. As noted in Chapter four, the physical surface has clear limitations and depends on the interactions in an already actualised environment. To this extent it is an actualisation of the ideational surface. It is a solution or expression of an extensive problematic field. The ego or the organism and its environment are able to emerge, given the existence of this field. The physical surface may be considered as a limit imposed upon the ego. It limits the manner in which the outside can be experienced by the introduction of a clear separation. The physical surface limits the possibility of engagement with events, while the

---

[30] I allude to: '*Mais la distinction n'est pas entre deux sortes d'événements, elle est entre l'événement, par nature idéal, et son effectuation spatio-temporelle dans un état de choses.*' (LdS 69), (LoS 53).

[31] I have in mind: '*Il appartient comme tel a une surface idéelle sur laquelle il est produit comme effet, et qui transcende l'intérieur et l'extérieur, puisqu'elle a pour propriété topologique de mettre en contact « son » cote intérieur et « son » cote extérieur pour les déplier en un seul cote.*' (LdS 246), (LoS 211).

ideational surface precedes such limitations. The subject is never only actual in nature. He emerges out of interactions within a problematic and changing environment and participates in its construction. It is a product of events.[32]

Phantasm-event is hence subject to a double causality.[33] On the one hand, the phantasm is an expression of internal and external physical causes. On the other it is equally dependent on a quasi-cause that is spiritual in nature. What is a quasi-cause, more precisely? According to Deleuze, the quasi-cause mobilises the phantasm. It allows for its continuous engagement with the problematic field. It allows for a communication with other phantasm-events. The quasi-cause has previously played a role in the dynamic genesis, although in a more limited form.[34] In the depressive position, the role of quasi-cause was played by the good object of the heights: the object was a quasi-cause that allowed for the emergence of the surface of the body. This surface could not emerge without its previous existence. The transcendent object allowed the subject not only to overcome the paranoid-schizoid fears but, more importantly, to subsequently strengthen its narcissism and belief in reparative capacities. The quasi-cause has also appeared in the oedipal phase of the sexual position. There, the image of the phallus was the quasi-cause of the emergence of the metaphysical

---

[32] In 'Fifteenth Series of Singularities', Deleuze makes the following statement about events and sense proper to the ideational surface: '*Les deux moments du sens, impassibilité et genèse, neutralité et productivité, ne sont pas tels que l'un puisse passer pour l'apparence de l'autre. La neutralité, l'impassibilité de l'événement, **son indifférence aux déterminations de l'intérieur et de l'extérieur**,* (emphasis P.S.) *de l'individuel et du collectif, du particulier et du général, etc., sont même une constante sans laquelle l'événement n'aurait pas de vérité éternelle et ne se distinguerait pas de ses effectuations temporelles.* (LdS 122, LoS 100) (...) *Nous cherchons à déterminer un champ transcendantal impersonnel et pré-individuel, qui ne ressemble pas aux champs empiriques correspondants et qui ne se confond pas pourtant avec une profondeur indifférenciée. Ce champ ne peut pas être déterminé comme celui d'une conscience (...) Ce qui n'est ni individuel ni personnel, au contraire, ce sont les émissions de singularités en tant qu'elles se font sur une surface inconsciente et qu'elles se font sur une surface inconsciente et qu'elles jouissent d'un principe mobile immanent d'auto-unification par distribution nomade, qui se distingue radicalement des distributions fixes et sédentaires comme conditions des synthèses de conscience.*' (LdS 125), (LoS 103). The difference between the physical and ideational or metaphysical surface will be elaborated later in the chapter.

[33] I am referring to: '*C'est pourquoi le phantasme-événement est soumis à la double causalité, renvoyant d'une part aux causes externes et internes dont il résulte en profondeur, mais d'autre part à la quasi-cause qui l' « opère » à la surface, et le fait communiquer avec tous les autres événements-phantasmes.*' (LdS 246), (LoS 211).

[34] I refer to: '*A deux reprises, nous avons vu comment la place était préparée pour de tels effets différant en nature de ce dont ils résultent: une première fois dès la position dépressive, lorsque la cause se retire en hauteur, et laisse le champ libre au développement d'une surface à venir; puis dans la situation œdipienne, lorsque l'intention laisse le champ libre pour un résultat d'une tout autre nature, où le phallus joue le rôle de quasi-cause.*' (LdS 246), (LoS 211).

surface.[35] This image is not to be considered as a real or physical cause. The image of the phallus is a spiritual construction that emerges as a result of a multiplicity of events, both public and private in nature. The metaphysical surface can only liberate itself from the physical one given the existence of the image of the phallus and the subsequent real events. The image of the phallus was the quasi-cause that allowed for narcissistic actions. The real events, on the other hand, have subsequently challenged the inflated self-confidence of the ego.

The quasi-cause gains more importance after the event of castration and after the separation of the metaphysical surface from the physical one. Elsewhere in *The Logic of Sense*, Deleuze discusses this topic by referring to the philosophy of the Stoa.[36] For those ancient philosophers too, human action was not only characterised by physical causes. It is not submitted to the laws of material causality, but is characterised by an orientation to spiritual quasi-causes. For the Stoa, an event expresses physical causes, but is at the same time not a necessity.[37] Human behaviour is dependent on quasi-causes and can overcome the laws of causality and fate. Such an orientation does not always lead to physically different behaviour but does effectuate a different relationship towards material events. Deleuze gives an example here of a stoic sage who attains more freedom by an orientation to a quasi-cause.[38] The

---

[35] I comment on: '*puis dans la situation œdipienne, lorsque l'intention laisse le champ libre pour un résultat d'une tout autre nature, où le phallus joue le rôle de quasi-cause.*' (LdS 246), (LoS 211).

[36] For a thorough analysis of the influence of Stoa on Deleuze see Sellars (2006), or Sean Bowden (2011). Deleuze himself bases his analysis primarily on Emile Brehier (1907), *La théorie des incorporels dans l'ancien stoicisme*, Paris: Picard.

[37] I have in mind this passage from the 'Twenty-Fourth Series of the Communication of Events': '*Une des plus grandes audaces de la pensée stoïcienne, c'est la rupture de la relation causale: les causes sont renvoyées en profondeur à une unité qui leur est propre et les effets entretiennent à la surface des rapports spécifiques d'un autre type. Le destin, c'est d'abord l'unité ou le lien des causes physiques entre elles; les effets incorporels sont évidement soumis au destin, dans la mesure où ils diffèrent en nature de ces causes, ils entrent les uns avec les autres dans des rapports de quasi-causalité, et tous ensemble ils entrent en rapport avec une quasi-cause elle-même incorporelle, qui leur assure une indépendance très spéciale, non pas exactement à l'égard du destin, mais à l'égard de la nécessité qui devrait normalement découler du destin.*' (LdS 198), (LoS 169).

[38] Deleuze describes this as follows in 'Twentieth Series on Stoic Philosophy': '*Le sage stoïcien s'identifie' à la quasi-cause: il s'installe à la surface, sur la ligne droite qui traverse celle-ci, au point aléatoire qui trace ou parcourt cette ligne. Aussi est-il comme l'archer. Toutefois, ce rapport avec l'archer ne doit pas être compris sous l'espèce d'une métaphore morale de l'intention, comme Plutarque nous y invite en disant que le sage stoïcien est censé tout faire, non pas pour atteindre le but, mais pour avoir fait tout ce qui dépendait de lui pour l'atteindre. Une telle rationalisation implique une interprétation tardive, et hostile au stoïcisme. Le rapport avec l'archer est plus proche du Zen: le tireur à l'arc doit atteindre au point où le visé est aussi le non-visé, c'est-à-dire le tireur lui-même, et où la flèche file sur sa ligne droite en créant son propre but, où la surface de*

sage is similar to a bowman who develops a particular relationship toward his activity. The sage-bowman does not intend to shoot precisely at his goal. Neither does he want to approach perfection. He does not wish to maximise his own already actualised potential.[39] The freedom of the bowman is found elsewhere. He does not aim at an external goal. However, the sage must be directed at an event and not its spatio-temporal actualisation. Rather, he must reach a point of depersonalisation, as occurs in the practice of Zen. This can be attained by the construction of a particular phantasm of shooting. In this phantasm the sage is not the narcissist capable of shooting precisely at the goal. He reaches the point of depersonalisation by becoming the shooter, the shot and the goal at the same time. Only such a phantasm can be a quasi-cause of his activity. The sage becomes one with the world. He is oriented towards an event, an instance that is not an already actualised past but also a future that is yet to come. This does not mean that the sage aims entirely to escape the concrete circumstances in which he is acting. The orientation to an event is not a form of escapism.[40] The physical circumstances, in which he truly aims at a goal, are of fundamental importance. The depersonalisation is reached within concrete circumstances. The incorporeal event must be materialised. The sage bowman will always aim precisely because he is able to abandon the realm of the actual and of the physical causes. He is able to become directed at a quasi-cause.

From this example it becomes clear that the phantasm does not only express the active or passive attitude of a subject.[41] It does not primarily concern his internal or external life. Moreover, the phantasm has little to do with the power of imagination or with the real events it supposedly represents. The phantasm separates itself from the subject and his intentions. It represents an

---

la cible est aussi bien la droite et le point, le tireur, le tir, et le tire. Telle est la volonté stoïcienne orientale, comme pro-airesis. Là le sage attend l'événement. C'est-à-dire: il comprend l'événement pur dans sa vérité éternelle, indépendamment de son effectuation spatio-temporelle, comme à la fois éternellement à venir et toujours déjà passé suivant la ligne de l'Aiôn.' (LdS 172), (LoS 147).

[39] I comment on: *'Toutefois, ce rapport avec l'archer ne doit pas être compris sous l'espèce d'une métaphore morale de l'intention, comme Plutarque nous y invite en disant que le sage stoïcien est censé tout faire, non pas pour atteindre le but, mais pour avoir fait tout ce qui dépendait de lui pour l'atteindre.'* (LdS 172), (LoS 147).

[40] I refer to: *'Mais, aussi et en même temps, du même coup, il veut l'incarnation, l'effectuation de l'événement pur incorporel dans un état de choses et dans son propre corps, dans sa propre chair: s'étant identifié à la quasi-cause, le sage veut en « corporaliser » l'effet incorporel, puisque l'effet hérite de la cause … La quasi-cause ne crée pas, elle "opère", et ne veut que ce qui arrive.'* (LdS 172), (LoS 147).

[41] I am referring to: *'Ni actifs ni passifs, ni internes ni externes, ni imaginaires ni réels, les phantasmes ont bien l'impassibilité et l'idéalité de l'événement. Face à cette impassibilité, ils nous inspirent une attente insupportable, l'attente de ce qui va résulter, de ce qui est déjà en train et n'en finit pas de résulter.'* (LdS 246), (LoS 211).

event that surpasses its own material causes. The phantasm is characterised by an impassibility and an ideality. Intrinsically, it introduces a particular change in the subjective relation toward the world. The impassibility introduces what Deleuze calls an unbearable waiting (*attente*). We wait for that which is to come. We wait for 'that which is going to come about as a result and for that which is already in the process of coming about and never stops coming about', he states.[42] The ego aims at the unexpected. It awaits the uncertain results of its own actions.

This particular kind of waiting cannot be understood by means of the concept of the possible. This concept already forces us to acknowledge that the conditions for the emergence of an event have been specified in advance.[43] We can state that the state of waiting for an event is impossible in those positions. The relationships with objects from the previous positions are merely possible relationships. In the schizoid position, the ego is overwhelmed by the events that happen to it. In fact it lives in a state of fear with respect to the events that are to come. The ego awaits the future with much tension. But this state does not presuppose a true openness towards an event. The conditions of possibility for its appearance are already determined and are in fact very limited. The events can only appear to the ego as threatening or nonthreatening. The new objects can only be the sources of pleasure or fear. They will only offer a temporary diminishment or increase of tension. Thus, an event does not pose any challenge to the present structure of desire. The body without organs is not an exception in this respect. The tormented subject can in this case only await the end of continuous attacks by bad partial objects. What the subject waits for is not unexpected. The state of rest is considered to be a possibility within this position. An event may either succeed or fail in realising this possibility.

The depressive and sexual positions also limit the possibilities for the appearance of an event. Any event occurring in the depressive position in the end will concern the object of the heights. It will threaten or strengthen the order guaranteed by this object and either contribute to protection of the ego or will be perceived as a direct attack. Within the pre-genital phase of the sexual position an event will also either generate a state of pleasure or prevent it from occurring. The subject is not open towards any other experience. In the genital phase the events will be experienced through the prism of narcissism. They will nurture it or undermine it. In all of these cases the subject is confronted with possible events. The only events that may occur are those that will threaten

---

[42] I allude to: '*ils nous inspirent une attente insupportable, l'attente de ce qui va résulter, de ce qui est déjà en train et n'en finit pas de résulter.*' (LdS 246), (LoS 211).

[43] Deleuze analyses such an open relationship towards the unknown among others in *Difference and Repetition*. (See a.o. DR 272, DRE 211) and in Bergsonism (B 17), (BF 6).

the very structure of those positions. Only a sudden emergence of the object of the heights, of the image of the phallus or castration can be characterised as a true event. These fundamentally reshuffle the psychic coordinates of the positions within which they emerge. A continuous receptivity towards events, however, emerges only on the metaphysical surface.

By means of the orientation to events, the phantasm directly liberates desire from actualised patterns of behaviour.[44] The phantasm allows for an orientation to an instance that will never be actualised. It aims at events that transcend their own causes. In the case of the phantasm the ego truly becomes excessive. This is visible in the example of Ahab. His excessive actions are not only outrageous and destructive; he also goes on to liberate himself from the physical causes that have brought him to his current state. He ceases to be a disappointed captain, unable to live the life of an industrial whale hunter. The loss of his leg ceases to be the source of his suffering. Ahab becomes the offspring of the phantasm he constructs. His ego dissolves in the phantasm. He becomes the unknown product of the excess he himself brings about.[45] He hunts the white whale in order to produce a new world for him and his crew. This orientation to the quasi-cause is also called counter-effectuation. According to Deleuze, only this form of resistance to the actual can be depicted as the true source of freedom.[46] Counter-effectuation liberates the subject from a subjection to material circumstances. A subject can learn to accept the physical causes of her own behaviour, but can nevertheless also learn to limit their impact. Due to counter-effectuation she can gain distance from the laws of physical causality and cease to have partial control over the material circumstances.[47] Counter-effectuation allows for a choice of one of the possible

---

[44] I allude to: '*Crime parfait, vérité éternelle, splendeur royale de l'événement, dont chacun communique avec tous les autres dans les variations d'un seul et même phantasme: distinct de son effectuation comme des causes qui le produisent, faisant valoir cette éternelle part d'excès par rapport à ces causes, cette part d'inaccompli par rapport à ses effectuations, survolant son propre champ, nous faisant fils de lui-même.*' (LdS 247), (LoS 212).

[45] In the next part of the chapter I discuss the role of the ego in the phantasm in relation to psychoanalysis more extensively.

[46] I am referring to: '*Et si c'est bien dans cette part que l'effectuation ne peut pas accomplir, ni la cause produire, que l'événement réside tout entier, c'est là aussi qu'il s'offre à la contre-effectuation et que réside notre plus haute liberté, par laquelle nous le développons en le menons à son terme, à sa transmutation, et devenons maître enfin des effectuations et des causes. Comme science des événements purs, la psychanalyse est aussi un art des contre-effectuations, sublimations et symbolisations.*' (LdS 247), (LoS 212).

[47] This point is also alluded to by Žižek who distances himself from the claims of both Hallward (2006) and Badiou. The concept of counter-effectuation does not reveal Deleuze as a dogmatic and religious philosopher of the One. Žižek states: 'Hallward is right to emphasise that, for Deleuze, freedom "isn't a matter of human liberty but of liberation from humanity," of fully submerging oneself in the creative flux of the absolute Life.

pasts. It does not lead to a form of escapism; the material conditions that have led to the construction of a phantasm are not irrelevant. Ahab accepts his past and chooses how to respond. He constructs a problematic field and solutions that are proper to it. The becoming-animal is possible only given the existence of the process of counter-effectuation. Only this process allows him to choose between the events that determine his life. Counter-effectuation allows him to gain more than a conceptual insight into his own past and into the physical causes of his own suffering. It allows him to act. The reconfiguration of the past is directly a production of the future. Ahab constructs a new world and becomes one of the ocean's forces. In this way he regains control of his own future.

In this way we understand that the counter-effectuation allows the ego to transcend its physical interactions. It opens it up towards a yet unknown environment. This process leads to a perpetual state of loss of identity. The ego finds itself in a state of perpetual disintegration. This loss of identity is contrasted by Deleuze with the one found in the depths. Deleuze discusses this topic in the 'Twenty-fourth series on the communication of events.'[48] The ego of the depths is in a state of disintegration. It lacks power. It continually disintegrates, but only due to the attacks of the bad partial objects. The only means of acting against this disintegration is the development of what Deleuze calls an infinite identity. This identity suspends the differentiation between the inside and the outside. The ego incorporates all partial objects that are within its reach. All distinctions characterising reality are suspended.[49] In Chapter two

---

His political conclusion from this seems too facile (...) Hallward ignores the retroactive movement on which Deleuze also insists, the way this eternal pure past (this pure past or the virtual is named the metaphysical or ideational surface in *The Logic of Sense* - PS) which fully determines us is itself subjected to retroactive change. (...) I can retroactively determine which causes will determine me: we, subjects, are passively affected by pathological objects and motivations; but, in a reflexive way, we ourselves have the minimal power to accept (or reject) being affected in this way, in other words, we retroactively determine the causes allowed to determine us, or, at least the mode of this linear determination. "Freedom" is thus inherently retroactive: at its most elementary, it is not a free act which, out of nowhere, starts a new causal link, but a retroactive act of endorsing which link/sequence of necessities will determine me.' (Žižek 2004: 314). I return to this topic in the conclusion of this book.

[48] I refer to: '*Et il faut distinguer deux manières dont l'identité personnelle est perdue, deux manières dont la contradiction se développe. En profondeur, c'est par l'identité infinie que les contraires communiquent et que l'identité de chacun se trouve rompue, scindée: si bien que chaque terme est à la fois le moment et le tout, la partie, le rapport et le tout, le moi, le monde et Dieu, le sujet, le copule et le prédicat.*' (LdS 205), (LoS 175).

[49] Deleuze writes: '*chaque terme est à la fois le moment et le tout, la partie, le rapport et le tout, le moi, le monde et Dieu, le sujet, le copule et le prédicat.*' (LdS 205), (LoS 175).

we have already observed how the ego of the depths masters this splintered experience of the depths, by means of the simulacrum of the body without organs. The empty body without organs is equal to a radical rejection of the environment. The ego closes itself off from all possible tension. It reaches a state of infinite identity that is equal to a state of absolute emptiness. This state is aimed at, for example, in cases of anorexia. The full body without organs, on the other hand, is a simulacrum of a body that resolves the splintered experience by welding all the loose and threatening pieces into a unity. This simulacrum accompanies the attempt to create a state of perfect unity. The various experiences can no longer be separated. The ego dissolves in an infinite identity. It overcomes all limitations and now encompasses the whole reality.

It must be stressed that counter-actualisation leads to a different kind of loss of identity.[50] The separate experiences do not meld together. A phantasm constructed on the metaphysical surface leads to an orientation towards infinite events. Each of these events communicates with others but is at the same time kept at a distance; the various events are not welded into a unity. Rather, they are arranged in relation to one another. The metaphysical surface is characterised by a disjunctive synthesis. This synthesis does not produce a higher entity.[51] The ego no longer attempts to impose a unity upon the diverse experiences, as was the case with the conjunctive synthesis, or with the construction of the body without organs. The loss of identity occurs because the ego follows the movement of the disjunctive synthesis. The ego emerges as a result of the interactions of the divergent series. It loses its central place but does not entirely disappear: it becomes a point of view. It continually emerges out of events generated by the physical experience and allows for their transformation. The ego of Ahab is also such a point of view. It is produced by the disjunctive synthesis of divergent series. His experience is no longer an expression of a neatly organised structure. The ego emerges out of a new reality, characterised by Deleuze as chaosmos. The states he is going through are not expressing a higher order.[52] The ego is directed at a quasi-cause or an

---

[50] I remark on: '*Mais, à la surface où ne se déploient que les événements infinitifs, il en va tout autrement: chacun communique avec l'autre par le caractère positif de sa distance, par le caractère affirmatif de la disjonction, si bien que le moi se confond avec cette disjonction même qui libère hors de lui, qui met hors de lui ses séries divergentes comme autant de singularités impersonnelles et préindividuelles. Telle est déjà la contre-effectuation: distance infinitive, au lieu d'identité infinie. Tout se fait par résonance des disparates, point de vue sur le point de vue, déplacement de la perspective, différenciation de la différence, et non par identité infinie.*' (LdS 205), (LoS 175).

[51] I will analyse this topic more extensively below.

[52] I refer to the following passage from 'Twenty-Fourth Series on the Communication of Events': '*La divergence des séries affirmées forme un « chaosmos » et non plus un monde; le point aléatoire qui les parcourt forme un contre-moi, et non plus un moi: la disjonction posée comme*

'object=x'. It continually becomes a counter-ego, a de-centred centre or a point of pure movement. It continually follows a changing point of view. The world ceases to be experienced as stable. The counter-effectuation or orientation to a counter-ego is only possible when a subject can understand itself as an event, contends Deleuze.[53] He or she must understand that events, effectuating themselves inside him, originate in another individual. An individual must realise that change in another individual is continually possible. This change is only possible when new events are allowed to continually become part of changing identity. All other individuals – everything that he or she can become – must be encountered as events. The other individuals become a mirror that reflects all the existing possibilities for the ego.

The statements about counter-effectuation and orientation towards events have been criticised by many philosophers.[54] Badiou characterises Deleuze as a pre-critical metaphysician and a vitalist. His conceptualisation of event leads to a noncritical orientation to a metaphysical One. Deleuze does not systematically differentiate between various kinds of events and even less between various forms of subjective participation in an event. The metaphysical surface is undifferentiated. It does not consist of clearly distinguished events and clearly defined persons. This critique is unjustified. We have already observed that the metaphysical surface consists of a multiplicity of series and of various events.[55] These events are always synthesised and represented in an individual phantasm. The phantasm is hence never an expression of a deeper-lying

---

synthèse troque son principe théologique contre un principe diabolique. Ce centre décentré, c'est lui qui trace entre les séries et pour toutes les disjonctions l'impitoyable ligne droite de l'Aiôn, c'est-à-dire la distance, où s'alignent les dépouilles du moi, du monde et de Dieu: grand Cañon du monde, fêlure du moi, démembrement divin.' (LdS 206), (LoS 176).

[53] I have in mind this passage from 'Twenty-Fifth Series of Univocity': 'Le problème est donc de savoir comment l'individu pourrait dépasser sa forme et son lien syntaxique avec un monde pour atteindre à l'universelle communication des événements, c'est-à-dire à l'affirmation d'une synthèse disjonctive au-delà non seulement des contradictions logiques, mais même des incompatibilités alogiques. Il faudrait que l'individu se saisisse lui-même comme événement. Et que, l'événement qui s'effectue en lui, il le saisisse aussi bien comme un autre individu greffé sur lui. Alors, cet événement, il ne le comprendrait pas, ne le voudrait pas, ne le représenterait pas sans comprendre et vouloir aussi tous les autres événements comme individus, sans représenter tous les autres individus comme événements. Chaque individu serait comme un miroir pour la condensation des singularités, chaque monde une distance dans le miroir. Tel est le sens ultime de la contre-effectuation.' (LdS 209), (LoS 178).

[54] See for example: Badiou (2000) and Badiou (2006: 403), (2009: 381) or Hallward (2006).

[55] This topic is analysed extensively in literature on the Badiou's book on Deleuze. In a very interesting text, Daniel Smith, - Smith, D., (2003), 'Mathematics and the Theory of Multiplicities: Deleuze and Badiou Revisited,' Southern Journal of Philosophy, 41, pp. 411-449 – argues that the One discussed by Deleuze is always a multiplicity. The One is not a substance and implies an activity. See also Roffe (2011) and Bowden (2011).

vitalist force. It is always a construction within a given problematic environment that is always submitted to change.[56] This point will be elaborated on further below.

4. Psychoanalysis as science of events

The conception of the phantasm discussed above may be of great importance for psychoanalysis, which can allow for the construction of phantasms. Psychoanalysis can become a science of events and it is able to engage a subject with a problematic field. As we have already noticed, psychoanalysis speaks of events when it analyses murder-incest-castration or devouring-eventration-adsorption.[57] Psychoanalysis can contribute to the overcoming of the limits of a narrowed down experience. To become a science of events psychoanalysis must nevertheless meet certain conditions. Events and the phantasms representing them should not be interpreted by means of a pre-given structure. They should not be treated as something that must be given sense.[58] The events, and therefore also phantasms, carry their own sense within themselves. They are quasi-causes that produce reality. Their sense cannot be determined by means of their effectuation or actualisation. An interpretation by means of an actualised structure narrows the sense of the phantasm. It directly limits its engagement with the problematic field. According to Deleuze, a phantasm never reveals a hidden truth about individual desire. It is not a representation of a hidden core, but rather a construction. It expresses a problematic field and offers solutions that can be worthy of this field.

Deleuze criticises psychoanalysis for its attempts to prevent such an engagement with the problematic field. The attempts to construct phantasms that refer only to oedipal sexuality unnecessarily limit desire. They lead to construction of solutions to an inadequately explored problematic field. They impose an unnecessary limit on the unconscious and are frequently doomed to fail. A correct procedure on the other hand recognises the importance of events visible in a phantasm. Here Deleuze first of all criticises Freud who

---

[56] I will return to these points in the conclusion of the book.

[57] I have in mind: 'Et de quoi nous parle la psychanalyse avec la grande trinité meurtre-inceste-castration, dévoration-éventration-adsorption — sinon d'événements purs?' (LdS 246), (LoS 211).

[58] As Deleuze states: 'Tous les événements en Un, comme dans la blessure? Totem et tabou est la grande théorie de l'événement et la psychanalyse en général la science des événements: à condition de ne pas traiter l'événement comme quelque chose dont il faut chercher et dégager le sens, puisque l'événement, c'est le sens lui-même, en tant qu'il se dégage ou se distingue des états de choses qui le produisent et où il s'effectue.' (LdS 246), (LoS 211).

has limited the scope of his analysis of the unconscious to a limited number of problems. He also criticises Melanie Klein. According to him, in the end it is not enough to strengthen the identification with the good object of the heights or to strengthen the development of the reparative capacities. The analysis must allow for an open attitude towards events. Even an idol must eventually receive the characteristics of a phantasm. The figure of Joan of Arc, initially experienced as a good object of the heights, must allow for an openness towards events. The ego must discover the ideational character of such a figure. It should come to realise that Joan of Arc does not possess universal characteristics. It does not only strengthen the feminine tendencies of the subject, for example, by strengthening the reparative capacities or by allowing for the development of a phantasm of a feeding breast. A phantasm does not refer to the problems concerning human sexuality only, nor does it strengthen narcissism. Such phantasm is singular in nature. In each case it allows for a synthesis of various events. The figure of Joan of Arc does allow for the process of becoming-woman and for the development of a feminine relation to the environment. Moreover, this process is still very different in nature for different women and men. It always emerges differently given specific problematic fields.

Historically speaking, psychoanalysis has primarily been a source of knowledge about the state of affairs characterising the body and the depths.[59] It has revealed the unconscious part of the conscious passions and actions, increasing our control over the unconscious. It has allowed the ego to understand the impact of the id and the super-ego on its own actions. According to Deleuze, psychoanalysis should, nevertheless, not stop at the famous statement '*Wo Es warr, soll Ich werden*' ('Where Id was, there shall ego be'). In the end it must enable a continuous construction of phantasms that properly engage a problematic field.[60] Psychoanalysis can enable an anticipatory attitude towards an event. Freud opened up this possibility in his analysis of the original fantasy but did not make sufficient use of it. In fact he was overly focussed on the conflict within the psychoanalytic movement. He was too engaged in the discussion with the esoteric theories of Jung to pay sufficient attention to concerns other than that of sexuality. According to Freud, sexuality, and primarily that of the oedipal, must be considered to be the royal way into the unconscious. For Freud an engagement with a too

---

[59] I allude here to: '*Sur les états de choses et leur profondeur, leurs mélanges, leurs actions en passions, la psychanalyse jette la plus vive lumière; mais pour en arriver à l'émergence de ce qui en résulte, l'événement d'une autre nature, comme effet de surface.*' (LdS 246), (LoS 211).

[60] I refer to: '*mais pour en arriver à l'émergence de ce qui en résulte, l'événement d'une autre nature, comme effet de surface.*' (LdS 246), (LoS 211).

extensive problematic field would only destroy psychoanalysis as a practice by undermining its scientific status. Some limit hence had to be imposed upon the process of construction of fantasy. Unforeseen problems can never be constitutive.

The limitation of this stance is visible in the analysis of the Wolf-Man. Freud unnecessarily confines the problems of his patients to oedipal sexuality only. In *A Thousand Plateaus*, Deleuze and Guattari demonstrate that other problems are of equal importance for this case. These are social and political in nature.[61] The wolves in the tree in the dream of the Wolf-Man cannot merely express the fear of a castrating father. The dream does not only reveal hidden fears tormenting a young boy confronted with the problems of emerging sexuality. Deleuze and Guattari emphasise that wolves always live in packs. The little boy must have known that. The pack of wolves cannot be reduced to a single wolf. Freud's patient comes from a wealthy bourgeois family that fled communist Russia. The wolves may just as well have been related to the Bolsheviks who threatened his family. Wolf-Man's phantasm refers to a larger field of problems.[62] It is produced in a field of changing relationships and always represents an event. Freud is unable to perceive that this phantasm carries the possibility of a solution to such a shifting problematic field. His phantasm is not a failed attempt to respond to the setbacks faced by the boy. The Wolf-Man does not only fail. His dream not only induces fear but also refers to events that could allow for the development of an affirmative stance.[63] The Wolf-Man participates in events. He is not only scared of the pack of the Wolves, but equally affected by its force. Becoming-animal allows him to experience pride, vitality but also the independence and hostility towards humans that is expressed by these animals. The phantasm makes his suffering bearable.

---

[61] See MP 38, ATP 26.

[62] Deleuze and Guattari remark: '*On ne séparera pas chez l'Homme au loups le devenir-loup du rêve, et l'organisation religieuse et militaire des obsessions. Un militaire fait le loup, un militaire fait le chien. Il n'y a pas deux multiplicités ou deux machines, mais un seul et même agencement machinique qui produit et distribue le tout, c'est-à-dire l'ensemble des énoncés qui correspondent au « complexe ». (...) Soit le second rêve de l'Homme aux loups, au moment de l'épisode dit psychotique: dans une rue, un mur, avec une porte fermée, et à gauche une armoire vide; le patient devant l'armoire, et une grande femme à petite cicatrice qui semble vouloir contourner le mur; et derrière le mur, des loups qui se pressent vers la porte. Mme Brunswick elle-même ne peut pas s'y tromper: elle a beau se reconnaître dans la grande femme, elle voit bien que les loups sont cette fois les Bolcheviks, la masse révolutionnaire qui a vidé l'armoire ou confisqué la fortune de l'Homme aux loups. Dans un état métastable, les loups sont passés du côté d'une grande machine sociale.*' (MP 48), (ATP 38).

[63] CeC: 84, ECC: 94. See also Freud 1918 in 1955: 50.

According to Deleuze, psychoanalysis should amend its understanding of the procedure of construction of a phantasm. It is able to help to construct phantasms that can be an expression of a problematic field. The machinery of the unconscious can allow for the production of sense.[64] Each phantasm must indeed first be reconnected with its material causes. The symbols and phantasms indeed always have a physical history and refer to experiences determined by the schizoid, depressive and sexual positions.[65] As a nuclear complex, Oedipus indeed is of great significance because it marks the internal development of any individual who engages his world. But the Oedipus complex is also fundamental because it allows for the opening towards the metaphysical surface.[66] Oedipus is the condition enabling the formation of a phantasm that can allow for a distance towards those material causes.[67] Each phantasm should become such a quasi-cause. It must allow for an opening towards that what is to come. It must allow for a construction of new ways of being.

On the first view, during their collaboration Deleuze and Guattari seem to be distancing themselves from Deleuze's earlier more positive engagement with the work of Freud. Psychoanalysis does not allow for an orientation to events. It is a practice of a priest that limits desire and its open relation to the world. It stimulates feelings of guilt and a reactive stance towards the world.[68]

---

[64] In 'Eleventh Series of Nonsense' Deleuze states: '*Il est donc agréable que résonne aujourd'hui la bonne nouvelle: le sens n'est jamais principe ou origine, il est produit. Il n'est pas à découvrir, à restaurer, ni à re-employer, il est à produire par de nouvelles machineries. Il n'appartient à aucune hauteur, il n'est dans aucune profondeur, mais effet de surface, inséparable de la surface comme de sa dimension propre. (...) Nous ne cherchons pas en Freud un explorateur de la profondeur humaine et du sens originaire, mais le prodigieux découvreur de la machinerie de l'inconscient par lequel le sens est produit, toujours produit en fonction du non-sens. (...) bref produire le sens, est la tâche aujourd'hui.*' (LdS 91) (LoS 72).

[65] I refer here to: '*Aussi, quelle que soit l'importance des positions précédentes, ou la nécessité de rattacher toujours l'événement à ses causes, la psychanalyse a raison de rappeler le rôle d'Œdipe comme « complexe nucléaire » – formule de même importance que le « noyau noématique » de Husserl.*' (LdS 247), (LoS 212).

[66] Akin to Freud, Deleuze therefore recognises the central status of this complex. Laplanche puts this as follows: '*En fait, chez Freud, la conception de l'Œdipe est marquée de réalisme: qu'il soit représenté comme conflit interne (« complexe nucléaire ») ou comme institution sociale, le complexe reste une donnée; le sujet le rencontre, « tout être humain se voit imposer la tâche de la maîtriser ».*' Laplanche and Pontalis, (1985: 49), Laplanche and Pontalis (1986) 'Fantasy and the origins of sexuality' in Burgin *et al.*, (eds.), (1986), *Formations of Fantasy*, London: Methuen, pp. 5-34.

[67] I am referring to: '*Car c'est avec Œdipe que l'événement se dégage de ses causes en profondeur, s'étale à la surface et se rattache à sa quasi-cause du point de vue d'une genèse dynamique.*' (LdS 247), (LoS 212).

[68] See: Chapter two of *Anti-Oedipus* and chapter two of *A Thousand Plateaus*, (MP 39), (ATP 26).

Psychoanalysis is one of the many discourses forcing contemporary subjects to embrace the structure of power characterising capitalism. It confines each subject to a narrowly defined field of subjective problems and leads subsequently to the development of inadequate solutions. Psychoanalysis limits human desire to a state of perpetual striving towards a discharge, a state of perpetual lack that can be soothed only by continuous incorporation of various objects. It is unable to understand desire as possessing possible social and political dimensions. The differences between the earlier work of Deleuze on desire and his collaboration with Guattari are according to me nevertheless not fundamental in nature. As I have indicated above, already in *The Logic of Sense,* Deleuze emphasises the importance of the opening of psychoanalysis towards the notion of the event. Deleuze claims that only in such case psychoanalysis will be able to contribute to a construction of desire on a more broadly defined problematic field. The interpretation of the unconscious by means of already established categories – categories that are indeed provided by the current regime of representation proper to the capitalist mode of production – prevents psychoanalysis from achieving this goal.

5. The phantasm and the ego in psychoanalysis

Deleuze continues to analyse the differences between his understanding of the phantasm and psychoanalysis in the chapter 'Thirtieth Series of the Phantasm.' He particularly refers to the analysis of the Freudian notion of original fantasy by Laplanche and Pontalis. Original fantasy visualises the most important events of our lives and displays the sources of subsequent psychic problems generated by those events. Deleuze acknowledges the positive aspects of this discovery but also disagrees, in his account, with several points. According to Deleuze, psychoanalysis is in the end not only unable to fully understand the nature of the events expressed in a phantasm but is moreover, incapable of correctly understanding the role of the ego within it.[69] Psychoanalysis does not critically distance itself from the idea of autoeroticism and does not properly explore the metaphysical surface. It limits itself to the history of the ego and of the body. In the following discussion I will first expound the position

---

[69] I refer to: '*Le second caractère du phantasme est sa situation par rapport au moi, ou plutôt la situation du moi dans le phantasme lui-même. Il est bien vrai que le phantasme trouve son point de départ (ou son auteur) dans le moi phallique du narcissisme secondaire. Mais si le phantasme a la propriété de se retourner sur son auteur, quelle est la place du moi dans le phantasme, compte tenu du déroulement ou du développement qui en sont inséparables?*' (LdS 247), (LoS 212).

taken by Laplanche and Pontalis, including their critique of Melanie Klein.[70] Subsequent to that, I analyse Deleuze's description of the nature of the drives that invest the metaphysical surface, a topic that unveils the critique of the notion of autoeroticism.

According to Deleuze the text 'Fantasy and the Origins of Sexuality' by Laplanche and Pontalis (1964, 1986) is the most sophisticated account of fantasy and the role of the ego within it, developed within psychoanalysis.[71] According to Laplanche and Pontalis, the ego always appears in the fantasy at various places. It is an instance that acts, that is being acted upon or that perceives the whole situation revealed in the fantasy. The ego's place within it is never fully determined. It is present in the scene but it is unclear where exactly it should be located. The ego might appear in all places and at all moments. The original fantasy is hence characterised by the absence of a clear point of subjectivation. Ahab's phantasm of catching a white whale can be understood as having the structure of an original fantasy. Ahab's ego may be found in the person of the whale hunter, the hunted whale or, equally, the place of a person who observes the whole aggressive scene. In their article, Laplanche and Pontalis take the fantasy of seduction, represented by the formulation 'a father seduces a daughter,' as an example.[72] This fantasy is a scenario with multiple entries. The subject may be located in the place of the daughter, the father or even in the verb 'seduce'.

---

[70] Here, I mainly concentrate on Deleuze's description of Laplanche and Pontalis. Laplanche has, in his later work, distanced himself from some of the statements of his influential article; for example, by pointing to the cultural aspects contributing to the emergence of a fantasy. See Laplanche (2000), 'The other within', in *Radical Philosophy* (102), pp 33. In this way, Laplanche has partially responded to the critique by, for example, Deleuze.

[71] Deleuze writes: '*Laplanche et Pontalis ont particulièrement posé ce problème, dans des conditions telles qu'ils récusent d'avance toute réponse facile: bien que le moi puisse apparaître dans le phantasme à tel ou tel moment comme agissant, comme subissant une action, comme tiers observant, il n'est ni actif ni passif et ne se laisse à aucun moment fixer à une place, fût-elle réversible.*' (LdS 247), (LoS 212).

[72] I base this on Deleuze's interpretation of this article and from which he cites a passage « *Fantasme originaire, fantasme des origines, origine du fantasme* » (1964) in *The Logic of Sense*: '« *Un père séduit une fille, telle serait par exemple la formulation résumée du fantasme de séduction. La marque du processus primaire n'est pas ici l'absence d'organisation, comme on le dit parfois, mais ce caractère particulier de la structure: elle est un scénario à entrées multiples, dans lequel rien ne dit que le sujet trouvera d'emblée sa place dans le terme fille; on peut le voir se fixer aussi bien en père ou même en séduit* ».' (LdS 248, Laplanche and Pontalis 1985: 62, 1986: 22), (LoS 354).

The remarks of Laplanche and Pontalis have two important benefits, according to Deleuze.[73] The original fantasy or the phantasm is no longer considered to be a direct representation of an action or passion. It does not directly express a desiring body and its conscious or unconscious emotions. Secondly, the original fantasy also allows for a different understanding of the nature of the drive that invests the fantasy. The drives investing it are no longer considered to be directly reversible.[74] Here Laplanche and Pontalis criticise the theory of Klein and Isaacs, who claim that the ego can assume only the active role or a reverse passive one.[75] As already noted, Deleuze prefers an analysis that reserves the possibility of such a reversal only to the drives characterising the depths. According to Deleuze, Laplanche and Pontalis are able to go beyond the analysis of fantasy in terms of reversible drives because they make use of the pronominal model (*modèle du pronominal*).[76] Laplanche and Pontalis's point of departure is the ego connected to what they call an autoerotic 'this-side' (*en-deçà*).[77] What does it mean? This state of autoeroticism does not refer to an original state of libido, one that is not yet oriented to external objects. As I have briefly mentioned in the previous chapter, autoerotic satisfaction they speak of must be considered to be a secondary phenomenon. Autoeroticism develops in a later stage of development of desire, at the moment when a separation between real needs and the pleasure principle is established. Fantasy, Laplanche and Pontalis speak of, originates in a libido that ceases to

---

[73] I comment on: '*Ces remarques ont deux avantages: d'une part elles soulignent que le phantasme n'est pas représentation d'action ni de passion, mais appartient à un tout autre domaine; d'autre part elles montrent que, si le moi s'y dissipe, ce ne peut être en vertu d'une quelconque identité des contraires, d'un renversement où l'actif deviendrait passif — comme cela arrive dans le devenir des profondeurs et l'identité infinie qu'il implique.*' (LdS 248), (LoS 213).

[74] I have in mind: '*d'autre part elles montrent que, si le moi s'y dissipe, ce ne peut être en vertu d'une quelconque identité des contraires, d'un renversement où l'actif deviendrait passif — comme cela arrive dans le devenir des profondeurs et l'identité infinie qu'il implique.*' (LdS 248), (LoS 213).

[75] Deleuze cites Laplanche and Pontalis' text on fantasy: '*C'est même l'essentiel de la critique que Laplanche et Pontalis adressent à la thèse de Susan Isaacs (« Nature et fonction du phantasme » in* Développements de la psychanalyse*): celle-ci, modelant le phantasme sur la pulsion, donne au sujet une place déterminée active, même si l'actif se retourne en passif et inversement. A quoi ils objectent: « Suffit-il de reconnaître dans le fantasme d'incorporation l'équivalence de manger et d'être mangé? Tant qu'est maintenue l'idée d'une place du sujet, même si celui-ci peut y être passive, sommes-nous dans la structure du fantasme le plus fondamental? »*' (LdS 248, Laplanche and Pontalis 1985: 67), (LoS 354).

[76] I refer to: '*Toutefois, nous ne pouvons pas suivre ces auteurs lorsqu'ils cherchent cet au-delà de l'actif et du passif dans un modèle du pronominal qui fait encore appel au moi, et même se rapporte explicitement à un en-deçà auto-érotique.*' (LdS 248), (LoS 213).

[77] It must be noted that Deleuze bases his argument here on brief remarks made by Laplanche and Pontalis, found at the end of their analysis of original fantasy.

be oriented to external real objects.[78] The autoerotic satisfaction that produces fantasy is the product of the anarchic activity of the partial drives. These drives are closely linked to the excitations of the various erotogenic zones. The fantasy emerges given the dominance of such a fragmented pleasure rather than given the existence of a global, unified and functional form of desire.

According to Deleuze's reading Freud nevertheless underestimates the importance of this chaotic and free energy in his analysis of fantasy.[79] He emphasises that the mentioned autoerotic state can best be understood by means of a difference between a noun and a reflexive pronoun.[80] The ego of autoeroticism can attain a position within a fantasy only because a noun is replaced with a reflexive pronoun. A sadistic or masochist fantasy, described by the formulation 'A child is being beaten', is an example of the working of the pronominal model. The opposition between punishment (the active, sadistic position) and being punished (the passive, masochist position) is extended by the use of the reflexive pronoun form: to punish *oneself* (*se punir*). To punish *oneself* is considered here to be a more primordial and autoerotic scenario that only subsequently expresses itself in the masochist or sadist positions.[81] Initially, the subject is not playing an active or passive role, turning only secondarily to one of these positions. The model of the reflexive pronoun reveals that the ego is able to distance itself and reflect upon these positions. Another example of the use of a reflexive pronoun is found in the voyeuristic fantasy. Without a reflexive pronoun a subject can assume either the active or passive role. In the case where he assumes a passive role, he is the instance that is being looked at, leading, for example, to the feeling of shame. When

---

[78] Laplanche and Pontalis devote the end of their article to this topic, stating: '*L'idéal, si l'on peut dire, de l'auto-érotisme, ce sont « des lèvres qui se baisent elles-mêmes »*' (LP cite Freud from *Trois essais sur la théorie de la sexualité*, op. cit., p. 75): '*ici, dans cette jouissance apparemment fermée sur soi, comme au plus profond du fantasme, ce discours qui ne s'adresse plus à personne, toute répartition du sujet et de l'objet est abolie.*' (Laplanche and Pontalis 1985: 73, 1986: 26).

[79] Concurring with Monique David-Ménard, I can claim that Deleuze's description of Freud is in this respect limited (see David-Ménard 2005: 179).

[80] I comment here on Deleuze's representation of Laplanche and Pontalis; he states: '*La valeur du pronominal — se punir au lieu de punir ou d'être puni, ou mieux encore se voir soi-même au lieu de voir ou d'être vu — est bien attesté par Freud, mais ne semble pas dépasser le point de vue d'une identité des contraires, soit par approfondissement de l'un d'eux, soit par synthèse des deux.*' (LdS 248), (LoS 213).

[81] This reading is supported by the statements by Laplanche and Pontalis in note 71: '*Cf. aussi dans « Pulsions et destins des pulsions » l'analyse des couples d'opposés sadisme-masochisme, voyeurisme-exhibitionnisme. En deçà de la forme active ou passive de la phrase (voir-être vu, par exemple), il faudrait supposer une forme réfléchie (se voir soi-même) qui serait, selon Freud, primordiale. Sans doute faudrait-il chercher ce degré primordial là où le sujet ne se situe plus dans les différents termes du fantasme.*' (Laplanche and Pontalis 1985: 85, 1986: 34, note 64).

he assumes the active role, he is enjoying the act of observing. He controls his environment and fully enjoys the activity of introjection. These two positions can nevertheless be preceded by a more originary one, made visible by a reflexive pronoun. Laplanche and Pontalis speak of a reflexive pronoun, 'seeing oneself' (*se voir soi-même*), that precedes 'seeing' (*voir*) and 'being seen' (*d'être vu*). In this case, the subject is not yet identified with either of the two sides of the fantasy. Nevertheless, according to Deleuze 'seeing oneself' does not refer to a free and chaotic energy of the libido. This position is rather constructed only in order to be subsequently developed into one of the two eventual possibilities. The reflexive pronoun directly contains both positions that will be secondarily differentiated. By seeing itself, the subject takes a step back. He is able to reflect upon the two positions he will have to subsequently occupy. He discovers the primary mutual ground of these positions.

Deleuze is not satisfied with the solution he has attributed to both Freud and Laplanche and Pontalis. He dismisses the idea that the autoerotic primordial desire has to be transformed into one of the two opposite positions. In Deleuze's interpretation the opposition between the subject's active and passive role in a fantasy is not sufficiently engendered by the mentioned writers. On the contrary, their approach provides only for the notion that the ego is allowed only to reflect upon its position within a fantasy. The ego is left with a very limited set of choices. In the case of sadomasochistic fantasy, the ego is in the end only able to choose to direct its aggression either towards the outside or the inside. According to Deleuze the central role attributed to autoeroticism in Freud's account of the fantasy takes the identity of contraries (*identité des contraires*) as its point of departure.[82] The ego must make a choice for one of the two parts of the fantasy (*par approfondissement de l'un d'eux*) or at best reach a synthesis of both options. The active and the passive parts remain intertwined. For Deleuze, Freud's account of fantasy is in fact deeply Hegelian in nature.[83] Deleuze supports his description by referring to Freud's analysis of the meaning of primal words.[84] According to Freud, just as in dreams, these supposedly existing words carry two opposing meanings. An example of such

---

[82] I am referring to: '*mais ne semble pas dépasser le point de vue d'une identité des contraires, soit par approfondissement de l'un d'eux, soit par synthèse des deux.*' (LdS 248), (LoS 213).

[83] I refer to: '*Que Freud soit resté attaché à un tel point de vue « hégélien » n'est pas douteux, comme on le voit dans le domaine du langage à propos d'une thèse sur les mots primitifs pourvus d'un sens contradictoire.*' (LdS 248), (LoS 213). For a critique of this description of Freud, refer: David-Ménard (2005: 179).

[84] Deleuze and Benveniste refer to Freud, S. (1910), 'Antithetical meaning of primal words,' in S. Freud (1957), *The Standard Edition of the works of Freud, Volume XI*, transl. James Strachley, London: The Hogarth Press, pp. 153-161.

a word is the German *bass*. This supposedly historically existing word has been split into two opposing ones that we use on daily basis, *besser* and *bös* (better and bad). The original and historic *Bass* would convey the characteristics of both. Deleuze dismisses this idea. He supports his critique by referring to the work of the structuralist linguist Benveniste.[85] Benveniste denies the existence of originary words that could carry two opposite meanings. The theory about the existence of primitive words is false. No such originary words could have ever existed. Freud has committed an etymological mistake. The origin of the word *bös* is different from the word *besser*.[86] An originary language never existed. For Benveniste, the meaning of words is always determined by the structural relations in a network of signifiers. Their meaning can be only determined by an analysis of the whole network of signifiers.[87]

Deleuze naturally does not entirely agree with Benveniste's structuralist analysis of the working of language and considers it to be too rationalist in the description of its functioning.[88] The relations between various terms – the visible (manifested) organisation of language – are according to Deleuze accompanied by various paradoxes. Sense is produced by non-sense. What then is Deleuze's answer to Freud's model of the pronominal?[89] What allows him

---

[85] I discuss: '*Le texte de Freud sur les sens opposés dans les mots primitifs a été critiqué par Emile Benveniste (« Remarques sur la fonction du langage dans la découverte freudienne », Problèmes de linguistique générale), Benveniste montre qu'une langue peut fort bien ne pas comporter telle ou telle catégorie, mais non pas lui donner une expression contradictoire.*' (LdS 248), (LoS 355).

[86] Benveniste writes: '*Abel fournit une série de correspondances entre l'anglais et l'allemand, que Freud a relevées comme montrant d'une langue a l'autre des sens opposes, et entre lesquels on constaterait une « transformation phonétique en vue de la séparation des contraires ». Sans insister pur le moment sur la grave erreur de raisonnement qui se dissimule dans cette simple remarque, contentons-nous de rectifier ces rapprochements. L'ancien adverbe allemand* bass, *«bien », s'apparente a* besser, *mais n'a aucun rapport avec* bös, *« mauvais », de même qu'en vieil anglais* bat, *« bon, meilleur », est sans relation avec* badde *(aujourd'hui bad), « mouvais ».*' (Benveniste 1966: 81).

[87] As Benveniste states: '*Un langage est d'abord une catégorisation, une création d'objets et de relations entre ces objets. Imaginer un stade du langage, aussi « originel » qu'on le voudra, mais néanmoins réel et « historique », ou un certain objet serait dénommé comme étant lui-même et en même temps n'importe quel autre, et ou la relation exprimée serait la relation de contradiction permanente, la relation non relationnante, ou tout serait soi et autre que soi, donc ni soi ni autre, c'est imaginer une pure chimère.*' (Benveniste 1966: 83).

[88] Deleuze remarks: '*Toutefois, à lire Benveniste, on a l'impression qu'une langue se confond nécessairement avec de purs processus de rationalisation; le langage n'implique-t-il pas pourtant des procédés paradoxaux par rapport à son organisation manifeste, bien que ces procédés ne se laissent nullement réduire à l'identification des contraires*' (LdS 249), (LoS 355).

[89] I refer to: '*En vérité, le dépassement de l'actif et du passif, et la dissolution du moi qui lui correspond, ne se font pas dans la direction d'une subjectivité infinie ou réfléchie. Ce qui est au-delà de l'actif et du passif, ce n'est pas le pronominal, mais le résultat — résultat d'actions et de passions, l'effet de surface ou l'événement.*' (LdS 249), (LoS 213).

to go beyond autoeroticism? Can phantasm allow for more than a reflection on the position each subject is destined to assume in real life? These questions have been partially answered above. The dissolution of the ego, reached when going beyond the active and the passive in a phantasm, does not have to lead to the emergence of an infinite or reflective subjectivity. We are not required to assume the existence of a subject who incorporates the whole world, neither do we have to speak of a subject who is able to withdraw himself from the material world, only in order to reflect upon his position. According to Deleuze, beyond the active and the passive we do not find any form of subjectivity, but rather the events of the metaphysical surface. These events separate themselves from the actions and passions from which they result. The phantasm does not allow for a reflection upon the possible positions. Rather, it accompanies the movement of the ego on the metaphysical surface. I have discussed the nature of this movement in the example of little Hans's case study. The little boy develops a new relationship to the world. He loses his narcissism and is affected by the suffering, courage and determination of horses. The phantasm of the falling horse is not a representation of his inner life. The boy does not merely reach a state that allows him to reflect upon the obstacles that limit his creative energy. He is not obliged only to assume either a passive or an active role. Becoming-horse allows the child to sympathise with the problems encountered by the horse in its life. It embodies all the possible affects that are fundamental for the boy. He is proud and independent, but he also suffers and is not protected against external power. He can now relate to his environment by means of these affects. He is continually engaging different aspects of the phantasm of the falling horse and opens towards new possibilities for action.

6. Neutral energy and disjunctive synthesis

As an answer to Freud we, nevertheless, still have to reflect on the nature of the libido that invests the metaphysical surface. How can libido not be autoerotic in nature? In the previous chapter the differences between the metaphysical and the physical surface were introduced. The physical surface is a membrane that connects the organism with its environment. It both serves as a protective shield and allows for interaction. The physical surface is characterised by what Deleuze calls the individual and personal singularities. Following Simondon, he claims that an individual always emerges in a particular environment. An organism is a response to this environment. The physical surface that protects this organism is a solution to encountered problems. It emerges in the process of actualisation. The metaphysical surface, on the other hand, is different in nature. It is not actual but virtual. The singularities that characterise it concern incorporeal events. The movement that is visible in the phantasm implies an opening towards liberated a-cosmic, impersonal and pre-individual singularities (*singularités acosmiques, impersonnelles et pré-individuelles*). These singularities are released like spores and burst as they get jettisoned, in Deleuze's terms.[90] This analysis of the nature of the metaphysical surface is in fact far from being severely abstract.[91] As already emphasised, Deleuze is not a vitalist. The phantasm is not bringing the subject into connection with a deeper 'a-cosmic' source of life energy, but rather leads to the demise of the dominance of the ego. The subject no longer perceives the world from an already actualised perspective. The phantasm allows the ego to open up towards the world that it cannot control. The singularities proper to the metaphysical surface are liberated from an actualised form structures.[92] These singularities express an opening towards virtual events that are not yet included in the ego.

As was indicated in the previous chapter, Deleuze clarifies such statements by referring to the energy that invests the metaphysical surface. This energy differs from the libido, proper to the physical surface.[93] This energy is, as he states, neutral. Neutral energy differs from the negative force of the death drive, found in the depths.[94] The neutral energy, or what we have called the speculative death-drive, does not strive towards a bottomless abyss. It does not aim at a direct removal of tension. Neutral energy is pre-individual and impersonal. It is proper to the problems characterising the environment of the organism. This energy refers to singularities liberated from the actual form. It is an energy that is liberated, given the adsorption of the physical

---

[90] I refer to: '*A la lettre, il les lâche comme des spores, et éclate dans ce délestage.*' (LdS 249), (LoS 213). A comparable disparity between Simondon and Deleuze's approaches towards this aspect of genesis has also been noted by Toscano (2006: 197).

[91] I return to the critique of similar passages by Badiou and Hallward below.

[92] I am referring to: '*Ce qui apparaît dans le phantasme, c'est le mouvement par lequel le moi s'ouvre à la surface et libère les singularités acosmiques, impersonnelles et pré-individuelles qu'il emprisonnait.*' (LdS 249), (LoS 213).

[93] I comment upon: '*Il faut interpréter l'expression « énergie neutre » en ce sens: neutre signifie alors pré-individuel et impersonnel, mais ne qualifie pas l'état d'une énergie qui viendrait rejoindre un sans-fond, il renvoie au contraire aux singularités libérées du moi par la blessure narcissique. Cette neutralité, c'est-à dire ce mouvement par lequel des singularités sont émises ou plutôt restituées par un moi qui se dissout ou s'adsorbe à la surface, appartient essentiellement au phantasme: ainsi dans « Un enfant est battu » (ou encore « Un père séduit une fille », suivant l'exemple invoqué par Laplanche et Pontalis).*' (LdS 249), (LoS 213).

[94] For an interesting defence of Freud against Deleuze's arguments, see Monique David-Ménard (2005), Chapters seven and eight. According to David-Ménard, Deleuze does little justice to Freud's idea of the death drive when he equates it with the idea of negation and destruction. According to her, Freud has paid sufficient attention to a number of aspects of the neutral energy that have been discussed for example, in *The Logic of Sense*.

surface.[95] According to Deleuze, the fantasies analysed by Freud, such as 'a child is being beaten' – characterising sado-masochism – or 'a father seduces his daughter' – revealing the origins of sexuality, testify to the presence of similar kinds of energy.[96] Sadism and masochism are as we have seen more than just a choice for an active or passive position. They are not grounded in a more originary form described by the formula 'to punish oneself'. According to Deleuze, both perversions actualise an entirely different virtual and problematic field. Firstly, the two perversions originate in different bodily positions. Sadism belongs to the schizoid position and masochism to the depressive position. Secondly, the perversions emerge as a response to different social and political environments. Deleuze analyses this point in *Coldness and Cruelty*. Masochism is not a reversal of sadism. Both forms of perversion are radically different, despite being described by the same formula. Both emerge out of a synthesis of different social and political factors. They concern different pre-individual singular points. Deleuze distinguishes ten major points of difference between these two practices.[97] Sadism is, for example, characterised by the dominance of the so-called demonstrative faculty. A sadist wishes to reveal what he considers to be the true nature of reality. He wants to demonstrate the existence of the destructive power of the so-called primary nature and achieves this goal by means of negation. He intends to destroy the humane and sentimental secondary nature that merely serves as a veil to cover the primary nature. Similarly, a masochist is also endeavouring to establish a relationship with the primary nature, but makes use of different, far less violent means. A masochist

---

[95] I have in mind: '*Cette neutralité, c'est-à-dire ce mouvement par lequel des singularités sont émises ou plutôt restituées par un moi qui se dissout ou s'adsorbe à la surface, appartient essentiellement au phantasme.*' (LdS 249), (LoS 213).

[96] I am referring to: '*Cette neutralité, (…) appartient essentiellement au phantasme: ainsi dans « Un enfant est battu » (ou encore « Un père séduit une fille », suivant l'exemple invoqué par Laplanche et Pontalis).*' (LdS: 249), (LoS 213).

[97] I briefly refer here to the summary given by Deleuze at the end of *Coldness and Cruelty*: '*Sado-masochisme est un de ces noms mal fabriqués, monstre sémiologique. Chaque fois quand nous nous sommes trouvés devant un signe apparemment commun, il s'agissait seulement d'un syndrome, dissociable en symptômes irréductibles. Résumons: 1 la faculté spéculative-démonstrative du sadisme, la faculté dialectique-imaginative du masochisme; 2 le négatif et la négation dans le sadisme, la dénégation et le suspensif dans le masochisme; 3 la réitération quantitative, le suspens qualitatif; 4 le masochisme propre sadique, le sadisme propre au masochisme, l'un ne se combinant jamais avec l'autre; 5 le négation de la mère et l'inflation du père dans le sadisme, la « dénégation » de la mère et l'annihilation du père dans le masochisme; 6 l'opposition du rôle et du sens du fétiche dans les deux cas; de même pour le phantasme; 7 l'antiesthétisme du sadisme, l'esthétisme du masochisme; 8 le sens « institutionnel » de l'un, le sens contractuel de l'autre; 9 le surmoi et l'identification dans le sadisme, le moi et l'idéalisation dans le masochisme; 10 les deux formes opposées de désexualisation et de resexualisation; 11 et, résumant l'ensemble, la différence radicale entre l'apathie sadique et le froid masochiste.*' (PSM 115), (CC 134).

does not make use of negation but of imagination. He denies and suspends. He does not, for example, wish to violently reveal the existence of a lack that is a sign of the imperfection of the object of his desire. Instead, he disavows its existence. In the case of a woman, the lack is disavowed by means of a fetish. His mistress must wear specific clothes, for instance, furs, and act in a very precise manner to mask her lack of perfection. Both practices are also characterised by a different relationship towards the law. A sadist is attached to institutions. He incorporates the paternal law and punishes himself and others in its name. A masochist, on the other hand, attempts to distance himself from the law and the institutions imposing it. He mocks the paternal law by means of an independent contract with the mistress.[98] He laughs at the law by making it an object of a game. Institutions are successfully kept at a distance. From this brief summary we can only conclude that both perversions emerge out of a synthesis of entirely different events and provide a response to different social and political problems.

The phantasm 'a father seduces his daughter' also establishes a particular synthesis of the pre-individual singularities. The two supposedly opposing tendencies – seducing and being seduced – manifest in the phantasm are not grounded in a more primordial scenario described by the formula 'to seduce oneself'. Certainly, a woman can take on the passive role and be the one seduced. She can also take on an active role. Her phantasm can in that case mutate into forms such as: 'I am seducing myself', 'I am seducing others' or 'I am placing others in a position in which they cannot resist'. These two opposing positions are nevertheless reached in different manners. They concern different quasi-causes and are answers to different problems. The phantasm will play an entirely different role in a society where free sexuality may still have an emancipatory potential. A woman's assuming a passive position might only express her submission to patriarchal rules and her inability to behave in a narcissistic fashion. Nevertheless, given a different problematic field, for example in a contemporary form of patriarchal society where it is taken for granted that women assume an active role, the same passive position might be an entirely different solution. Assuming the role of being seduced might be considered a form of retreat from the compulsory participation in pre-established gender relations.

---

[98] I lack space here to analyse the differences between both practices more extensively. An interesting aspect of the differences between Sade and Masoch can be found i.a. in Geyskens, (2006), 'Gilles Deleuze over Sacher-Masoch. Literatuur als symptomatologie', *Tijdschrift voor Filosofie*, pp. 779. Geyskens emphasises the importance of the rational and destructive side of sadism as well as the role of imagination and the production of non-genital sexuality in masochism.

In his analysis of the operation of fantasy, Freud does not only make use of the model of pronominal. In some case studies he analyses the possible grammatical transformations of each fantasy. Schreber's fantasy can be represented by the formula '*I* (a man) *love him* (a man).'[99] According to Freud the major forms of paranoia can be seen as a protest against this one sentence. Freud understands paranoia as an expression of an unwillingness to become conscious of one's own homosexual feelings towards the father. The grammatical transformations of this formula express various forms of a protest against homosexuality. In the case of the paranoia of persecution the sentence is first transformed into a formula '*I* do not *love* him – I *hate* him.'[100] Freud stresses that this formulation can nevertheless be too threatening to the ego. It still implies a recognition of homosexuality. The internal perception of the feeling of love or hate is therefore subsequently replaced by a perception of something external by means of a projection. The expression 'I hate him' is made into a sentence: '*He hates* (persecutes) *me*, which will justify me in hating him.' This projection onto the outside world may still have negative consequences for the ego. The person who experiences being persecuted does not need to become aware of the fact that he hates the other. In the instance of Schreber, for example, it leads to a false conviction that the hate of the son towards the father is caused by the more original hatred of the father towards the son himself. The eventual form of the fantasy becomes: 'I do not *love* him, I *hate* him, because he persecutes me.'[101] Just as in the previous cases, Deleuze does not agree with this reading of the nature of grammatical transformations characterising a phantasm.[102] The transformations cannot be caused by the reversal of the drives. They are not governed by any higher order, but are a consequence of a communication within a multiplicity of events on the metaphysical surface. In the spirit of Deleuze, we can, for example, declare that the negation of one's own homosexual drives – visible in the phantasm 'I (a man) love him (a man)' – must be caused by a variety of events. A person with strong narcissist tendencies will be less likely to negate its existence compared to a person with strong depressive or schizoid tendencies. Here in *The Logic of Sense*, Deleuze is already suggesting that the role of the environment is

---

[99] Freud 1911 in 1958: 63.
[100] Freud 1911 in 1958: 63.
[101] Freud 1911 in 1958: 63.
[102] As Deleuze states: '*Et les célèbres transformations grammaticales (comme celles du président Schreber, ou bien celles du sadisme ou du voyeurisme) marquent chaque fois des assomptions de singularités réparties dans des disjonctions, toutes communicantes dans l'événement pour chaque cas, tous les événements communiquant en un, comme les coups de dés dans un même lancer.*' (LdS 249), (LoS 214).

of fundamental importance for a similar phantasm. The resistance towards homosexuality in a tolerant environment will naturally be far less strong than in one where homosexuality is a taboo. The problematic field is different in each case. In the latter case, the events that will strengthen the resistance towards this sentence are far more likely to take place. The construction of the phantasm of becoming-woman that truly explores the problematic field and offers it a solution might be a far more difficult task.[103]

I have already argued that the orientation towards the phantasm becomes intertwined with the event of the phantasm itself.[104] The ego is now oriented to a series of various individuals. It is allowed to take on different roles. Deleuze states that the phantasm stages a game of chance.[105] The dissolved ego (*moi dissous*) is enabled to see itself in all possibilities. It is able to continually engage in a new disjunctive synthesis and develop a new relationship towards the structures of sense that have been already actualised. The new synthesis differs greatly from the previous ones. The first positions are characterised by a rather rudimentary connective synthesis. In this case the separate experiences are related just to one another. The ego accompanies the pleasurable interactions with various objects. It is at the same time entirely subjected to its environment and is unable to exercise any influence upon it. The role of the ego is entirely determined by the actualised structures. As was made clear in Chapters four and five, the conjunctive synthesis goes beyond the connective synthesis. The distinct experiences are brought into a unity. The ego starts to exercise an influence upon its environment.[106] The divergent series that

---

[103] See AO 17, LAO 24.

[104] I refer to: '*Alors l'individualité du moi se confond avec l'événement du phantasme lui-même; quitte à ce que l'événement représenté dans le phantasme soit saisi comme un autre individu, ou plutôt comme une série d'autres individus par lesquels passe le moi dissous.*' (LdS 249), (LoS 214).

[105] I allude to: '*Le phantasme est ainsi inséparable des coups de dés ou des cas fortuits qu'il met en scène.*' (LdS 249), (LoS 214).

[106] I comment here on the following passage from the 'Twenty-Fourth Series of the Communication of Events': '*Non pas que la disjonction soit ramenée à une simple conjonction. On distingue trois sortes de synthèses: la synthèse connective (si..., alors) qui porte sur la construction d'une seule série; la synthèse conjonctive (et), comme procédé de construction de séries convergentes; la synthèse disjonctive (ou bien) qui répartit les séries divergentes.*' (LdS 203), (LoS 174). These three syntheses also play a central role in *Anti-Oedipus*. Deleuze and Guattari analyse the synthesis in a different order. The connective synthesis is followed by a disjunctive synthesis. The conjunctive synthesis contributes to the emergence of a unified experience only in particular cases and seems to be of lesser importance than the disjunctive synthesis. In their collaborative work, Deleuze and Guattari pay less attention to the role of the physical surface and to the emergence of unified experience. The conjunctive synthesis is an attempt to impose partial order upon the separate and chaotic experience of the body without organs. I lack the space here to fully analyse the difference between both books concerning this topic.

organise experience start to converge around a central point. The ego aims at constructing of a stable and secure environment. The originally unrelated experiences gain a place within a coherent world. The ego constructs a sound narrative about its own life. This narrative might be presented in a linear, if not a teleological, form. The ego becomes the centre of the world's structures and perceives itself as capable of transforming them.

This relationship with the actualised structures alters with the introduction of the castration complex. The loss of the image of the phallus and emergence of the metaphysical surface allows for the emergence of the disjunctive synthesis. This synthesis no longer produces a coherent experience and narrative. The separate series cease to converge around a central point.[107] The ego is no longer capable of controlling the environment and its structures, and begins to affirm diversity. From now on it accompanies the construction of partial temporary structures. The constructed narrative is partial and dependent on the various temporary points of view assumed by the ego. The presence of disjunctive synthesis is visible in the structure of the phantasm. A phantasm allows for the communication between hitherto unrelated events. It is a scenario that does not impose a rigid order on experience but, rather, allows for a continuous affirmation of chance.

According to Deleuze, the disjunctive synthesis may be used in various ways.[108] An affirmative use of this synthesis, one that allows for an affirmation of chance, is uncommon. Deleuze criticises the possible restrictive use of the disjunctive synthesis.[109] In this case, one directly selects the predicates that will

---

[107] I have in mind: '*Nous retrouvons ici l'illustration d'un principe de la distance positive, avec les singularités qui la jalonnent, et d'un usage affirmatif de la synthèse disjonctive (et non pas synthèse de contradiction).*' (LdS 249), (LoS 214).

[108] This topic also plays a crucial role in *Anti-Oedipus* and is analysed extensively in the second chapter. I lack the space here to discuss the differences between the approaches taken in both books.

[109] I refer here to the following passage from 'Twenty-Fourth Series of the Communication of Events': '*Les conexa, les conjuncta, les disjuncta. Mais, justement, toute la question est de savoir à quelles conditions la disjonction est une véritable synthèse, et non pas un procédé d'analyse qui se contente d'exclure des prédicats d'une chose en vertu de l'identité de son concept (usage négatif, limitatif ou exclusif de la disjonction). La réponse est donnée pour autant que la divergence ou le décentrement déterminés par la disjonction deviennent objets d'affirmation comme tels. La disjonction n'est pas du tout réduite à une conjonction, elle reste une disjonction puisqu'elle porte et continue à porter sur une divergence en tant que telle. Mais cette divergence est affirmée de sorte que le ou bien devient lui-même affirmation pure. Au lieu qu'un certain nombre de prédicats soient exclus d'une chose en vertu de l'identité de son concept, chaque « chose » s'ouvre à l'infini des prédicats par lesquels elle passe, en même temps qu'elle perd son centre, c'est-à-dire son identité comme concept ou comme moi*. A l'exclusion des prédicats se substitue la communication des événements.*' (LdS 204), (LoS 174).

be attributed to an object or an event. A horse that fascinates little Hans would in that case represent the father. The horse could also be straightforwardly interpreted as courageous and strong. One is tempted to simply interpret the phantasm by means of preselected attributes. The boy becomes active and strong. The phantasm strengthens his active forces. An affirmative use of the synthesis on the other hand resists such a direct interpretation and does not attempt to impose any order upon the phantasm.[110] The ego must have the capacity to open up towards the possible future scenarios that are visible in the phantasm. The divergence, made possible by the disjunctive synthesis, must be acknowledged. The ego opens up towards chance.[111] For Deleuze, only such an affirmative use will enable true counter-actualisation. The horse possesses an infinity of characteristics and expresses an infinity of events. It makes noise and is insubordinate. At the same time it is clearly suffering and is unable to liberate itself from subjection. The horse is first of all a paradoxical instance, an 'object = x'. It allows the ego to participate in the disjunctive synthesis of divergent series.[112] It opens it up to different scenarios and allows it to construct solutions that are worthy of the problems proper to its environment. Hence little Hans is not only obedient but also capable of biting back and of enduring the various punishments.[113] His phantasm does not express the existence of a deeper lying life force. It must rather be considered as a precise construction that is developed within a given problematic field.

---

[110] I am referring to: '*Au lieu qu'un certain nombre de prédicats soient exclus d'une chose en vertu de l'identité de son concept, chaque « chose » s'ouvre à l'infini des prédicats par lesquels elle passe, en même temps qu'elle perd son centre, c'est-à-dire son identité comme concept ou comme moi.*' (LdS 204), (LoS 174).

[111] I refer to: '*Nous avons vu quel était le procédé de cette disjonction synthétique affirmative: il consiste dans l'érection d'une instance paradoxale, point aléatoire à deux faces impaires, qui parcourt les séries divergentes comme divergentes et les fait résonner par leur distance, dans leur distance. Ainsi le centre idéal de convergence est par nature perpétuellement décentré, il ne sert plus qu'à affirmer la divergence. C'est pourquoi il a semblé qu'un chemin ésotérique, excentré, s'ouvrait à nous, tout à fait différent du chemin ordinaire. Car ordinairement la disjonction n'est pas une synthèse à proprement parler, mais seulement une analyse régulatrice au service des synthèses conjonctives, puisqu'elle sépare les unes des autres les séries non convergentes; et chaque synthèse conjonctive à son tour tend elle-même à se subordonner à la synthèse de connexion, puisqu'elle organise les séries convergentes sur lesquelles elle porte en prolongement les unes des autres sous une condition de continuité.*' (LdS 204), (LoS 175).

[112] I allude to: '*il consiste dans l'érection d'une instance paradoxale, point aléatoire à deux faces impaires, qui parcourt les séries divergentes comme divergentes et les fait résonner par leur distance, dans leur distance.*' (LdS 204), (LoS 174).

[113] See DRF 82, TRM 92.

7. Love and nationalism

Can other common human experiences be elevated to the level of the phantasm? I wish to refer briefly to two examples, discussed in the previous chapters. One of those instances was the experience of love. It was argued that a person experiencing love out of the genital phase of the sexual position considers herself capable of complementing and restoring the other. This person considers herself as healing the disintegrated body of the partner. We have, nevertheless, also noticed that such a person can be quickly deprived of his good intentions. A narcissist leaves little space for the other. The other frequently does not want to be rescued or completed. What are the other possibilities? Deleuze does not follow here the road taken by Levinas or Jean Luc Marion.[114] Narcissism will not be lost at the moment when the other starts to play a more fundamental role. To Deleuze the question 'Does the other love me?' is far less fundamental than for the authors mentioned. The metaphysical surface transcends the separation between the ego and the other. Both instances are considered to be a result of, or a solution to, pre-individual interactions. The phantasm does not only allow for a true opening up towards the other, but also for becoming-other. The ego can be affected by character, posture, attitude or the kind of movement of the other. Little movements, perseverance, attentions and care are of fundamental importance here. The other must nevertheless, first of all, become the source of events that are able to take the ego by surprise and continue to change it. To use the concept of Deleuze and Guattari, the two persons form first of all an assemblage, a unity in diversity. They continually construct a new life and become an entity they have not been before. In this case, the other ceases to be an imperfect object in need of being restored. The relationship of mutual dependence is also different in nature from the depressive one. The other ceases to be an idealised object. He or she no longer has to be perfect in order to protect the ego. The phantasm leads to an acceptance of the other's existing imperfections. It leads to constructions in which these very imperfections actually in fact play a fundamental role for the relationship. The loss of the object of love is traumatic, but for reasons different from those in the case of the depressive position. The ego that has constructed a phantasm does not lose its sole foundation. The loss is traumatic for a person who was able to construct a phantasm for a different reason. His or her life becomes simply less thrilling and more predictable. The events made possible by the other can no longer be revealed. A mutual problematic field evaporates. An entire world disappears.

---

[114] See i.a. Marion (2003), *Le phénomène érotique*, Paris: Grasset 2003.

Similar characteristics can also be attributed to the experience of national or ethnic identity. A schizoid nationalist experiences his national identity merely as a partial good object. This identity temporarily allows the ego to alleviate tension. The sign expressing its identity might nevertheless quickly become the source of suffering. In that case it will quickly be replaced by another sign of identity. The depressive relation to one's national identity, on the other hand, implies that it is elevated to the status of the good object of the heights. The identity becomes an idealised object that must be protected against all possible attacks by bad partial objects aiming to deprive it of its purity. Every person that doubts or criticises the idealised object is kept at a distance or treated with aggression. Conflicts with threatening objects inevitably emerge. Yet another form of nationalism, more common in northern Europe, is narcissistic in nature. A narcissist does not have to continually endure the states of threat that continually disrupt the life of a depressive nationalist. Identification with a nation provides only a large sense of self-confidence. The narcissistic nationalist possesses knowledge and other qualities that allow him to act purposefully, convinced that the world improves as a consequence of his own actions. He is absolutely persuaded that he belongs to a better category of humans, one that is capable of changing the world. He is convinced that the others can and must become more like him. His trust in good intentions allows him to act violently upon others without even considering his own actions as violent in nature. In this case conflicts can emerge only when the narcissistic nationalist is confronted with and affected by the consequences of his own actions.

Can national identity be elevated to the level of the phantasm and lose even its narcissistic qualities? This might be possible, but only within very limited parameters. In that case, the embracing of the national identity must lead to a non-narcissistic opening towards the outside. It should lead, for example, to a process of becoming-minoritarian, a process that is still unknown to most of the inhabitants of the so-called civilised North. It should lead to a profound opening towards, for instance, minorities and to an acknowledgement of their contribution to one's own identity. 'I am a Dutchman' must in that sense become a phantasm that is brought about by a disjunctive synthesis. It must also imply statements such as 'I am a woman, Surinamese, Chinese, Turkish, Moroccan, Jew and a Pole'. The development of such a phantasm is not self-evident. It is only possible when, as also stressed by Laplanche and Pontalis, the sexual drives are liberated from the 'alimentary model,' when desire no longer pursues natural objects necessary for its direct survival.[115] Symbolisation and the phantasm are only attainable when the schizoid and depressive positions no longer dominate. Furthermore, it is solely possible once the destructive drives of the depths are left behind and once narcissism has been left behind.[116]

8. Conclusion

In this chapter the dynamic genesis of sense has been analysed firstly as a psychoanalytic theory about the nature of human desire, secondly as a philosophical theory analysing the emergence of the structures of sense and finally, as a specific development of Deleuze's thought about desire. In this chapter I have furthermore discussed several characteristics of the concept of the phantasm. We have seen that the phantasm belongs to the metaphysical surface. It is produced by the body and is at the same time also separated from it. It represents incorporeal events that cannot be determined by the laws of causality. The phantasm is virtual in nature. It has become apparent that for Deleuze the phantasm does not express an engagement of the subject with most fundamental and universal questions and problems of human existence. The problems encountered by the subject during his or her life are a multiplicity. Phantasm refers to events generating a variety of problems. It cannot be narrowed down to a limited number of questions. We have seen that a phantasm gives direction to action, and noticed that Deleuze once again implicitly criticised structuralist psychoanalysis. The unconscious cannot be interpreted by means of a pre-established structure, referring only to problems concerning sexuality. Deleuze criticises a restrictive use of disjunctive synthesis. A phantasm emerges out of an engagement with a problematic field and chance. Patients of psychoanalysts are not always afforded this possibility and are subjected to s limited system of representation. This situation is nevertheless reversible. Psychoanalysis can become a science of events. It can allow for the construction of a proper form of phantasm. To reach this goal it must cease to interpret desire. A psychoanalyst must allow for an affirmative use of disjunctive synthesis. He must allow for an orientation to an 'object = x'

---

[115] I discuss: '*Laplanche et Pontalis fondent le phantasme avec auto-érotisme, et le lient au moment où les pulsions sexuelles se dégagent du modèle alimentaire et abandonnent « tout objet naturel » (d'où l'importance qu'ils accordent au pronominal, et le sens qu'ils donnent aux transformations grammaticales comme telles dans la position non localisable du sujet).*' (LdS 252), (LoS 216).

[116] I refer to: '*Précisément, il nous semble que le phantasme à proprement parler ne trouve son origine que dans le moi du narcissisme secondaire, avec la blessure narcissique, avec la neutralisation, la symbolisation et la sublimation qui s'ensuivent.*' (LdS 252), (LoS 216).

or the quasi-cause, and strengthen the process of counter-actualisation. In that manner he can allow further sublimations and symbolisations. In the chapter I have also briefly stated that the phantasm does not express a hidden vitalism, supposedly characterising Deleuze's philosophy. Phantasm does not establish a connection with a hidden life force. It is always a construction, providing a solution adequate to a particular problematic field.

CHAPTER 7

Conclusion

1. Psychoanalysis

This book has been devoted to an *ad litteram* analysis of a relatively short part of Deleuze's work, *The Logic of Sense,* devoted to the analysis of the dynamic genesis of sense. The objective of this approach was to do justice both to the high degree of complexity of the arguments, regarding the nature of desire, developed in his book, and to give a reader who is relatively unskilled in both philosophy and psychoanalysis, a comprehensible reading of Deleuze's text. I claim that the dynamic genesis of sense is of crucial importance for a complete understanding of his attempts to understand the nature of desire and the unconscious. In the text I have analysed he not only reveals himself as greatly influenced by psychoanalysis but also develops several points of critique that are known from his later work. Guattari contributed greatly to both volumes of *Capitalism and Schizophrenia,* but a large part of the conceptual framework for those books was previously developed in *The Logic of Sense.* In this book it is apparent that Deleuze has already distanced himself from structuralist psychoanalysis. Desire cannot be interpreted by means of one single structure: structures are a multiplicity. They are constructions emerging in virtual and problematic fields.

The alternative to structuralist psychoanalysis is developed by referring to the ideas of Melanie Klein, a point hardly recognised in the reception of Deleuze and Guattari's work. Deleuze is particularly interested in her analysis of the bodily nature of unconscious phantasies. Her work supports his claim that desire may be thought of outside of the influence of language and the actualised structures of sense. For both Deleuze and Klein, psychopathology is primarily a bodily affair. The body experiences the most traumatic events of life and is of fundamental importance for the subsequent production of sense. Klein's work allows Deleuze to describe the unconscious as a dynamic system, consisting of various positions. In this book I have analysed the organisation of the schizoid, depressive and sexual positions, including their respective topology and phantasmatic objects. I have also analysed the process of the genesis of the subsequent positions. Chapter three addressed the way in which the central object of the depressive position – the idol – evolves out of the initial simulacrum of the body without organs, that is proper to the previous schizoid position. The idol itself also appears to be of fundamental importance during the genital period of the sexual position, topic analysed in Chapter four. The idol is a quasi-cause that allows for the emergence of the image of the phallus.

The idea of genesis allows Deleuze to criticise the structuralist psychoanalysis's approach to desire. The images or simulacra are not signifiers. They are not inscribed upon the body by an external structure or the symbolic order; for example, the emergence of the image of the phallus is a logical consequence of the process of genesis. It is an image of a reparative organ whose emergence is dependent upon the defusion of the drives, a process that occurs solely in the sexual position, and upon the previous existence of the idol. This image emerges when the ego is capable of distancing itself from both aggression and the self-preservation drives. His analysis of the role of good intentions in the sexual position moreover allows Deleuze to develop an alternative analysis of the Oedipus complex. According to him, Oedipus is driven by good intentions. Even in his unconscious, he does not wish to possess his mother, nor does he feel any kind of aggression towards his father. On the contrary, he wants to restore the disintegrated body of the mother and make the absent father present.

The fact that Melanie Klein's work allows Deleuze to develop a critique of the structuralist psychoanalysis does not mean that her theories are unreservedly embraced. We have observed that during the analysis of the castration-complex, Deleuze in the end distances himself from parts of her work. The fears of castration are not to be understood as only a symptom of a regression to the previous schizoid position. Castration is not merely proper to the depths and not only refers to a fear of attacks by bad partial objects. In addition a castration exists that is proper to the sexual position itself. It is characterised by the loss of the image of the phallus and the disintegration of the physical surface. The possible regression to the schizoid position is only one of the consequences of this castration by adsorption. In the final two chapters it was also argued that this final form of castration conveys a particular kind of possibility. According to Deleuze, it is possible to escape the terror of the castration complex. The loss of narcissism is not the end of the dynamic genesis. Castration by adsorption also leads to the liberation of a metaphysical or spiritual surface, one that allows for the development of a proper form of the phantasm and for an orientation to the various symbols.

The characteristics of the metaphysical surface have been discussed in Chapters five and six. In those chapters, I have briefly analysed the differences between the characteristics of this surface and the idea of the symbolic order, as described in structuralist psychoanalysis. According to Deleuze, sense is a multiplicity and is organised by means of various series that are never fused together into one rigid structure. Structures are always partial and virtual in nature. We have noticed that the scenes visible in phantasms constructed by the patients of Freud cannot be understood by referring merely to one problem and one structure. They express a continual search for solutions within a varying problematic field. The fears generated by the appearance of horses or of wolves in these patients' dreams and fantasies are not only an expression of a confrontation with the problems of (oedipal) sexuality, but also, and equally, concern other experiences and problems that are also social and economic in nature. Moreover the analysis by Deleuze allows us to rethink the nature of the relation of each subject towards its desire. The phantasm is not a source of knowledge about the fundamental and universal problems of existence. Desire should not be interpreted. Any act of interpretation is highly artificial. It can only subjugate the unconscious to an external structure of meaning. As such it will always impede a proper development of desire in its own problematic field. Phantasms are solutions that must be worthy of the problematic field in which they emerge. Desire must be continually produced.

Deleuze's conceptual step beyond Klein's work, found in the analysis of the castration complex and in the analysis of the phantasm, may be perceived as highly problematic by many psychoanalysts. Melanie Klein has a reason for being extremely careful in her analysis of a liberated sexuality. Viewed from her perspective, the attempt to go beyond sexuality can only lead to an undermining of the strength of the reparative tendencies and can only be understood as completely unreasonable. Her understanding of the nature of desire does not allow for any speculation about the proper form of the phantasm or about a possible orientation to events. The struggle of the libido against destructive drives is central to human nature. It is a battle that will never be concluded. The strengthening of the libido and the reparative tendencies is the only option. Monique David-Ménard (2005), a psychoanalyst and philosopher interested in the work of Deleuze, is of a similar opinion: Deleuze has unrealistic expectations with respect to clinical practice.[1] The psychic suffering of her patients cannot be eliminated. It is impossible to undertake attempts that will direct patients towards infinite events. It is not possible to claim the capacity of reaching joy and active affects, about which Spinoza writes. Suffering and continual sabotage of one's own happiness continually destabilise each subject. Negation and the destructive drives are the basic material with which each psychoanalytic practitioner has to work.

---

[1] See David-Ménard 2005: 147.

In her book, David-Ménard discusses the case study of a girl suffering from anorexia. According to her, we cannot expect that her patient will suddenly construct a phantasm. She cannot proceed to counter-effectuation or counter-actualisation. An anorexic patient will continue to suffer; she will prolong her own destructive behaviour by every means within her reach. A psychoanalytic practitioner can do nothing else but diminish the degree of her suffering. A patient will never become master of her own drives.[2] For David-Ménard, the most important goal of a therapy is nevertheless different from that of Klein. The latter aims to strengthen the ego by increasing belief in the existence of the complete good object and by development of the reparative tendencies. David-Ménard, on the other hand, trusts in the capacity of transformation allowed for during the psychoanalytic transference.[3] The analysis allows the patients to develop new perspectives towards their own suffering. They can develop new interpretations of their actions and challenge the old ones. The causes of suffering may be slowly removed only by such cognitive capacities. Transference introduces uncertainty that allows the patient to begin to doubt her own rigid interpretations. Only a re-interpretation will be able to introduce small changes of behaviour and make the desire less destructive.

Both critiques touch the very core of Deleuze's relationship to psychoanalysis. We can merely stress here that for Deleuze too, the complete annihilation of psychic suffering is absolutely unattainable. As with David-Ménard, he also stresses the importance of gaining distance towards one's own suffering. The

---

[2] As Monique David-Ménard writes: '*Cet exemple* (of anorexic patient – PS) *me paraît souligner qu'il est inexact d'opposer en bloc une conception du désir comme manque-à-être à cet autre thème selon lequel le désir ne manque rien. Car une cure analytique n'a pas affaire à une essence du désir, dont il s'agirait de se demander si elle relève d'une négation ontologique ou d'une affirmation. Une cure met en jeu des souffrances, des phénomènes de répétition que Freud rapportaient à une pulsion de mort; mais, justement, faire l'hypothèse que c'est par les répétitions que la pulsion de mort travaille, c'est la concevoir comme indissociable de ce dispositif du transfert.*' (David-Ménard 2005: 150).

[3] David-Ménard makes the following remark about the possibilities for the anorexic patient: '*Aller voir une analyste, pour Anne-Marie, c'était pouvoir se dire en détresse en s'adressant à une inconnue qu'elle avait, dans son économie interne, des raisons d'admirer. Il y avait donc là, en vertu même de sa souffrance, le déploiement de ce qu'on nomme, en psychanalyse, en transfert: cette délégation à un(e) autre du pouvoir de transformer un désespoir rampant en … autre chose d'inconnu. (…) Écouter cette analysante er laisser résonner dans le lieu de transfert quelques phrases concernant la teneur fantasmatique de sa détresse, c'est une initiative de l'analyste qui ouvre un autre espace que celui de la malédiction dans laquelle Anne-Marie se trouvait enfermée sans le savoir: l'alerte donnée par la confrontation au risque de sa propre mort se liait magiquement pour elle à sa folle idée d'une revanche, exercée contre le mari, par la maladie. Mais seul le fait de formuler cette angoisse auprès d'une analyste qui y cherchait autre chose que la réalisation magique d'une haine lui permit de faire le pari du fantasme, au lieu de s'enfermer dans la certitude d'une malédiction.*' (David-Ménard 2005: 149).

road to reach this point is nevertheless different. A patient has more options than are allowed for within the hermeneutic vocabulary used by David-Ménard. Transference must allow for more than only a distance from, and a possible reinterpretation of, the causes of psychic problems. The confrontation with the rigid interpretations, the opening towards chance, cannot be reached merely by an open conversation and the activity of questioning. For Deleuze, the goal of analysis must be defined in a different manner. Psychoanalysis must strengthen the process of constructing phantasms. The simulacrum of the body without organs is already fulfilling such a role in the case of anorexia. It can serve as a shield against the attacks by bad partial objects. Nevertheless the solution to anorexia cannot be found in the depths only. The simulacrum must be replaced by an idol and, if possible, by the image of the phallus. The strengthened good intentions may allow an anorexic patient to transform the rejection of food into a more creative activity. Her strengthened narcissism could make her condition manageable by an active repression of the destructive tendencies. As has been established, Deleuze goes further than this Kleinian alternative. Good intentions, supported by the narcissistic image, are not enough. An anorexic patient might, for example, develop the phantasm of Joan of Arc or becoming-woman discussed previously. She could start to believe in the force of her own femininity. The phantasm may enable a constructive resistance towards the environment. It is able to allow for a counter-effectuation. The suffering may become an opportunity. Anorexia, elevated to the surface of sense, can become a social practice that is full of sense. It might enable a meaningful relation towards the continuous flow of consumption products. It could also allow for an escape from the demands imposed upon women by the society. The opening to the metaphysical surface might in the end contribute to the development of a phantasm that is less destructive in nature than the simulacrum of the body without organs.[4] Nevertheless, this does not mean that one can easily overcome the limitations imposed by Melanie Klein on psychoanalytic practice. The strengthening of the reparative tendencies, in order to counterbalance the destructive urges, might still be the best option available for any psychoanalytic practitioner, a patient or in fact, any subject.

---

[4] It must be noted here that the therapies, developed in the experimental clinics such as *La Borde,* by amongst others, Guattari, are similar to the strategy discussed here. Additionally, in *La Borde,* interpretation of a patient's own desire was of minimal importance; and more emphasis was put on the constructions of new symbols. This goal was reached for example, by the patients to participate in artistic projects. See a.o. Dosse 2007.

2. Philosophical implications

The analysis of the dynamic genesis of sense also has more general philosophical implications, allowing us to draw a general picture concerning Deleuze's immanent ontology. God, Ideas, universal structure or a subject are not a fundament of knowledge. All these instances are constructions, emerging on an immanent problematic field. There exists no universal structure of sense that always expresses itself in human behaviour. A subject, too, is a construction or a solution emerging within immanence. The subject reflects the continuous movement proper to this virtual field. Furthermore, the materialist point of departure adopted by Deleuze does not mean that he considers thought to be fully determined by its physical base. The metaphysical surface or the surface of sense not only expresses the physical reality, but is also able to submit it to change. It was shown that the notion of event and quasi-causality plays a crucial role within the ontology of Deleuze. Sense, too, emerges in the communication between events proper to the metaphysical surface. We have examined the way in which this idea is applied to the analysis of the phantasm. A phantasm represents a variety of events. It allows for the construction of a particular problematic field with corresponding solutions. One of the crucial aspects of Deleuze's critique of structuralism and of any idealist philosophy, such as hermeneutics, is that phantasms allow for more than interpretation of the encountered problems. Production of sense is an activity that exceeds the activity of interpretation. Phantasms allow the ego to act and to transform itself instead of enabling the activity of understanding.

We have also observed that despite it not being a rigid structure, sense is not equal to complete chaos. Sense emerges out of the material interactions of the body with its environment as well as out of the communications between events. The environment in which it emerges is not chaotic but, rather, highly determined. We are seldom confronted with continually changing patterns of sense. An individual is capable of establishing new connections between the actual material entities only under very strict conditions. I have tried to show that the analysis of the dynamic genesis is an attempt to specify such conditions. We have realised that the ego, engaged in a free production of simulacra, characterising the schizoid position, is far removed from the production of sense. Such a weak ego is yet unaware of the existence of the already existing and actual structures and merely produces unengaged simulacra; in the end it is simply interested in minimising the potentially negative influence of the environment. Despite living in a self-created universe, the ego is not constructing sense. The depressive position introduces a very limited change.

The ego begins to perceive itself as a part of a larger whole. It starts to realise that it is restrained by external structures. Nevertheless, as in the case of previous position, we can hardly speak of any kind of independence with respect to those structures. The ego is incapable of understanding their nature. It subordinates itself to an organisation it does not comprehend. The language and sense fully transcend and determine the subject.

We have also observed that the sexual position leads to an important change. This position changes the nature of the orientation of a subject towards structures. The ego is no longer blindly submitting itself to the external structures. It increasingly gains independence. In the pre-genital phase, it starts to engage the environment, although still in a fully dependent manner. The various egos aim at experiences of pleasure, but do not exercise any kind of influence on the structures of sense. This state alters in the genital phase. Upon the emergence of the image of the phallus, the ego starts to perceive itself as a full-fledged member of the environment. The ego claims the capacity to change those structures. It presumes that the environment may be amended to its own wishes. It claims the capacity to unify the fragmented experience. The subject constitutes the structures of sense and starts to function as the fundament of knowledge. We have nevertheless noticed that the attempts of the ego to establish such a unity are doomed to fail. No unified structure of sense can emerge; the subject cannot be the ultimate ground of reality. A naive belief in his own control of the world is quickly ruined. The transformation of the actualised patterns is not easy to reach. The loss of narcissism may nevertheless potentially lead to a new perception of the nature of the structures of sense: the ego may start to realise that it emerges out of a multiplicity. Sense constructed on the metaphysical surface is always partial. It is a dynamic system of relationships that are both expressing the material circumstances and freely communicating between each other. Only an ego that comes to realise this, can engage in the construction of new patterns. An orientation to infinite events – the acceptance of the contingent nature of sense – alone, allows for an escape from the grip of the actual. Construction of sense is solely possible once its virtual nature is acknowledged. The virtual alone serves as the ground of the actual.

The analysis of the notion of event and of the virtual has been a subject of a broad and ongoing philosophical debate. One of the most interesting critiques of Deleuze has been expressed by Alain Badiou and Peter Hallward.[5] Both philosophers try to demonstrate that Deleuze's philosophy is metaphysical, impractical and escapist in nature. It provides barely any ground for a subject

---

[5]   See Badiou (2000), (2006), (2009) and Peter Hallward (2006).

who is willing to act in order to change its world. According to both, no socially and politically engaged organisation can make use of the concepts developed by Deleuze. Hallward focuses his critique on the concept of counter-effectuation, which is supposedly typical of the escapist tendencies characterising Deleuze's philosophy.[6] According to Hallward Deleuze is not interested in the process of actually changing contemporary world's social and political problems. The immense degree of social and political inequality or the true psychic suffering of psychoanalytic patients would be of no interest to him. Deleuze's goal is transformation for the sake of transformation. His whole philosophical oeuvre is a boring repetition of an analysis of attempts to escape the imposition of an external order on the desiring body. Hallward's premise is that this is exactly the reason why the phantasm can never gain a precise formulation. It must allow for continuous change to occur and should therefore never be precisely determined. Deleuze's philosophy is vitalist and escapist in nature.

Hallward contends that the philosopher Alain Badiou, who has analysed the conditions under which a subject can become an active participant in the construction of concrete reality, alone provides contemporary subjects with conceptual tools to think about political action. In books such as *The Logics of the Worlds,* Badiou attempts to analyse conditions under which a subject can leave an eventless or atonal world. A free subject can be faithful to an event and a universal truth revealed by it. He is consequently able to make stepwise attempts to construct a world made possible by an event. Badiou's famous example is Spartacus. The event – the slaves rising against their masters – is represented by a phrase, *'Nous, esclaves, nous voulons retourner chez nous.'*[7] This phrase refers to an unrealised new world without slavery, one where achievement of equality between humans has become possible. It is a world that was unthinkable before this particular event and the subsequent revolt initiated by Spartacus. This precise phrase opens a world of possibilities. A new world can be realised by subjects faithful to an event and the truth revealed in it. The event forces the subjects to act in a precise manner in order to realise the new world. Such profound will and faithfulness to an event seem entirely incomprehensible from the perspective of Deleuze's philosophy.[8] Deleuze recognises the importance of events but does not connect them directly to the idea of truth, nor does he reveal how an event can contribute to the emergence of a new world. According to Badiou and Hallward, Deleuze is uninterested in

---

[6] See Chapter six of *Out of this World* (Hallward 2006).
[7] See Alain Badiou 2006: 59, 2009: 51. 'We slaves, we want to return home.'
[8] See Hallward 2006: 161.

the necessity of organising political and individual action. An event exists for itself; as an ultimate goal of action, it is always ahead of a subject. It is posed as always unreachable. Making of normative statements becomes impossible. Both philosophers contend that Deleuze preaches about change for the sake of change and does not offer any concepts that might help us to guide our public and private lives.

Our analysis of the dynamic genesis of sense allows us to partially dismiss this critique. It has been made clear that Deleuze is not a vitalist. He does not analyse the conditions of possibility for the expression of a deeper-lying life force. Deleuze is not interested in change for the sake of change, even in his account of counter-effectuation. Each phantasm can and must be formulated in a concrete manner, always emerging in precise circumstances and providing a solution that must be adequate to the constructed problematic field. The notion of counter-effectuation specifically allows for the construction of such a field and for the development of a precise response. It continually establishes communication between events. Counter-effectuation facilitates the development of adequate solutions to the encountered problems. Holding on to just one formulation of the phantasm and to just one supposedly clearly defined problem, as in the case of Badiou, is impossible. It unjustly limits the problematic field. Viewed from the perspective of the dynamic genesis, each attempt to construct the phantasm that is as limited as Badiou wants it to be, can solely possess a narcissistic character. Badiou presupposes that it is possible to have a complete grip on the process of production of sense. He wrongly assumes that the structures of sense can be unified or that the encountered problems are as narrow as he defines them. Viewed from our perspective, the phrase that facilitates the subjective orientation to an event may alone be treated as an image of the phallus. It is an image that supports narcissism, an instance that must be lost by adsorption in order to allow for a different relationship to the world.

As the later books of Deleuze and Guattari, *The Logic of Sense* is also not asserting an escapist position and reveals a true interest in practical and normative questions and choices made in real life. Each phantasm must be very carefully constructed. The problematic field in which it emerges, can change its nature. He emphasises that each phantasm may suddenly facilitate the expression of destructive drives of the depths. This is the reason why Deleuze stresses the importance of counter-effectuation. A subject must always be responsive to the newly emerging problems. Contemporary politics provides us with enough examples of ideas that quickly modify their nature by beginning to function in a completely different, problematic, field.

In contemporary Europe, the idea of freedom of speech has been entirely separated from its initial problematic field. It has suddenly become a notion in the service of the most conservative, if not racist, forces on the continent. It has become a false solution, entirely unrelated to the initial problem of the inequality it aimed at resolving. Only flexibility, introduced by Deleuze to his analysis of the phantasm, can prevent similar scenarios from occurring. The French new philosophers, who were briefly mentioned in Chapter five, are an uncomfortable example in this respect. Some of the former French Maoists have become the most fervent defenders of the contemporary conservative status quo. They no longer attempt to challenge the tremendous power-differences and exploitation shattering the contemporary world. The new philosophers have become disenchanted. They have lost their narcissistic belief in their capacity to create a righteous world by a rigid application of the thoughts of Marx, Lenin and Mao. In fact, they went through an irreversible regression and are now doomed to continue their manic attempts to veil the loss of the good object. Badiou's philosophy, in fact, faces a similar challenge. Its rigid appeal to a transcendent truth and subjective faithfulness to an event does not constitute an answer to the defenders of the false democracy that veils the exploitation generated by contemporary for of capitalism.[9] Deleuze makes an attempt to develop a more profound alternative than the one developed by Badiou. He attempts to conceptualise a far more profound form of engagement with the politics of public and individual life, than that envisaged by his critics. Deleuze's point of departure is a critique of the drawbacks of an engagement that takes the depressive or narcissistic positions as a starting point. Phantasms, guiding individual and collective actions, must be freed from such depressive and narcissist elements. I have tried to indicate that the concepts building on the idea of the phantasm in particular, and further developed in the work with Guattari, such as becoming-minoritarian, becoming-women, becoming-invisible, serve such a goal. They have been developed out of the initial analysis of the various positions analysed in *The Logic of Sense*.

3. The Logic of Sense *and the collaboration with Guattari*

The analysis of desire in *The Logic of Sense* has been unjustly overlooked in the reception of the work of Deleuze. It is of considerable significance for the systematic understanding of both the collaboration between Deleuze and

---

[9] For a fierce critique of the new philosophers see Deleuze 1977, 'A propos des nouveaux philosophes et d'un problème plus général', in DRF, pp. 127-135, TRM 139-147.

Guattari as well as Deleuze's earlier texts. In Chapter three, I have for example indicated that the analysis of the positions distinguished in the dynamic genesis is relevant for a proper understanding of the earlier analysis of masochism; developed in *Coldness and Cruelty*. In this earlier book, Deleuze is already making implicit use of Melanie Klein's terminology and speaks, for example, of the phantasm of 'good mother'. I have also come to the conclusion that the differences between the individual work by Deleuze and that arising from the cooperation with Guattari, should not be overestimated.[10] The cooperation is a continuation of the former's earlier work, despite the fact that a large number of the concepts developed by Guattari greatly enhance our understanding of the social and political dimensions of desire.[11] The rhetoric used to write about psychoanalysis changes radically and becomes aggressive in tone. In their common work, Deleuze and Guattari also develop concepts that replace analysis in terms of depths, heights and the physical and metaphysical surfaces. They write about various desiring machines and assemblages.[12] Nevertheless, the earlier concepts continue to play a fundamental role. In *Anti-Oedipus*, both thinkers use the concepts of the body without organs and speak of the schizoid, paranoid, narcissistic and miraculating machines. They also continue to work on the connective, disjunctive and conjunctive synthesises that have been analysed in this text.

The importance of *The Logic of Sense* for Deleuze's later work, is for example particularly apparent in the analysis of Freud's writing about Schreber in the introduction to *Anti-Oedipus*. Deleuze and Guattari dismiss the Freudian interpretation of Schreber's paranoia, which makes extensive use of oedipal terminology and emphasises the latter's relationship with the father. According to Freud, the origin of the paranoia can only be found in Schreber's repressed homosexual desire towards his father. He represses this desire and becomes anxious about all fatherly figures, among which is his psychiatrist. Deleuze and Guattari, on the other hand, demonstrate that the paranoia of Schreber cannot be traced to oedipal bodily desire. The paranoia emerges primarily due to the impact of social machines on Schreber. He fears his father, not for being his father, but because of his ideas about the upbringing of children. Schreber's father has been an inventor of all kinds of sadistic machines, amongst which

---

[10] The break between the two periods of his work is stressed among others by Žižek (2004: xi).

[11] For the analysis of the influence of the earlier work of Deleuze on Guattari, see Dosse (2007: 15, 233, 269). For analysis of the impact of Guattari on Deleuze, see also Berardi (2008: 43).

[12] Deleuze observes the following about the shifts occurring in the collaboration with Guattari: '*Je crois que nous avons cherché d'autres directions parce que nous en avions le désir. L'Anti-Œdipe n'a plus ni hauteur, ni profondeur, ni surface. Là tout arrive, se fait, les intensités, les multiplicités, les événements, sur une sorte de corps sphérique ou de tableau cylindrique: corps sans organes.*' (DRF: 60), (TRM: 66).

is a particular kind of chastity belt. He enforced 'correct' behaviour upon his son. Schreber's delirium is consequently greatly influenced through the experiments by his father that were carried out on him and other children. His delirium concerns the educational system and the sadistic behaviour exercised in the name of this system.

The analysis of the impact of the social machines on the individual desire can be carried out partially well also with the conceptual framework developed in *The Logic of Sense*. We have also understood that Deleuze has criticised Freud's analysis of the various grammatical transformations, proper to a phantasm. Reversal of a drive cannot explain the emergence of paranoia. We have perceived that the phantasm constructed on the metaphysical surface, not only concerns the bodily problematic but also engages the environment of a subject. The concepts by means of which both Deleuze and Guattari conceptualise a subsequent transformation of the suffering of Schreber into a new form of desire do not differ greatly from the earlier individual work of Deleuze. In *Anti-Oedipus* Deleuze and Guattari emphasise that Schreber's suffering is overcome by means of the process of becoming-woman. Schreber constructs a solitary machine.[13] He transforms the negative experiences of the past into a new machine by dressing as a woman. We have seen that becoming-woman can be understood as a phantasm. It is a solution to a properly constructed problematic field, Deleuze writes about in his earlier work. It depends on counter-effectuation, on a particular way of synthesising events.

Nevertheless, the interaction between individual desire and the social and political machines has not been the central part of the current analysis. Rather, I have concentrated on the analysis of the different ways in which individual desire may relate to these machines, without sufficiently discussing the mechanisms governing these very machines. To develop a full image of the working of desire, such an analysis of various institutions and discourses

---

[13] In *Anti-Oedipus* they make the following point: 'Freud is more specific when he stresses the crucial turning point that occurs in Schreber's illness when Schreber becomes reconciled to becoming-woman and embarks upon a process of self-cure that brings him back to the equation Nature = Production (the production of a new humanity). As a matter of fact, Schreber finds himself frozen in the pose and trapped in the paraphernalia of a transvestite, at a moment when he is practically cured and has recovered all his faculties: "I am sometimes to be found, standing before the mirror or elsewhere, with the upper portion of my body partly bared, and wearing sundry feminine adornments, such as ribbons, trumpery necklaces, and the like. This occurs only, I may add, when I am *by myself*, and never, at least so far as I am able to avoid it, in the presence of other people." Let us borrow the term "celibate machine" to designate this machine that succeeds the paranoiac machine and the miraculating machine, forming a new alliance between the desiring-machines and the body without organs so as to give birth to a new humanity or a glorious organism.' (AO: 17).

governing them is indispensable. Only such an analysis can lead to a fully critical understanding of the role of psychoanalysis in contemporary society. In their common endeavours, Deleuze and Guattari analyse the impact of the various economic modes of production on desire. Basing their argument on the work of Marx, they differentiate between the primitive, despotic (feudal) and capitalist modes of production.[14] According to both philosophers, the structure of the economy exercises a profound influence on the nature of the structures of sense and therefore on the nature of desire. The economic base produces different regimes of representation that subsequently develop different social practices and systems of thought. These regimes of representation understand the individual desire only in ways that contribute to a smooth functioning of the corresponding economic modes of production. Given the analysis of *The Logic of Sense,* we are simply able to emphasise that for example, the despotic mode of production – presupposing a strict hierarchy of social and economic relations – functions in the most productive manner when the depressive tendencies in individual desire are being strengthened. The corresponding regime of representation will thus generate conditions under which the orientation to an idol will be of fundamental importance. Such a regime will minimise the development of both the schizoid and narcissistic tendencies that might unnecessarily challenge the stable functioning of the function of authority and therefore destabilise the equilibrium of the economic relations.

The critique of psychoanalysis developed in *Anti-Oedipus* is motivated by the analysis of the production of desire under the capitalist mode of production, a topic hardly covered in this book. According to Deleuze and Guattari, capitalism functions most smoothly given an organisation of desire that corresponds with what I have analysed as the schizoid and narcissistic positions.[15] The subjects are in that case either doomed to consume in an uncritical manner or to believe in their own reparative powers. They must think of themselves as independent of the hierarchic structures of power. The regime of representation, proper to the capitalist mode of production, is capable of directly imposing limits upon this independence. It thrives only if limitations are imposed upon desire. According to Deleuze and Guattari, psychoanalysis is one of the institutions that enables the imposing of such limitations. It conceptualises desire as physical and not social in nature, subsequently analysing it by means of a very limited conceptual framework.

---

[14] For the analysis of the three modes of production and the corresponding regimes of production see Chapter three. LAO (163-324), AO: (139- 272).

[15] Deleuze and Guattari analyse the influence of capitalism on the psyche, for example in LAO: 292, 298. AO: 245, 251. They nevertheless emphasise that the determination by the economic modes of production is always partial.

Psychoanalysis prevents its patients from discovering the social and political aspects of their phantasms. In this text, I have indicated that anorexia can be understood by means of a broader field of references. Anorexia has nothing to do with Oedipus. The major causes of anorexia can be found in a society that values limitless consumption, one that directs limitless flow of consumption products on the vulnerable bodies of women, men and particularly young girls.

Do Deleuze and Guattari offer us suggestions about the manners in which the construction of desire should be exercised? Philosophers such as Žižek have criticised both writers for overemphasising the positive aspects of schizophrenia.[16] They supposedly perceive the possibility of a critical engagement with reality in a limitless production of desire alone, one that is unbothered by boundaries imposed upon it by external structures.[17] For Žižek, such an approach would be a mistake. A schizophrenic can never be a role model for a contemporary critical philosopher, a political activist, or for a psychoanalytic patient. Schizophrenia does not allow for a critical engagement with reality. It does not liberate anybody from the negative effects of some of the social and political machines. In their common work, Deleuze and Guattari have neglected the importance of the notion of event and the phantasm, initially developed in *The Logic of Sense*. At first sight Žižek seems to be correct in his claim that *The Logic of Sense* might be more interesting for his goals. An uncritical endorsement of schizophrenia is indeed absent in this book. Schizophrenia belongs to the depths. The engagement with the work of Klein forces Deleuze to point towards the suffering and tension proper to this state. The schizoid position is characterised as uncritical and disconnected from the structures of sense. It should be overcome at all costs. Any mechanism that might trigger it must be denounced. Only the phantasm offers a solution to the ego by allowing it to orient itself to infinite events. The difference in the use of the concept of schizophrenia in the individual work of Deleuze and his common work with Guattari has only been partially analysed here. We can, nevertheless, rehearse the argument developed above. The opposition between the earlier and later statements is merely superficial. The differentiation between the schizophrenia of the depths and the phantasm of the surface is actually also present in the later work. I have pointed to this fact in the brief analysis of Schreber's case. Deleuze and Guattari differentiate between machines capable of an engagement with an event and machines incapable of reaching it. In their later work they also make a distinction between the

---

[16] Žižek 2004: 21.
[17] LAO: 292, AO: 245. See Žižek (2004: 183).

processes of re-territorialisation on the one hand and relative and absolute de-territorialisation on the other. All these processes have to be approached with a sense of prudence. Deleuze and Guattari are fully aware of the dangers of assemblages that are too destructive in nature and that never reach any kind of internal coherence. In the terminology of *The Logic of Sense,* also in their mutual work the philosophers continue to warn against phantasms that are too excessively oriented towards events. They warn against phantasms that are not related to a carefully constructed problematic field and that do not allow for the development of solutions that would be adequate to this field.[18]

---

[18] In *A Thousand Plateaus* Deleuze and Guattari point to the dangers of excessive de-territorialisation. See i.a. MP: 201, 205, ATP: 162.

References

Badiou, Alain, (2000), *Deleuze: The clamour of being*, Cambridge: MIT Press.

_____. (2006), *Logiques de Mondes,* Paris: Seuil.

_____. (2009), *Logics of Worlds: Being and Event II*, London: Continuum.

_____. (2012), *The Rebirth of History: Times of Riots and Uprisings*, London: Verso.

Bednarek, Joanna, (2012), 'Logika sensu – najbardziej lacanowska z książek Deleuze'a?,' *Praktyka Teoretyczna*, nr 5/2012.

Bégoin, Jean, (1974), 'L'Anti-Œdipe ou la destruction envieuse du sein', in Privat, Edouard, (ed.), (1974), *Les chemins de l'anti-œdipe*, Toulouse: Bibliothèque de Psychologie Clinique, pp. 139-159.

Benveniste, Jacques, (1966), *Problemes de linguistique générale*, Paris: Gallimard.

Berardi, Franco, (2008), *Felix Guattari, Thought, Friendship and Visionary Cartography*, New York: Palgrave.

Bergson, Henri, (1919), *L'Energie spirituelle*, Paris: PUF.

Boundas, Constantin, (2005), 'Virtual/Virtuality,' in Adrian Parr, (ed.), *The Deleuze Dictionary*, Edinbourgh: EUP, pp. 296-299.

Bowden, Sean, (2011), *The priority of Events – Deleuze's Logic of Sense*, Edinburgh: EUP.

Brehier, Emile, (1907), *La théorie des incorporels dans l'ancien stoicisme*, Paris: Picard.

Bryant, Paul Levi, (2009), 'Individuering', in van Tuinen *et al.*, (eds), *Deleuze Compendium*, Amsterdam: Boom, pp. 372.

David-Ménard, Monique, (2005), *Deleuze et la psychanalyse*, Paris: PUF.

Deleuze, Gilles, (1953), *Empirisme et Subjectivité*, Paris: PUF.

_____. (1962), *Nietzsche et la philosophie*, Paris: Les Éditions de Minuit.

_____. (1963), *La philosophie critique de Kant*, Paris: Les Éditions de Minuit.

_____. (1966), *Le Bergsonisme*, Paris: PUF.

_____. (1967), *Presentation de Sacher Masoch*, Paris: Les Éditions de Minuit.

_____. (1968), *Spinoza et le problème de l'expression*, Paris: Les Éditions de Minuit.

_____. (1968), *Différence et Répétion,* Paris: PUF.

_____. (1969), *Logique du Sens*, Paris: Les Éditions de Minuit.

_____. (1970), *Spinoza – Philosophie pratique*, Paris: Les Éditions de Minuit.

_____. (1973), 'A quoi reconnaît-on le *structuralisme*,' in François Châtelet, (dir.), *Histoire de la philosophie VIII. Le XXe siècle,* Paris: Hachette, 1973 [édition de poche: coll. 'Pluriel', 2000].

_____. (1977), *Dialogues*, Paris: Flamarion.

_____. (1986), *Foucault*, Paris: Les Éditions de Minuit.

_____. (1988a), *Le pli*, Paris: Les Éditions de Minuit.

_____. (1988), *Bergsonism*, New York: Zone Books.

_____. (1988b), *Périclès et Verdi: La philosophie de François Châtelet*, Paris: Les Éditions de Minuit.

_____. (1989), *Coldness and Cruelty*, New York: Urzone, Inc.

_____. (1990), *The Logic of Sense*, New York: CUP.

_____. (1993), *Critique en Clinique*, Paris: Les Éditions de Minuit.

_____. (1994), *Difference and Repetition*, New York: CUP.

_____. (1997), *Essays Critical and Clinical*, Minneapolis: University of Minnesota Press.

_____. (2002), *L'île Déserte*, Paris: Les Éditions de Minuit.

_____. (2003), *Deux régimes de fous*, Paris: Les Éditions de Minuit.

_____. (2004), *Desert Islands*, Los Angeles: Semiotext(e).

_____. (2006), *Two regimes of Madness*, Los Angeles: Semiotext(e).

Deleuze, Gilles & Guattari, Felix, (1972), *L'Anti-Œdipe*, Paris: Les Éditions de Minuit.

_____. (1980), *Mille Plateaux*, Paris: Les Éditions de Minuit.

_____. (1983), *Anti-Oedipus*, Minneapolis: University of Minnesota Press.

_____. (1987), *A Thousand Plateaus*, Minneapolis: University of Minnesota Press.

_____. (1991), *Qu'est-ce que la philosophie?*, Paris: Les Éditions de Minuit.

_____. (1994), *What is Philosophy?*, London: Verso.

Derrida, Jacques, (1982), *Margins of philosophy*, Brighton: The Harvest Press.

_____. (1987), *The Post-card. From Socrates to Freud and beyond*, Chicago: The University of Chicago Press.

_____. (1990), 'Force of law', *Cardozo Law Review*, vol 11: 919, pp. 943.

Dosse, François, (2007), *Gilles Deleuze et Félix Guattari, Biographie Croisée*, Paris: La Découverte.

_____. (2010), *Gilles Deleuze and Felix Guattari, intersecting lives*, New York: CUP.

Fink, Bruce, (1997), *Lacanian Psychoanalysis, theory and technique*, Cambridge: HUP.

Foucault, Michel, (1966), *Les mots et les choses*, Paris: Gallimard.

_____. (1970), 'Teatrum Philosophicum,' *Critique* 282, pp. 885-908.

_____. (1978), *History of Sexuality, vol. 1, The will to knowledge*, New York: Pantheon Books.

Freud, Sigmund, (1905a), 'Fragment of an analysis of a case of Hysteria (1905[1901]),' in Freud, S. (1953), *The Standard Edition of the complete psychological works of Sigmund Freud, volume VII, (1901-1905)*, London: The Hogarth Press Ltd, pp. 3-124.

_____. (1905b), 'Three Essays on the Theory of Sexuality,' in Freud, S. (1953), *The Standard Edition of the complete psychological works of Sigmund Freud, volume VII, (1901-1905)*, London: The Hogarth Press Ltd, pp. 130-248.

_____. (1908), 'Character and anal erotism', in Freud, S. (1959), *The Standard Edition of the complete psychological works of Sigmund Freud, volume IX, (1906-1908)*, London: The Hogarth Press Ltd, pp. 167-177.

_____. (1909), 'Analysis of a phobia in a five-year-old boy', in Freud, S. (1955), *The Standard Edition of the complete psychological works of Sigmund Freud, volume X, (1909)*, London: The Hogarth Press Ltd, pp. 5-152.

_____. (1910), 'Antithetical meaning of primal words,' in Freud, S. (1957), *The Standard Edition of the works of Freud, Volume XI (1910)*, London: The Hogarth Press, pp. 153-161.

_____. (1911), 'Psycho-analytic notes on an autobiographical account of a case of paranoia (Dementia Paranoides),' in Freud, S. (1955), *The Standard Edition of the complete psychological works of Sigmund Freud, volume XII, (1911-1913)*, London: The Hogarth Press Ltd, pp. 3-84.

_____. (1915), 'Instincts and their Vicissitudes,' in Freud, S. (1955), *The Standard Edition of the complete psychological works of Sigmund Freud, volume XIV, (1914-1916)*, London: The Hogarth Press Ltd.

_____. (1918), 'From the history of an infantile neurosis,' in Freud, S. (1955), *The Standard Edition of the complete psychological works of Sigmund Freud, volume XVII, (1917-1919)*, London: The Hogarth Press Ltd., pp. 7-124.

_____. (1919), 'A Child is being beaten: A contribution to the study of the origin of sexual perversion,' in Freud, S.(1955), *The Standard Edition of the complete psychological works of Sigmund Freud, volume XVII (1917-1919)*, London: The Hogarth Press Ltd., pp. 175-204.

_____. (1923), '*The Ego and the Id*', in Freud, S., (1989), *The Freud Reader*, New York: Norton & Company.

_____. (1961), *Beyond Pleasure Principle*, New York: Norton & Company.

_____. (1962), *Civilization and its discontents*, New York: Norton & Company.

_____. (1989), *The Freud Reader*, New York: Norton & Company.

Geyskens, Tomas, (2006), 'Deleuze over Sacher-Masoch – Literatuur als symptomatologie,' *Tijdschrift voor Filosofie* 68, pp. 779-801.

Gross, Jan, (2006), *Fear: Anti-Semitism in Poland after Auschwitz: An Essay in Historical Interpretation*, New Jersey: Princeton University Press.

_____. (2011): *Złote żniwa. Rzecz o tym, co się działo na obrzeżach zagłady Żydów*, Kraków: Znak.

Grossman, Evelyne & Jacob Rogozinski, (2008) 'Deleuze lecteur d'Artaud', *Rue Descartes* 59(1), pp. 77-91.

Grossman, David, (2007), 'interview', 15 sept 2007,
http://www.guardian.co.uk/books/2007/sep/15/featuresreviews.guardianreview2 (seen October 2011).

Hallward, Peter, (2006), *Out of this World*, London: Verso.

Heidegger, Martin, (2008), *Nietzsche*, Stuttgart: Klett-Cotta Verlag.

Heimann, Paula, (1952), 'Notes on the Theory of the Life and Death Instincts,' in Klein *et al.,* (eds.), *Developments in Psycho-analysis*, London: The Hogarth Press.

Holland, Eugene, (1999), *Deleuze and Guattari's Anti-Oedipus*, London: Routledge.

Isaacs, Susan (1948), 'The Nature and Function of Phantasy,' *International Journal of Psychoanalysis* 29, pp. 73-97.

_____. (1952) 'The Nature and Function of Phantasy,' in Klein, Heiman *et al.,* (eds.), *Developments in Psycho-Analysis*, pp. 67-121.

Kerslake, Christian, (2006), *Deleuze and the Unconscious*, London: Continuum.

_____. (2009), *Immanence and the Vertigo of Philosophy: From Kant to Deleuze*, Edinburgh: Edinburgh University Press.

de Kesel, Marc, (2009), 'Logique du Sens' in van Tuinen *et al.*, (eds.), *Deleuze Compendium*, Amsterdam: Boom.

Klein, Melanie, (1930), 'The importance of symbol formation in the Development of the Ego, in Mitchell, Juliet, (ed.) 1986, *The Selected Melanie Klein*, (1986), New York: The Free Press, pp. 95-114.

_____. (1935), 'A contribution to the psychogenesis of manic-depressive states,' in Mitchell, Juliet, (ed.), *The Selected Melanie Klein*, (1986), New York: The Free Press, pp. 115-145.

_____. (1940), 'Mourning and its relation to manic-depressive states', in Mitchel, Juliet, (ed.), *The Selected Melanie Klein*, (1986), New York: The Free Press, pp. 146-174.

_____. (1947) 'Notes on some Schizoid Mechanisms?' in Mitchell, Juliet, (ed.), *The Selected Melanie Klein*, (1986), New York: The Free Press, pp. 175-200.

_____. (1997), *The Psychoanalysis of Children*, London: Vintage.

Klein, Melanie, Heiman, Paula et al., (eds.), (1952), *Developments in Phycho-Analysis*, London: The Hogarth Press Ltd.

Klossowski, Pierre, (1997), *Nietzsche and the vicious circle*, London: The Athlone Press.

Kristeva, Julia, (2001), *Melanie Klein*, New York: CUP.

Lacan, Jacques, (1953), 'Some Reflections on the Ego,' *International Journal Psycho-Analysis* 34, p. 11.

_____. (1953-1954), *Le Séminaire I*, unpublished version.

_____. (1956-57), *Seminar 1956-1957, La relation d'objet*, unpublished version.

_____. (1966), *Écrits I*, Paris: Seuil.

_____. (1966), *Écrits II*, Paris: Seuil

Laermans, Rudi, (2009), 'Verlangen', in van Tuinen (et al), (eds), *Deleuze Compendium*, Amsterdam: Boom.

Lampert, Jay, (2006), *Deleuze and Guattari's Philosophy of History*, London: Continuum.

Lear, Jonathan, (2005), *Freud*, New York: Routledge.

Laplanche, Jean, (1976), *Life and Death in Psychoanalysis*, Baltimore: The Johns Hopkins University Press.

_____. (2000), 'The other within,' *Radical Philosophy* 102, pp 33.

Laplanche, Jean and Jean-Bertrand Pontalis (1967), *Vocabulaire de psychanalyse*, Paris: PUF.

_____. (1973), *Language of Psycho-Analysis*, London: The Hogarth Press.

_____. (1985), *Fantasme originaire, fantasmes des origines, origine du fantasme*, Paris: Hachette.

_____. (1986), 'Fantasy and the Origins of Sexuality,' in Burgin, V. *et al.*, (eds)., *Formations of Fantasy*, London: Methuen.

Leder, A., (2014), *Prześniona Rewolucja*, Warszawa: Krytyka Polityczna.

Marion, Jean Luc, (2003), *Le phénomène érotique*, Paris: Grasset.

Massumi, Brian, (1987), 'Realer that real, The Simulacrum According to Deleuze and Guattari,' in *Copyright* no.1.

Meillassoux, Quentin, (2007), 'Subtraction and Contraction, Deleuze's remarks on *Matter and Memory*,' in *Collapse III,* pp. 63-108.

Miłosz, Cz., (1953), *Captive Mind*, London: Vintage Books.

Mitchel, Juliet, (ed.), *The Selected Melanie Klein,* (1986), New York: The Free Press.

Patton, Paul and John Protevi, (eds), (2003), *Between Deleuze & Derrida*, London: Continuum.

Pearson, Keith Ansel, (2007), 'review of Jay Lampart, Deleuze and Guattari's Philosophy of History, *Notre Dame philosophical reviews* (2007.03.06).

Plato, (1989), *Sophist*, Amsterdam: Uitgeverij de Driehoek.

Privat, Edouard, (ed.), (1974), *Les chemins de l'anti-œdipe*, Toulouse: Bibliothèque de Psychologie Clinique.

Roffe, J., (2011), *Badiou's Deleuze*, Montreal: McGill-Queen's University Press.

Rogozinski, Jacob, (2008), 'Deleuze lecteur d'Artaud,' *Rue Descartes* 59 (1), pp. 77-91.

Simondon, Gilbert, (1964), *L'Individu et sa genèse physico-biologique*, Paris: PUF.

Sellars, John (2006), 'An Ethics of the event, Deleuze's stoicism,' in *Angelaki,* Vol 2: 3, pp. 157-171.

Smith, Daniel, (2003), 'Mathematics and the Theory of Multiplicities: Deleuze and Badiou Revisited,' *Southern Journal of Philosophy* 41, pp. 411-449.

Stengers, Isabel, Didier Debeise, (et al), (2004), 'Majeure: Politiques de l' individuation. Penser avec Simondon', in *Multitudes* 2004 (18), pp. 15-106.

Toscano, Alberto, (2006), *The Theatre of Production – Philosophy and Individuation between Kant and Deleuze*, London: Palgrave.

Tort, Michel, (2005), *Fin du dogme paternel*, Paris: Éditions Flammarion.

van Tuinen, Sjoerd, Ed Romein, Marc Schuilenburg, (eds.), (2009), *Deleuze Compendium*, Amsterdam: Boom.

van Haute, Philippe, (2001), *Against Adaptation*, New York: Other Press.

_____. (2008) 'Lacan reads Klein: some remarks on the body in psychoanalytic thought,' *Philosophy Today*, pp.54-62.

van Haute, P. and Geyskens, T, (2004), *Confusion of tongues. The primacy of sexuality in Freud, Ferenczi and Laplanche*, New York: Other Press.

_____. (2007), *From death instinct to attachment theory: the primacy of the child in Freud, Klein, and Harmann*, New York: Other Press.

_____. (2012), *A non-oedipal psychoanalysis?: a clinical anthropology of hysteria in the works of Freud and Lacan*, Leuven: Leuven University Press.

Wambaq, Judith, (2008), 'Geleefde lichaam zonder organen,' *Estetica* 2008.

Widder, Nathan, (2009) 'From Negation to Disjunction in a World of Simulacra: Deleuze and Melanie Klein,' in *Deleuze Studies* 3(2), pp. 207-231.

Williams, James, (2008), *Gilles Deleuze's Logic of Sense: A Critical Introduction and Guide*, Edinburgh: EUP.

Žižek, Slavoj, (1991), *Looking Awry*, Cambridge, MIT Press.

_____. (2001), *The fright of real tears*, London: BFI publishing.

_____. (2004), *Organs without Bodies*, London: Routledge.

Zafiropoulos, Markos, (2003), *Lacan et Lévi-Straus, ou le retour à Freud 1951-1957*, Paris: Puf.

Index